THE NEW
COLOR
LINE

*How Quotas and
Privilege Destroy
Democracy*

THE NEW
COLOR
LINE

*How Quotas and
Privilege Destroy
Democracy*

PAUL CRAIG ROBERTS &
LAWRENCE M. STRATTON

REGNERY PUBLISHING, INC.
WASHINGTON, D.C.

JC
599
.U5
R56
1995

Library of Congress Cataloging-in-Publication Data
Roberts, Paul Craig, 1939–
    The new color line : how quotas and privilege destroy
democracy / Paul Craig Roberts & Lawrence M. Stratton.
    p.   cm.
    Includes bibliographical references (p.) and index.
    ISBN 0-89526-462-5 (hard : alk. paper)
    1. Reverse discrimination--United States. 2. Affirmative action
programs--United States. 3. Discrimination--United States.
4. United States--Social policy. I. Stratton, Lawrence M., 1963-
. II. Title.
JC599.U5R56 1995
323.1'73--dc20   95-31965
                                                        CIP

Published in the United States by
Regnery Publishing, Inc.
An Eagle Publishing Company
422 First Street, SE, Suite 300
Washington, DC 20003

Distributed to the trade by
National Book Network
4720-A Boston Way
Lanham, MD 20706

Printed on acid-free paper.
Manufactured in the United States of America

10 9 8 7 6 5 4 3 2

Books are available in quantity for promotional or premium use. Write to Director of Special Sales, Regnery Publishing, Inc., 422 First Street, SE, Suite 300, Washington, DC 20003, for information on discounts and terms or call (202) 546-5005.

C O N T E N T S

W hen I helped to organize civil rights protests as a college student, I did not expect the outcome to be racial quotas, racially gerrymandered congressional districts, government contract set-asides, or below-market interest rates on home mortgages for "protected minorities." As these privileges mount, it becomes increasingly difficult for young whites to comprehend the indignities blacks suffered because of the color of their skin. These indignities came both from laws that segregated public facilities and from behavioral responses or racial slights such as those catalogued in Ellis Cose's book, *The Rage of a Privileged Class*. Some white writers, such as novelist Lillian Smith, could empathize with blacks and convey a sense of the indignities to sensitive readers. One white, John H. Griffin, was not content to empathize. Desiring to directly experience blackness in order to report authoritatively what it was like, he ingested Oxsoralen to darken his skin pigmentation. The result was *Black Like Me*.

In the Atlanta, Georgia, of my youth, public segregation did not erect a wall of separation between blacks and whites. There was more to life than public institutions. Black and white kids played together—a fact that Thurgood Marshall emphasized when arguing for school desegregation before the Supreme Court—and many whites formed lifelong relationships with black household employees, who became de facto members of the families. It was as a college student that I began to experience the constraints that dark skin placed on a person. At Georgia Tech I was active in an organization that raised money to bring foreign students to Tech. I became friends with many, and it was my friendships with Ratan from India and Ibrahim, a dark-skinned Arab from Hebron, Jordan, that made me realize that my own choices were limited by my choice of friends. The only way we could get Ibrahim into the movie theaters was to make him wear his Arabic turban.

While at Tech, I met Lillian Smith. I later visited her in north Georgia, where she lived in a cabin on the side of a mountain. Her appeals resonated with me. It was ridiculous that I could attend classes at an elite engineering school with people that I couldn't take to the local movie. I became involved in organizing, as a representative from Tech, a civil rights march in Atlanta. At that time, white participation was appreciated because it was deemed to lend credibility to the protest.

All of this happened a long time ago before the discovery of "aversive racism," a doctrine that brands all whites as racists whether or not they will own up to it. White females have authority to speak on gender issues, but white males, as Charles Krauthammer has observed, have been stripped of all authority. Today their presence could lend no authority, moral or otherwise, to any civil rights demonstration. Even Jack Greenberg, the director-counsel of the NAACP Legal Defense and Educational Fund, who was handpicked by Thurgood Marshall to be his successor, found that his whiteness was reason for his course on civil rights to be picketed and boycotted by black law students at Harvard. In solidarity with blacks at Harvard, Stanford's black law students then blocked an effort to have Greenberg lecture at Stanford law school.

Critical Race Theorists have declared the Founding Fathers and the U. S. Constitution to be racist. Integration itself is said to be a racist plot to submerge blacks in white society. The once vaunted goal of color blindness is condemned today by Critical Race Theorists as "cultural genocide" for blacks.

The epithet, "racist," has been so overused that it has lost its sting. Critical Race Theorists have reduced an emotive term to a merely descriptive one by declaring all whites to be racist by definition. The determinism of the new Marxism allows whites no more escape from their racial consciousness than the old Marxism allowed the bourgeoisie to transcend their class consciousness. It is astonishing that the same theorists who have reduced mankind to a collection of disparate racial interests are demanding a multicultural society. Their assumption of disparate racial interests precludes the commonality of interests necessary for any society, much less a multicultural one. No social policy can construct a society out of irreconcilable interests.

In the United States today, white males don't have to read Lillian Smith and John Griffin to understand the affront of racial discrimination. As white males, many experience "reverse discrimination" in university admissions, law and medical school admissions, test scoring, employment, promotions, and access to training programs. The expansion of quotas has deprived white males of the protection of the Civil Rights Act. Preferment is replacing merit, and the institutions of liberal society are slowly giving way to a new feudalism based on race and gender estates. In pursuit of a moral cause, we let the ends justify the means and lost our way. We are in the process of losing our society along with the presumption of goodwill that is the basis of a democratic society in which law flows from a legislature accountable to the people.

This book is not about racism, segregation, or integration. It is about the suppositions that permit people to live together in harmony as equals under law. A liberal society is inconsistent with the assumption of disparate racial interests that undergirds civil rights policy in the United States today. This book is a defense of liberalism, which permits no special privileges for anyone.

Paul Craig Roberts
Washington, D.C.
1995

B orn a month before John F. Kennedy proposed what became the 1964 Civil Rights Act, I never encountered segregation. My great-grandmother helped organize the Duluth, Minnesota, chapter of the NAACP in the 1910s, but growing up in the rural town of Kutztown, Pennsylvania, where my father was president of Kutztown State College, I never experienced race as an issue.

Only a small percentage of Kutztown's five thousand students were black or minority, but in the mid-1970s the college had a black student government president and a Hispanic homecoming queen. Kristine Kenyatta, daughter of Kenyan leader Jomo Kenyatta, attended the college and became a family friend. Black athletes Doug Dennison and Bruce Harper were popular students who would have given the college national publicity on the Dallas Cowboys and New York Jets if ABC sports commentator Howard Cosell had been able to pronounce Kutztown correctly.

When I went away to college and entered the University of Pennsylvania in 1981, I learned that racism had taken over from segregation. In the integrated university most black students had voluntarily segregated themselves in the W.E.B. Du Bois College House on the other side of the campus. They had acquired the right to segregate themselves in order to form a support group against the racist environment.

My involvement with student government at Penn required that I attend a racism awareness seminar for student leaders. At this seminar I encountered the theories of institutional racism for the very first time. Jacqueline Wade, a black woman dressed in African garb with braided and beaded hair, told the audience that all whites are racists. I was amazed by her statement that integrated Penn was a racist institution because it was controlled by whites. Innocent of the imperatives of political correctness, I immediately raised my hand to challenge her statement. Noticing that Penn's newly hired provost, Thomas Ehrlich, now president of Indiana University, was sitting in the front row, I asked Wade if Penn was racist because it had just hired a provost who was white. "Yes," she said, Ehrlich's appointment was "compelling evidence" of institutional racism. Her reply seemed inconsistent with her own presence and name-calling authority.

I grew up with Sesame Street and black visitors in my home, but it was obvious from Wade's presentation that I would have no integrated experiences at Penn. My presence there and that of the other white students was "compelling evidence" of white racism. Truth by assumption had always left me cold, and it was a cold four years at Penn.

Soon after the racism awareness seminar, I observed a pattern that would be repeated. A fraternity was thrown off campus because one member allegedly shouted a racist epithet out of his window. Four-letter words were abundant in literature courses at Penn, and white students could freely employ fighting language in disputes among themselves. However, whites could be ejected from their hegemonic power structure if they spoke badly to blacks.

The pattern was repeated when the most popular professor in the Wharton School, Murray Dolfman, asked a black student in his business law class which constitutional amendment forbade slavery. Unknowingly, Dolfman was the first perpetrator of a heinous new crime—insensitivity. Penn President Sheldon Hackney, now Bill Clinton's chairman of the National Endowment for the Humanities, suspended Dolfman and sentenced him to sensitivity training. The persecution of Dolfman, a Jew whose ancestors were once owned by Egyptians, set the stage for Penn's infamous speech code and for the intimidation and harassment of white professors and students.

At Georgetown Law Center, I experienced the completion of another transformation—the reduction of constitutional law to sociologically based presumptions about racism. Introductory constitutional law courses traditionally began with a discussion of the famous 1803 Supreme Court case of *Marbury v. Madison* in which the Court grabbed the power of judicial review.[1] Today constitutional law courses begin with *Brown v. Board of Education.* Daniel A. Farber, William N. Eskridge, Jr., and Philip P. Frickey explain their decision to start their constitutional law text, *Cases and Materials on Constitutional Law: Themes for the Constitution's Third Century,* with *Brown,* instead of *Marbury,* by writing that *Brown* "has been the most important reference point for public-law thinking since the 1950s and has been an important testing case for the 'grand theories' of constitutional law." "Our thesis," the scholars state, "is that constitutional law generally, and dramatically after *Brown,* is incomprehensible without understanding social and political movements which shape its agenda."

By beginning with *Brown,* professors can debunk neutral legal principles and free the judiciary from the Constitution's text.

---

[1] See Robert H. Bork, *The Tempting of America: The Political Seduction of the Law* (New York: Free Press, 1990), 20–24.

In its place, judges are free to substitute their own views or those of social engineers—what Farber, Eskridge, and Frickey call "grand theories." *Brown* teaches students that constitutional law is not a body of law to be learned, but social policy decreed from the bench. Students learn that "good" social results are the proper aim of legal rulings, not "law by the books." Once protected by the Constitution's text, we are now dependent on the feelings of 846 federal judges. With the Constitution cast aside, the new clerisy has usurped legislative powers, calling into question the continuance of constitutional democracy, in which law flows from the people expressing their will through elected representatives. In this book we show the peril that the confusion over ends and means poses to American democracy.

Lawrence M. Stratton
Washington, D.C.
1995

The Demise of Liberalism

Forty years after *Brown v. Board of Education*, civil rights has lost its good name to quotas. As civil rights has come to be equated with preferential treatment based on race and gender, the public has withdrawn its support. This is not surprising. The civil rights movement was a popular and powerful democratic movement precisely because the vast majority of Americans stand unequivocally for equality under the law.

Outrage over preferential treatment for "protected minorities" has taken the place of guilt over segregation. Americans who hailed *Brown* are distressed and confused that *Brown* is now used to support privilege. Americans who supported desegregation and equal rights are astonished to find themselves governed by quotas despite the overwhelming rejection of quotas by the 1964 Civil Rights Act. Americans who marched, protested, and voted in favor of equal opportunity now discover that, in defiance of statutory law, race and gender preferences govern access to jobs, training programs, promotions, universities, and even home mortgages.

Where the opportunity is open to them, as in California, with its public referendum system, citizens are moving to take back their sovereignty over the law. Momentum is building in California for a 1996 initiative, modeled on the 1964 Civil Rights Act, to amend the state's constitution to prohibit the use of quotas by California public institutions. Polls indicate that the initiative's objective of ending affirmative action is enormously popular in California, even in traditionally liberal bastions such as Berkeley and San Francisco. And as California goes, so goes the country. Citizens in other states are following suit with their own grassroots efforts to place similar referenda on the ballot.

The hostility to race and gender preferments reflects a general sense that reverse discrimination violates fundamental norms of justice and fair play. Thomas Wood, a codrafter of the California initiative, and executive director of the California Association of Scholars, says that he has been denied a teaching job because he is a white male: "I was once told by a member of a search committee at a university, 'You'd walk into this job if you were the right gender.'" Glynn Custred, a California State University anthropology professor, says that he decided to join Wood in codrafting the initiative because of his concern about the destructive impact racial quotas were having on higher education, where the push for diversity overshadows academic merit.

The initiative has drawn support from across the political spectrum in California. Initiative supporter Charles Geshekter, a teacher of African history at Chico State University, wrote in the August 14, 1994, *Chico Enterprise Record*, "As a liberal Democrat, I despise those who advocate preferential treatment based on genitalia or skin color. Having taught university classes on the history of European racism towards Africa for twenty-five years, I am appalled to watch sexist and racist demands for equality of outcomes erode the principle of affirmative equality of opportunity." University of California regent Ward Connerly, a black businessman who supports the initiative, lamented in the August 10, 1994, *Sacramento Bee* that "we have institutionalized this preferential treatment."

Opposition to quotas was initially unfocused because their impact was not widely felt. The public was aware of a few celebrated cases, but they seemed to be the exception rather than the rule. Today this is no longer the case. Randy Pech, the owner of Adarand Constructors, lost the bid for a guardrail construction project in Colorado's San Juan National Forest because of his gender and skin color. Pech put in the lowest bid, but this wasn't enough to offset the disadvantage of being a white male. His competitor, a Hispanic-owned firm, was legally entitled to taxpayers' money in the form of a bounty paid by the U.S. Department of Transportation to the prime contractor for hiring minority-owned subcontractors. The bounty was greater than the difference in the bids, so it paid the prime contractor to hire the Hispanic-owned firm.

Pech filed a discrimination lawsuit, which worked its way to the Supreme Court in January 1995. There U.S. Solicitor General Drew S. Days III argued that Pech had no standing to be in court—despite the obvious fact that the U.S. government had paid the prime contractor $10,000 to discriminate against him.

The solicitor general's argument blatantly reveals the system of racial preferments that passes for civil rights. "Protected minorities" have been entitled to an automatic presumption of discrimination ever since the Supreme Court's *Griggs* ruling in 1971, and therefore have been able to sue in court without having to show that they have suffered from any discriminatory acts. Today's college-aged protected minorities were born into a legally privileged class and have never suffered from any legal act of discrimination. Yet U.S. policy assumes that they are victims of discrimination and provides remedies in the form of preferments. In contrast, victims of reverse discrimination find that they are disadvantaged in the law.

The anomaly of these divergent rights is having political repercussions. In the November 1994 congressional elections, white males deserted the Democratic party in droves, voting Republican by a margin of 63 percent to 37 percent. The *Wall Street Journal* has identified "angry white males" as an important new political group, which now sees that helping minorities means discriminating against white males.

Brown v. Board of Education and the Civil Rights Act of 1964 did not lead to the promised colorblind society, but to a system of racial preferments that an overwhelming majority of Americans finds very disturbing. In *The Scar of Race*, Paul Sniderman and Thomas Piazza report that 80 percent of Americans oppose busing and affirmative action in employment and education. Even the minority that is supposed to benefit from these policies is split 50-50 on busing and affirmative action. In our democracy, federal bureaucrats and federal courts have managed to impose a public policy that is overwhelmingly opposed by "We the People." A country that overwhelmingly supported civil rights thirty years ago now overwhelmingly opposes what they have become—race and gender preferments.

This book offers an explanation for these ironic outcomes; in short, democracy gave way to judicial and regulatory edicts, and persuasion gave way to coercion. This happened because democracy was seen as the problem and not the solution. The Supreme Court and elites generally were persuaded that Americans were so irredeemably racist that democracy would forever perpetuate segregation. The Court embarked on what has become a decades-long effort to reform society from the judicial bench instead of the legislative chamber. More is at stake than the plight of white males and the relative fortunes of political parties. At issue is equality before the law and the democratic process itself. As freedom of conscience, goodwill, and persuasion are supplanted by regulatory and judicial coercion, privilege reappears in open defiance of

Justice John Marshall Harlan's dictum: "There is no caste here. Our Constitution is color-blind." Privilege is incompatible with democracy, which depends on the notion of a common good. There is no common interest in a society where rights depend upon status and people do not stand equal under the law as citizens.

In one of the odder twists of American intellectual and political history, it was not an American but a Swedish sociologist who crystallized the belief that Americans were too irredeemably racist to be allowed to decide race questions democratically. Legal scholar Mark Tushnet has pointed out that "the intellectual atmosphere in which the Court operated enthusiastically received Gunnar Myrdal's critical study of the caste system, *An American Dilemma*," which argued that America was a deeply racist society. In *Brown*'s oral argument Justice Robert Jackson said, "I suppose that realistically the reason this case is here is that action couldn't be obtained from Congress."

Myrdal argued that it was unrealistic to expect a racist people to legislate the end of segregation. Therefore, the Court would have to end segregation by decree, which is what the Court did. Ironically, the widespread public support for the decision belied the assumption on which it was made.

If *Brown*'s result had been only to end public segregation, it would have been a victory. But more than that happened. *Brown* belittled democracy. The decision was based on the belief that democracy could not do the right thing and would not produce a moral outcome. The basis for the desegregation decision threw out the fundamental presumption of any democratic order—goodwill among citizens regardless of class, race, or gender. Without goodwill there is no basis for uniting different people in democratic self-rule.

The importance of goodwill to the case for democracy is not generally understood. Perhaps this is because the political philosophers of liberalism, like John Stuart Mill, wrote before Karl

Marx challenged them with the supremacy of class interests. Mill assumed goodwill and did not see any need to formulate explicitly its importance to the case for democracy. He simply took it for granted, as do in our opinion those who argue that democratic governance is simply a matter of contracts between people in pursuit of mutual benefits.

Marx challenged democracy on the grounds that its essential feature, goodwill among citizens, was an illusion. The truth about society, Marx said, is class interests, and the class interests of capitalists dominate. In Marx's analysis, law and democratic politics are just part of the "ideological superstructure" that serves the underlying dominant material interests. The brutal truth, Marx concluded, is that class consciousness results in each class serving only its own interest. Thus, no basis exists for uniting differing classes in a common interest. Marx solved the problem of governance by predicting the overthrow of the bourgeoisie and emergence of a classless society.

Marx's challenge to democracy was total. If class interests are supreme, people are unaffected by moral persuasion. The First Amendment is pointless, and freedom of conscience simply upholds class interests. Liberalism's self-image as a moral order replacing tyranny was reduced by Marx to a mere self-delusion.

Such views have gained a wider currency than is realized. The tyranny that democracy protects us against is long forgotten. It is commonplace today to hear democracy denigrated as a system that serves organized special interests. Critical Race Theorists and radical feminists reduce society to disparate race and gender interests. Even among libertarians there is a preoccupation not with the protections that democracy affords but with protecting dissenters, minorities, and those who are different from the will of the majority. There is danger in becoming too disillusioned with democracy. If we give up on "We the People," we will cease to be citizens and become subjects.

The process of giving up on democracy is further along than Americans imagine. The Supreme Court gave up on it in 1954. *Brown* was not just the end of public segregation, it was also the beginning of a judicial campaign to impose desirable racial outcomes. Neutral rules have been supplanted by social engineering. This outcome probably would have shocked much of the *Brown* court, even as judicial and bureaucratic subversions of the 1964 Civil Rights Act shocked congressional leaders who shepherded this legislation.

The more frequently courts step in to remedy the shortcomings of democracy, the less the presumption that self-rule is trustworthy. Courts, moreover, have gone beyond making the law to seizing the power of the purse from local and state governments. Scholars such as Ivan Hannaford have concluded that in the United States, race is crowding out politics altogether and that race and ethnicity have displaced citizenship as the badge of identity. This can only be worsened by the continuing struggle to garner as many race (and gender) privileges and preferments as possible.

Whatever the failures of democracy, they do not warrant substituting judicial and regulatory coercion for majority rule. The approach to race taken forty years ago has weakened our democracy and the concept of citizenship. It was done with good intentions and high hopes, but with disregard of the requirements and achievements of liberal society. Segregation could and should have been ended by legislative action.

Liberal society is a historic achievement. The mounting assaults on this achievement are the cause for the growing sense of unease about *Brown*. The unease is not with desegregation but with the manner in which it was done.

Many liberals have grown uneasy with *Brown* and its aftermath because of the pressures put on them to accept in *Brown's* name a hardening system of racial preferments and infringements on the First Amendment as necessary steps to complete the desegregation that *Brown* began. Conservatives are uneasy because *Brown* seems to have separated constitutional law from the Constitution and instead based it on sociology. Critical Race Theorists have dismissed *Brown* as, at best, a Cold War ploy to deflect communist propaganda, and, at worst, a plot to destroy black identity.

At the heart of all of this is the feeling that in *Brown* the Court substituted itself for the law. In the most important constitutional decision of our time, the Court rested its decisions neither on legal precedent nor constitutional interpretation, but on psychological experiments and a sociological analysis.

Many legal scholars have criticized *Brown* as an abandonment of law. Columbia Law Professor Herbert Wechsler, a prominent New Deal liberal, Nuremberg prosecutor, and NAACP litigation consultant, criticized *Brown* as an unprincipled decision that sacrificed neutral legal principles to the Justices' desired outcome. In his comprehensive study, *Government by Judiciary: The Transformation of the Fourteenth Amendment*, Raoul Berger accused the *Brown* decision of following the discredited doctrine that the end justifies the means when it usurped legislative power "on the ground that there is no other way to be rid of an acknowledged evil."

Even those primarily concerned with social results must find *Brown* lacking. In *The Burden of Brown: Thirty Years of School Desegregation*, Raymond Wolters concluded that in the wake of the decision education deteriorated even in the school districts that were the original defendants in the case. After surveying the results of *Brown*, University of Chicago Professor Gerald Rosenberg wrote in 1991 in his book, *The Hollow Hope*, that the judiciary is impotent to induce social change successfully. And in 1994, Irving Kristol wrote that *Brown*, "contrary to expectations, turned out to be the prelude to a major step backward in American race relations."

The unpopular and educationally disastrous aftermath of *Brown*—busing and racial quotas—has been laid at the decision's feet by no less a figure than Yale Law Professor Alexander Bickel, who as Justice Felix Frankfurter's law clerk was instrumental in both shaping and obtaining the *Brown* decision. University of Texas Law Professor Lino Graglia has stated that *Brown* turned the Supreme Court into a "seemingly omnipotent instrument for effecting fundamental social changes without obtaining the consent of the American people or their elected representatives." Political scientist Edward J. Erler says that the "legacy of *Brown v. Board of Education*" is "judicial oligarchy."

Many who have stood by *Brown* have become disaffected at some stage in its aftermath. Some believe the problems began with busing. Others accept busing but reject quotas. Still others believe that the civil rights movement went off track with assaults on free speech and academic freedom. For others the trouble began with racially gerrymandered congressional districts, race-weighted voting proposals, and a perceived shift in the civil rights movement toward separatist thinking.

None of the disaffected, however, have explained why bad came out of good only at their point of disaffection. Moreover people who accept *Brown* but reject its aftermath are confronted with the fact that the same lawyers who litigated *Brown* litigated its aftermath. For NAACP attorneys such as Jack Greenberg, busing, racial quotas, and gerrymandered districts are logical consequences of *Brown*. For the NAACP it was all part of litigating the revolution. What is undeniable is that the unpopular aftermath of *Brown* followed logically from the decision's assumption that an absence of racial goodwill precluded a democratic solution.

Conservative critics of judicial activism and libertarian critics of expansive government have accommodated themselves to *Brown* because they believe that segregation was unfair and unjust whatever its legal basis. Legal philosophers have long recognized equity as a necessary component of law and its interpretation. In the seventeenth century Grotius defined equity as "the correction of that, wherein the law is deficient." *Brown* could be seen as the use of interpretation to correct inequity in the law.

It would have been better for democracy if the Court had argued *Brown* on this basis rather than on Myrdal's assumption that democracy is unequal to the challenge of race. The renowned jurist William Blackstone said that there is a place for the moral conscience of judges in their interpretation of law in behalf of equity, but he warned of the dangers of letting the heart take over the law:

> The liberty of considering all cases in an equitable light must not be indulged too far, lest thereby we destroy all law, and leave the decision of every question entirely in the breast of the judge. And law, without equity, though hard and disagreeable, is much more desirable for the public good, than equity without law; which would make every judge a legislator, and introduce most infinite confusion; as there would then be almost as many different rules of action laid down in our courts, as there are differences of capacity and sentiment in the human mind.

Blackstone could have added that when judges become legislators democracy is preempted and law ceases to flow from the people. Georgetown Law Professor Peter B. Edelman, a Clinton administration candidate for the federal bench, has argued that *Brown* is the precedent that gives the judiciary the power to make the law whenever the legislature comes up short on equity. In the November 1987 *Hastings Law Journal*, he argues that *Brown* was a case "where the Court saw a political and legislative impasse regarding very basic and important rights, and decided to initiate a process of constitutional change." *Brown* is historic because the judiciary exercised its "affirmative obligation" to make the law serve a right that Congress was shortchanging, thereby establishing the principle of "judicial intervention to require legislative intervention."

Once this door is open, it is hard to close. Edelman wants the judiciary to use its four-decades-old power to instruct legislators "that they must do better than they have done" for the poor. He believes that just as Congress failed to meet its duty to blacks, it has failed to do right by the poor. Edelman sees a judicial mandate of a guaranteed income as the logical extension of *Brown*. Equity thus becomes a wedge for the judiciary to run away with the law.

Desegregation is an important accomplishment, but it loses its luster when it is done in a way that discredits democracy. As Friedrich Hayek said, majority rule is "the essential condition for the absence of arbitrary power and therefore of freedom." The power of the majority is not unlimited, but it is an absolute power over the imposition of government coercion. No government coercive power is legitimate in the pursuit of any end unless it is approved by at least a majority. In recent decades this power of democracy has been breached. Federal judges have imposed busing, quotas, and taxation on unwilling majorities. This governance by an extrademocratic clerisy is an atavistic throwback to a pre-American form of government.

Political philosophers and realists long ago made clear the perils of relying on a Charlemagne to protect us from ourselves. Today many see the Court as a Charlemagne whose function is to exercise veto power over democracy. They regard *Brown* as a good decision and the Civil Rights Act as good legislation, while deploring their distortion by subsequent judicial and regulatory rulings. Those who hold to this view are hard pressed to explain how we can rely on the Court to protect us from the tyranny of the majority when the Court only randomly does the right thing itself.

This book offers no plea for segregation or apology for racial discrimination. It is conceivable that *Brown* could have simply ended any government racial policy and stopped at that, and that the Civil Rights Act could have prohibited intentional racial discrimination in the workplace and stopped at that. These salutary outcomes were denied to American society because *Brown* gave up on goodwill and substituted judicial coercion for democratic outcomes. The Civil Rights Act gave up on freedom of conscience, preferring instead regulatory coercion. Both events took decision-making power away from the people on the grounds that they cannot be trusted to do the right thing if permitted to rule themselves.

Brown and the 1964 act did more than attack segregation and racial discrimination. They also attacked the presumption of goodwill and freedom of conscience, which are the foundations of civil society. *Brown* was based on the assumption that representative democracy cannot produce moral outcomes. Consequently, *Brown*'s aftermath is not only busing and racial preferments, but also judicial usurpation of legislative power. The Civil Rights Act extended *Brown*'s premise of inexorable racism from politics to private life. It reflects the belief that freedom of conscience would perpetuate racial discrimination in private affairs just as democracy would perpetuate segregation in public life.

We are still laboring under this heavy indictment of democracy. In the end it appears that Karl Marx won once the argument shifted from the supremacy of class interests to the supremacy of race interests. There is no way to govern a society composed of implacable separate interests except through coercion from above. If we continue the assaults on goodwill, we will lose our democracy.

C H A P T E R   T W O

Progress Redefined

I f asked to define the essence of modernity, most Americans would answer in terms of scientific, technical, and economic progress. Those who regard the Victorian era as ancient times might think of modernity in terms of the sexual revolution. Few would reply that what separates modern times from prior human history are equality before the law and the democratic process.

These two human achievements are the pillars of liberalism, a doctrine that until recent years has been synonymous with progress since the eighteenth century and the fount of our social and political institutions. Liberalism vanquished kings and destroyed feudalism—the status-based social system that had held sway for more than a millennium since the fall of the Roman Empire. In the modern era, equality before the law and the democratic process have represented the highest human hopes. Liberalism's confidence in the power of goodwill to change things for the better improved society with wave after wave of humanitarian reforms.

Equality before the law freed people from the constraints of birth, privilege, and class. The democratic process allowed people to decide their own fate by making them the source of the government's authority rather than subjects submitting to the decrees of an elite clerisy or a divinely appointed monarch. By demanding societal outcomes based on mutual consent derived from the interaction of individual opinions, liberalism liberated mankind from "the tyranny of the ends." Monarchs and inquisitors had justified tyrannical means by noble ends, but for liberals societal outcomes are no more ideal than the processes through which they are achieved. The ends cannot justify the means because there is no difference between what a society does and how it does it. In liberal society, ends cannot be defined independently of the means of achieving them. Liberalism's reliance on democratic outcomes closed the door to tyranny.

Alexis de Tocqueville captured the essence of this revolutionary change when he wrote more than 150 years ago that "aristocracy made a chain of all members of the community, from the peasant to the king; democracy breaks that chain and severs every link of it." Liberalism replaced the ancien régime "with a new social and political order, at once simple and more uniform, based on the concept of the equality of all men." Liberalism is summed up in a single word, "citizen," the enemy of class rank. In place of different courts with different laws for different classes of people— even legal restrictions on what clothes people of various ranks could wear and what food they could eat—the people of a country became united as citizens with equal standing under the law.

The disparate privileges of a status-based society are so long forgotten that it is useful to recall their injustice. Before the advent of liberalism, the legal requirement that judges weigh the distinctions of persons in dispensing justice made a person's status a threshold issue before the courts could address the merits of any legal claim. The status of the parties had to be determined first, because the set of legal burdens to which a person was then subjected depended on it. Status adjudication was also necessary because different courts had jurisdiction over different types of people. Freemen, for example, were permitted to file claims in the King's court, while villeins were not.

In order to determine the class into which a person was born, courts sometimes even had to determine the place where conception occurred. Bracton, a twelfth-century English jurist, set down the rule to determine the status of a child born from the union of a freeman and a serf. Whether the child's legal status was that of a freeman or a villein depended upon "whether the child was the result of intercourse in the villein tenement or outside it, in a free bed."

There were no First Amendment rights. Nobles were often protected against the verbal abuse of commoners by special provisions of the law. In places such as Lithuania, commoners who defamed nobles had their tongues cut out. The English privilege of *scandalum magnatum* gave nobles special privileges to sue their critics for slander and free rein to verbally harass others. Nobles were also legally entitled to command silence and respect when they entered and departed public buildings such as churches.

Criminal punishments depended on class. By paying a small fine, Eastern European nobles could be excused the death sentence if they murdered peasants. Nobles could not be tortured as a means of extorting evidence. In addition to having separate courts, nobles could bypass lower courts by appealing directly to the king. Commoners were usually precluded from bringing any legal action against nobles.

Wergild laws specified fines not by crime, but by the status of the victim. After the Norman conquest, William the Conqueror expanded upon this principle by increasing penalties for native English criminal defendants whose victims were of Norman descent. Attacks on Normans were worse in the eyes of the law than attacks on Englishmen. As a result, defendants used elaborate pedigrees, known as "presentations of Englishry," to prove that their victims were English.

Status-based legal distinctions were swept away by liberalism. For the first time in history, the liberal concept of individualism gave people an identity separate from their group status. According to the liberal ideal, rather than being a member of an estate, the vassal of a lord, or a slave, a person's legally relevant membership was as citizen of the nation, and all citizens were entitled to the same rights. Although the word citizen had been used in premodern monarchical societies to distinguish inhabitants of cities or towns from landed nobility or gentry, in the liberal era all members of the society became known as citizens.

The revolt against privilege embraced the democratic process because democracy gave all citizens the same share in making the law. Instead of the exercise of sovereign power by a privileged elite, sovereignty in democracy is summarized in the phrase, "We the People."

In his treatise, *On Representative Government*, English philosopher John Stuart Mill argued that democracy improved the overall character of society by encouraging a self-reliant and public-spirited people. In contrast, other forms of government, even rule by a wise and benevolent leader pursuing virtuous and moral ends, required a mentally passive people, which would stunt the development of virtue and intelligence within society and lead to national decay. "Everyone is degraded, whether aware of it or not, when other people, without consulting him, take upon themselves unlimited power to regulate his destiny." Mill argued that participation in self-government improved the quality of people, whereas the pursuit of just ends by a philosopher-king would be detrimental to the people themselves.

Mill praised democracy for drawing upon and expanding the talents of a multitude of people, not just the ruler and his entourage. Even if a private citizen rarely participated in public functions, such as someone who "drive[s] a quill, or sell[s] goods over a counter," democracy still performed a salutary moral function by having him "weigh interests not his own; to be guided, in case of conflicting claims, by another rule than his private partialities; to apply, at every turn, principles and maxims which have for their reason of existence the common good."

Liberalism ushered in a meritocracy that displaced family rank as the critical factor in determining lifetime opportunities. In the nineteenth century Henry Sumner Maine, a law professor at Cambridge and Oxford, observed that "the movement of the progressive societies has hitherto been a movement *from status to contract.*" Liberal societies had moved from "one terminus of history," in which all of a person's legal relationships flowed from his status, toward a new "social order in which all these relations arise from the free agreement of individuals."

In a meritocracy, individuals are free from feudal ties and can sell their services in the market. With the freedom to trade and move about, men can freely bargain and can advance themselves based on their own thrift, industry, and good fortune. During the French Revolution, this liberal theme was summarized in the rallying cry, "la carrière ouverte aux talents"—a career open to the talents. Every man had the right to push to his full potential. In America, liberalism's pathway for merit was called the opportunity society. In 1793, lexicographer Noah Webster proclaimed that "the road is open for the poorest citizen to amass wealth by labor and economy, and by his talent and virtue to raise himself to the highest offices of the State."

By unleashing talent from the tethers of feudal privilege, equality before the law not only freed the individual, but strengthened society by increasing economic activity and creating wealth. In 1776 Adam Smith described in *The Wealth of Nations* how competitive forces were matching opportunity with merit. Smith drew upon the ideas of the French physiocrats, especially François Quesnay, author of the 1758 classic, *Tableau économique*. The physiocrats helped set the French Revolution in motion by advocating an end to artificial impediments to the natural economic order, such as feudal dues, guild and manorial monopolies, and class privileges. According to Quesnay, France would become prosperous when all artificial restraints were removed.

Because the democratic process is built on persuasion rather than coercion, democracies favor free expression and a free press. Just as equality before the law promotes economic activity, free expression enhances the search for truth. When people feel comfortable positing ideas, the ideas can be tested and challenged. Liberalism holds that when human intellect is unshackled, creativity blossoms. The fecundity of free expression generates the ideas necessary for society to flourish. For this reason, free speech is the top listing in the Bill of Rights. Democracy suffers if elites can control the formation of opinion.

The confidence that liberals had in ordinary people was revolutionary. Thomas Jefferson and his contemporaries denied that philosopher kings and lettered elites had a monopoly on the ability to perceive truth. "State a moral case to a ploughman and a professor," Jefferson wrote, "the former will decide it as well, and often better than the latter, because he has not been led astray by artificial rules."

The democratic ideal is exemplified by the town meeting that originated in the New England colonies. Once a year the townspeople of all occupations would gather in a meeting hall to decide important local questions, such as whether to build a new bridge, repair a road, or expand a school. The citizens might not always agree and would engage in heated debate appealing to common values, but once the vote was taken, everyone consented to the will of the majority. The citizens would also choose a group of officers to govern the town until the next general gathering.

The citizens knew that civility was an important element in these meetings. Because they lived and worked with one another, they were loath to offend other members of the community. Former adversaries might need to be allies on other issues at future municipal gatherings. If a policy embraced at one meeting proved to be a failure, goodwill between citizens would make it easier to change course.

Participation in town meetings was part of the eighteenth-century ideal of free individuals engaging in collective action only by consent. Historian Edmund S. Morgan wrote in his book, *The Birth of the American Republic 1763–1789,* that in contrast to people everywhere else in the world, "standing on his own land with spade in hand and flintlock not far off, the American could look at his richest neighbor and laugh."

After the American Revolution, many political thinkers feared that independent Americans would be corrupted. Corruption did not refer solely to graft or bribery, but to the loss of the virtuous spirit of independence. Corruption meant free men becoming dependent upon privileges conveyed by the state. The safeguard against reenserfment was the invigorating democratic spirit. Those who lost elections were encouraged to marshal their arguments rather than to plot coups d'état. They could appeal to common societal values in order to persuade the majority of the population.

Today every one of these distinctive historical achievements of liberalism is endangered. The race, gender, and handicapped status of Americans has become a controlling factor in court cases, in the workplace, and at college. Where liberal government was once based on a deep trust in the wisdom and goodwill of citizens and the subordination of government to the consent of the governed, the ruling premise of government today is that race and gender interests have erected hegemonic discriminatory structures in law and employment that must be broken up by government coercion. We owe this loss of the liberal legacy to the way the issue of desegregation was decided.

Many Americans were uncomfortable and a few outraged with the injustices of segregation. And for good reason. Segregation was a moral abomination that demeaned black citizens on the basis of skin color. The damage done to the self-esteem and economic opportunities of blacks and to the conscience of whites was insufferable. The Cold War moreover brought new practical disadvantages to segregation. Moscow propaganda hammered away at American racial discrimination, portraying blacks as a brutally suppressed minority with no hope under the existing form of government. This provided pragmatic reasons as well as moral ones to speed the demise of segregation in order to remove a millstone from the neck of our foreign policy community, which was engaged in a protracted conflict to contain Soviet expansionism.

The new impracticality of segregation was quickly brought home when one of the first petitions presented to the recently established UN Commission on Human Rights was authored by W.E.B. Du Bois for the NAACP protesting American segregation. U.S. Attorney General Tom Clark was "humiliated" by the petition, and U.S. Delegate Eleanor Roosevelt refused to introduce it in order to protect America's international reputation.

Segregation was an affront to the liberal conscience, and the Soviet Union was a menace. Its large army, nuclear weapons, and definition of truth as what served its interest presented liberalism with a fearsome challenge. Impatience with segregation mounted. Something had to be done.

Lillian Smith had expressed impatience in her 1944 *New Republic* article, "Addressed to White Liberals." "I cannot endure the idea so many liberals hold that segregation must change slowly," she wrote. Nor was it enough to put "a ballot in everyone's hand." Indeed, liberals were arguing that the ballot itself was the problem.

Democracy Discredited

The thesis that democracy was the problem and not the solution to racial segregation was forcibly stated by Gunnar Myrdal in his magnum opus, *An American Dilemma*, published in 1944. Myrdal argued that democracy could not put right the injustice because the racist impulses of the electorate would forever perpetuate segregation. He envisioned the elimination of segregation in the United States by an educated elite using the coercive powers of the judiciary.

Myrdal's argument justified a new elitism that shaped the *Brown* decision and fundamentally altered liberalism's relationship to democracy, its own creation. More was involved here than an argument that the end justified the means. By dismissing the democratic process as unable to produce moral outcomes, Myrdal elevated coercion over persuasion and jettisoned liberalism's reliance on goodwill as the avenue to social progress.

Liberalism's confidence in goodwill among men as an effective force in history was also punctured by the persistence of seg-

regation in public accommodations, restaurants, and employment.
The result was the Civil Rights Act of 1964, which replaced freedom of conscience with governmental regulation of private behavior. Once statistical disparities became prima facie evidence of discrimination, quotas became unavoidable, and with quotas came
the reappearance of status-based legal rights. Today equality
before the law is giving way to demands for equality of result,
which is crowding out the liberal concept of a meritocratic society.
Liberalism's revolutionary demand, "a career open to the talents,"
is dismissed today as a segregationist ploy.

If we are going to hold on to democracy and equality before
the law, we have to rethink the paths that led to *Brown* and the
Civil Rights Act and regain liberalism's confidence in the goodwill
of free individuals to produce a just social order. This is especially true now that new schools of legal thought attack democracy
and equality before the law as hegemonic tools of white male
oppression.

Myrdal ensured that the democratic process would become
integration's first casualty, while setting in motion a way of thinking that, as it unfolded, would undermine integration as a goal. In
1937, he received a $300,000 grant from the Carnegie Foundation
to study the "Negro Problem" in the United States. As a leader of
Sweden's Social Democratic Party, Myrdal had helped to erect the
Swedish socialist welfare state, which was premised on the wisdom of bureaucratic social engineers to correct all social ills.

Myrdal had impressed many American intellectuals during
1929–30 when he had a Rockefeller Foundation fellowship
designed to introduce foreign scholars to American scholars.
During his fellowship, he visited several American universities,
including Chicago, Columbia, and Wisconsin, where he met faculty members and gave lectures. He wrote to his doctoral adviser at
the University of Stockholm, economist Gustav Cassel, that in
America he was being treated like a "golden child" and went

"around like a light from Nazareth with opinions ready on every-thing possible." When Carnegie Foundation President Frederick Keppel decided to finance a study on race relations, Beardsley Ruml, a New Deal Democrat and Rockefeller Foundation director, persuaded him to get Gunnar Myrdal to do it.

Growing up in a small town in the rural Swedish province of Dalarna, where his father was a successful building contractor, Myrdal was a child prodigy who was driven to succeed. In 1914 Myrdal became the first member of his family to be educated beyond grammar school when he went to Stockholm to study at the prestigious Norra Real gymnasium. To overcome the sneers of students who considered him a hick from Dalarna and to impress his teachers, Myrdal embraced elitist views.

At Norra Real, he became engrossed in Nietzsche's theme of the superman and in Swedish intellectual Rudolf Kjellen's political theories, which disdained the masses and argued that citizens had a moral duty to place the collective welfare of the nation above individual or group self-interest. In a gymnasium essay on the Enlightenment, Myrdal wrote that educated men should use rea-son to direct political development for the masses.

In 1918 he entered the University of Stockholm to study law. At law school he was an energetic debater. One classmate later recalled that Myrdal was "very loud-voiced and not exactly dis-pleased with his own talents, full of paradoxical ideas, cheeky and cocky." He expressed his disdainful attitude toward democracy, which stayed with him for the rest of his life, during a law school speech. According to Myrdal, "Democratic politics are *stupid*." The masses are "impervious to rational argument." Politicians could influence them only by making "intuitive appeals to emotion." He warned that the problem would get worse with suffrage for women, which would "increase the suggestibility [of the masses], lower the capacity for judgment—if that is possible," and even add an "erotic coloring" to political debate. "Great aims [and] original thoughts" were a political disadvantage in a democracy because popular sloganeering and the ability to appeal to the irrational mind of the masses was what counted.

To counter this state of affairs, Myrdal advocated a "party of intelligence" to guide the nation. "Precisely because the intelligent can think and not be defenseless against mass suggestion, one can expect that the future party of intelligence shall have the ability to defend the national interest against selfishness and class-egoism." To overcome objections that his proposal was impractical, Myrdal said that "men of intelligence" would have to learn the language of the masses in order "to translate the reasonable to the emotional, thought to slogan."

With extraordinary candor, Myrdal said that "the party [of intelligence] despises deeply the democratic principle but recognizes the driving idea [democracy] to be a powerful factor and is ready to work within this framework with suitable means." Men of intelligence could engage in sloganeering as long as they took pains to protect their capacity for clear thought. In the pursuit of intelligent government in the democratic era, "the end justifies the means."

After completing law school, Myrdal served as a law clerk for a Stockholm municipal court, as a magistrate in the town of Mariefred, and as a prosecutor in Norrsköping. But Myrdal found law to be boring. He longed to return to intellectual circles. At the encouragement of his wife Alva, he decided to study economics at the University of Stockholm.

In Stockholm's doctoral program, Myrdal developed a father–son relationship with his mentor, Gustav Cassel. Cassel was an internationally renowned economist who favored the free market and rejected economic planning because it inexorably led to dictatorship. Myrdal's doctoral thesis expanded upon Cassel's theory of price fluctuations. With his doctorate, he became a docent in political economy at the university.

Although Myrdal was admitted to Cassel's elite circle of intellectuals, he did not share his teacher's suspicion of government power. In a series of lectures at the University of Stockholm, he criticized neoclassical economics for its illusions. He later wrote that these lectures "became from a personal viewpoint a catharsis, a way of liberating myself from all that I had picked up as a precocious schoolboy and later in high school." With neoclassical economics cast aside, Myrdal soon began developing his theory of social engineering, in which elites substituted their judgments for democratic outcomes.

With his distrust of democracy and markets well ingrained, Myrdal began his Carnegie Foundation study in 1938. Alva and his three children moved into a New York City apartment on Riverside Drive near Columbia University. Alva participated in seminars at Columbia, and the children were enrolled in elite schools. The couple took the New York and Washington, D.C., social scene of intellectuals, politicians, diplomats, and European émigrés by storm. To many, the Myrdals seemed like oracles from a more advanced society. Although American social scientists were then reticent to inject values into their analyses, Myrdal proclaimed to his American friends that social engineering was "the supreme task of an accomplished social science." He was confident that he could unite American elites to eradicate America's racial ills.

Drawing upon his experience on the Swedish Royal Commission on population from June 1935 to June 1938, and using the generous Carnegie funding, Myrdal set out to win everyone who had ever written or done anything about race relations to the cause of his study. Myrdal made them collaborators and sought their contributions to his research. Chapel Hill sociologist Guy Johnson observed that this strategy was effective in producing a favorable response to Myrdal's book. Johnson wrote that Myrdal "was basically a politician... besides being a great scholar.... If [Myrdal] hadn't involved all these people and spent all this money and had a thousand names on the list of people that had helped, the reception might not have been as enthusiastic."

Activists also got involved. Sensing the potential impact of Myrdal's study, Roy Wilkins of the NAACP wrote to his colleague Walter White stressing the importance of getting the NAACP's line across to Myrdal: "As you have stated repeatedly, this survey probably will be the most important study of the Negro in the last 20 years. Unquestionably its findings will influence procedure along interracial lines for certainly the next ten years and perhaps longer." Wilkins thought that the study "would be used more or less as a Bible for Americans to guide them in their treatment of the Negro."

Myrdal's "Bible," *An American Dilemma*, was published in January 1944. It had over one thousand pages of text, ten appendixes, and 250 pages of notes. The book had the impact Wilkins predicted. In the 1960s, *Saturday Review* surveyed prominent intellectuals asking, "What books published during the past four decades most significantly altered the direction of our society?" Only Keynes' *General Theory* received more votes than *An American Dilemma*. Myrdal's book has been compared for its impact to Harriet Beecher Stowe's *Uncle Tom's Cabin* and Thomas Paine's *Common Sense*.

Upon its release, *An American Dilemma* was hailed for its insights as ranking with Alexis de Tocqueville's *Democracy in America* and James Bryce's *The American Commonwealth*. But whereas Tocqueville and Bryce celebrated American democracy, Myrdal denigrated it.

The central thesis of *An American Dilemma* was that America's racial problems were intertwined with the democratic process. America's "extreme democracy" fostered and legitimated racism. Myrdal argued that American racist impulses were so strong that segregation could not be overturned through the democratic process, leaving America caught in a dilemma between its creed of equality and the reality of segregation. Myrdal acknowledged that "an educational offensive against racial intolerance, going deeper than the reiteration of the 'glittering generalities' in the nation's political creed, has never seriously been attempted in America," but he believed that only the educated could be rescued from their racist instincts by reason.

Even here all was not assured. Anticipating what Critical Race Theorists would later call "aversive racism," Myrdal wrote that "there are few liberals, even in New England, who have not a well-furnished compartment of race prejudice, even if it is usually suppressed from conscious attention." Nevertheless, his biases in favor of rule by educated elites inflated his partisan readers with a sense of moral superiority and strengthened their belief that the moral imperative of ending segregation was above the rough-and-tumble of political debate. It was a job for the clerisy, the intelligentsia, to accomplish.

Myrdal concluded that if segregation was ever to end, America "has to do something big and do it soon." He put his hopes on the NAACP's litigation campaign attacking school segregation and hoped that one day soon the Supreme Court would apply the "spirit of the Reconstruction Amendments" to conclude that segregation was "flagrantly illegal."

The generous reception *An American Dilemma* received was not lost on Thurgood Marshall and his NAACP team of litigators, who were mounting an assault on segregation in the courts. Nathan Margold, a protégé of Harvard Law Professor Felix Frankfurter, was hired to draft the NAACP's strategy. Margold was a "legal realist." Legal realists downgraded precedent and original intent as tools of legal interpretation in favor of sociological approaches to law. They taught that law, even constitutional law, was simply an arm of social policy.

Myrdal's *An American Dilemma* gave the NAACP the confidence and ammunition it needed to push the legal realist argument in court. In his book, *The NAACP's Legal Strategy against Segregated Education, 1925–1950*, Mark Tushnet gave Myrdal credit for advancing the sociological approach to law. Tushnet wrote: "It was only natural for the NAACP lawyers to find satisfying an argument that allowed them to draw upon something as highly regarded as *An American Dilemma*."

CHAPTER FOUR

The Brown Decision

A t daybreak on Tuesday December 9, 1952, Washington, D.C., was covered in a cloud of fog so dense that National Airport was closed. Although much of the fog had lifted by early afternoon, it hung thick in the courtroom of the Supreme Court as the nine Justices took up the next case on their docket, an appeal by the NAACP of school desegregation suits it had lost in lower courts. Few in the courtroom, which was decorated with twenty-four marble columns that were a personal gift from Italian dictator Benito Mussolini, realized that this dispute would have far-reaching implications that would eventually devitalize American democracy. The item on the Court's agenda was actually a consolidation of five cases—from Delaware, the District of Columbia, Virginia, South Carolina, and Kansas—all addressing the constitutionality of racial segregation in public schools. It was the name of the Kansas lawsuit by which the entire set of cases would become known: *Brown v. Board of Education of Topeka*.

Brown has become such a powerful symbol of the end of segregation that it is now widely forgotten that after World War II the end of segregation was in sight as a democratic outcome. After *Brown*'s three days of argument had ended, the *New Republic* editorialized that postwar America was already poised to end segregation "in the onward rush of American history" from "the democratic heart of free men." "What the Supreme Court eventually decides will have little effect in altering the course of that history."

Ever since that journal of opinion had featured a special section, "The Negro: His Future in America," advocating segregation's abolition a decade earlier, America had been moving toward the end of segregation. Wartime labor shortages and postwar economic growth opened new opportunities for blacks, and many segregated workplaces became desegregated. In 1941 President Franklin Delano Roosevelt formed the Fair Employment Practices Committee to guard against racial discrimination by defense contractors. This trend was strengthened by the war against Hitler's regime that had reduced Jewish rights and then decimated the Jewish population. Later, the Cold War, which prompted Soviet attacks on U.S. segregation, provided another spur for change.

In 1946 President Harry Truman appointed a Committee on Civil Rights whose report, *To Secure These Rights*, called for the "elimination of segregation, based on race, color, creed, or national origin, from American life." Truman urged Congress to pass civil rights legislation and issued executive orders in 1948 to end segregation in federal employment and the military. Truman also eliminated the segregation requirements of federal housing mortgage insurance, and, as a *Washington Post* editorial noted the day *Brown*'s arguments began, President-elect Eisenhower promised during the 1952 campaign to end segregation in the District of Columbia.

Societal attitudes were also moving away from segregation. A July 1944 survey of college students found that 68 percent agreed that "our postwar policy should be to end discrimination

THE BROWN DECISION   31

against the Negro in schools, colleges and universities." Georgia's progressive governor, Ellis G. Arnall, accomplished the repeal of the poll tax in 1945 and thereby knocked down a barrier to black voting. Jackie Robinson broke the color line in baseball in 1947, and black entertainers such as Lena Horne found increased access to Hollywood and Broadway. In response to the Truman civil rights committee's report, ordinary people, such as citizens of Montclair, New Jersey, took community inventories to expose and challenge local segregation. The Red Cross eliminated the racial designation of blood donors in 1950. Oklahoma high school students ignored traditional prejudices and elected a seventeen-year-old black to lead the state's Hi-Y youth clubs in January 1952.

In the May 1991 *Virginia Law Review*, Professor Michael J. Klarman reports that by the late 1940s blacks in the upper South were occasionally winning local office with the help of substantial numbers of white votes. He cites the failure of the 1948 Dixiecrat ticket in the Southern states as evidence of growing Southern liberalism. National Opinion Research Center polls showed growing acceptance among white Southerners of integrated transportation and interracial residential proximity. He reports that some cities in the deep South were contemplating desegregating sporting contests and integrating the police force. He attributes the evolving racial attitudes to greater urbanization, industrialization, education, and prosperity and to persuasion by churches and universities. Klarman concludes in the June 1994 *Journal of American History* that "*Brown* was not necessary as an impetus to challenge the racial status quo."

Despite these advances, many were impatient that the social transformation wasn't coming fast enough. Thurgood Marshall was one of them when, in the climax of the NAACP's campaign to end segregation by judicial fiat, he stepped up to the Supreme Court's podium at 3:15 P.M. on December 9, 1952. It was strange that the great moral issue of the day was being debated in the

Supreme Court instead of across First Street in the U.S. Congress or in state legislatures. It was even stranger that the debate was not about the law but about sociological theories and the interpretation of doll experiments.

As Marshall was getting up, his colleague Robert Carter was sitting down. Carter had just been bruised by questions from the bench, especially from Justice Felix Frankfurter, a former Harvard law professor. Frankfurter had jumped on Carter's argument that the series of Supreme Court precedents mandating equal access and facilities under the Supreme Court's 1896 "separate but equal" doctrine implied an overturning of the *Plessy* ruling itself.

It is unclear why Frankfurter, who wanted to overturn the separate but equal doctrine, objected to Carter's line of legal argument. Perhaps Frankfurter was signaling the plaintiffs that the road to victory was not through the law. Frankfurter revealed his own approach to the case when he later asked Marshall whether the Court could "take judicial notice of Gunnar Myrdal's book."

In his argument, Marshall pled psychology, anthropology, and sociology. He did not base his appeal on an argument that the district courts had misread the law, but on the fact that the judges had rejected and ignored the social science data he had proffered. He complained that "the court completely disregarded" Kenneth Clark's research examining black schoolchildren and their perceptions of black and white dolls. A negative impression of black dolls was Marshall's evidence that segregation was unconstitutional.

John W. Davis, the opposing counsel, made short work of Marshall's argument. Davis had such a magnificent presence in court that a judge once commented that whenever he heard Davis argue a case, he closed his mind to Davis' argument for at least a week to let its magic subside. Oliver Wendell Holmes, who sat on the Supreme Court for thirty years, said that no advocate who ever appeared before him was "more elegant, more clear, more concise, or more logical" than John W. Davis.

Davis' oratory was honed in a brilliant career that included membership in the House of Representatives, service as the solicitor general in the Wilson administration, diplomacy as ambassador to Great Britain, defeat as the Democratic party's presidential nominee in Calvin Coolidge's 1924 landslide, and founder of a blue-chip New York City law firm that still bears his name—Davis, Polk & Wardwell. Davis so enjoyed lawyering that he declined an appointment to the Supreme Court. As a Wall Street lawyer, he literally wrote the book on appellate litigation. In this century, no one has argued as many cases before the Supreme Court. Among his many victories was one over President Truman in the Steel Seizure Case.

Never had two opponents been so mismatched as that day in 1952. Marshall himself regarded Davis as "the greatest solicitor general we ever had." Whenever Davis argued before the Supreme Court, Marshall would skip his classes at Howard University Law School to see the great man at work. It had left Marshall awed. "Will I ever, ever?" he asked himself, "No, never."

Davis was not a segregationist. As solicitor general he had persuaded the Supreme Court to strike down Oklahoma's voting statute that limited black voting. It was a historic case, marking the first time that the NAACP entered a Supreme Court case by filing an amicus curiae (friend of the court) brief in support of Davis' position. During his presidential campaign, he condemned the Ku Klux Klan for racial and religious bigotry.

Now seventy-nine and silver-haired, Davis was in command of the law. He was ecstatic when he read Marshall's brief and discovered that it relied on sociological rather than legal argument. Davis regarded the brief as "fluff" that could not move any court and confided to a lawyer friend, "I think I have never read a drearier lot of testimony than that furnished by the so-called educational and psychological experts." Davis confidently told an associate that "unless the Supreme Court wants to make the law over," something he thought no thoroughgoing jurist would do, "they must rule with me."

Marshall, younger, taller, and mustachioed, was fired by the morality of his cause. He handled the case more as a damage liability claim than a point of constitutional law. Harm had been done and was being done, and he had social scientists as witnesses. Law was not Marshall's strong point. William O. Douglas, with whom Marshall later served on the Supreme Court, regarded Marshall as "a fine individual" but one who is "extremely opinionated and not very well trained in the law." Judge Henry Friendly, with whom Marshall sat on the Second Circuit Court of Appeals, thought that Marshall took the law too lightly. He wrote to Justice Felix Frankfurter:

> I do not have the feeling that he realizes the difficulties of his job and is burning the midnight oil in an effort to conquer them; rather he seems convinced that the problems are pretty easy and that he is fairly well equipped to grapple with them—or rather to follow someone else's grapple. All this makes life fairly easy for him, save when he is confronted with a difference of opinion, and then he tosses a coin.

Davis found little legal argument to address in Marshall's presentation and after noting that fact before the Court—"the evidence offered by the plaintiffs... does not tread on constitutional right"—he turned to the doll experiments. Davis showed that this evidence, "be its merit what it may," actually contradicted Marshall's argument. Davis cited the results of Clark's surveys of children's preferences for white and black dolls: 62 percent of black children in the segregated South chose the white doll, as opposed to 72 percent in the nonsegregated North; when children were asked which doll was nice, 52 percent in the South chose the white doll as opposed to 68 percent in the North; when children were asked which doll was bad, 49 percent in the segregated

South said the black doll was bad compared to 71 percent of Northern children. Davis then revealed that Clark's court testimony was contrary to his published results. Obviously, a preference for white dolls among black Southern schoolchildren could not be interpreted as evidence of segregation's inimical effects when black schoolchildren in nonsegregated Northern states showed a stronger preference for white dolls. Clark's testimony that segregation produced negative, self-destructive tendencies among blacks resulting in self-hatred lay in ruins.

In his rebuttal, Marshall floundered. He responded to Davis merely by claiming the superiority of his social science experts. It was at this point that Frankfurter interjected Myrdal. Everyone knew that Justice Frankfurter was referring to the 1944 book, *An American Dilemma: The Negro Problem and Modern Democracy*, by his Swedish socialist friend, Gunnar Myrdal. During Myrdal's extended visits to the United States to work on his study, he had become a favorite of American intellectuals such as Frankfurter and his Harvard colleague, John Kenneth Galbraith. When Myrdal needed special State Department clearance for a wartime flight to Sweden in 1942, he listed Frankfurter as a reference. Upon the publication of Myrdal's study, Frankfurter swore that it was "indispensable."

Marshall's inability to convince the Court in 1952 was not due to any preference for segregation among the nine Justices. Segregation had no friend on the Supreme Court. Marshall's problem, and the one Frankfurter would overcome, was reluctance on the part of the majority of the Court to usurp legislative power and democratic process in the name of a just result, especially when the entire body of law on separate but equal stood in opposition to Marshall's goal. The legal problem greatly troubled Chief Justice Frederick M. Vinson, because the same Congress that had passed the Fourteenth Amendment had also segregated the schools in the District of Columbia. That fact made the argument unconvincing

that Congress intended the Fourteenth Amendment to abolish segregation.

When the Justices meet to settle cases, they shake one another's hands before sitting down by seniority in their leather chairs
surrounding the large table in the center of the Supreme Court's
oak-paneled conference room. They followed this routine on
Saturday, December 13, 1952. Oliver Wendell Holmes' small car-
riage clock, sitting atop the black marble mantle above the fire-
place, had just struck noon. With the great John Marshall, who
served from 1801 to 1835, staring down from an imposing portrait
hanging on the wall just above Justice Holmes' clock, Chief Justice
Frederick M. Vinson, Marshall's ninth successor, opened the meeting. Vinson had been President Franklin Roosevelt's "top utility-
man" for the New Deal and Harry Truman's Treasury secretary
before being appointed Chief Justice. He soberly noted that the
whole "body of law back of us on separate but equal" stood in
opposition to Thurgood Marshall's desired result. The Chief Justice
found it "hard to get away from" this conclusion.

Going by seniority, each Justice then spoke in turn. Hugo
Black had been appointed to the Court by President Roosevelt as a
reward for having deflected criticism of the New Deal by conduct-
ing a heavy-handed Senate investigation of alleged corruption in
the Hoover administration. Black hesitated to put the courts on the
"battle front," because it would lead to "law by injunction."

Stanley Reed, who had been appointed by Roosevelt in 1938
after defending the New Deal as solicitor general, said that he
would uphold the separate but equal doctrine. He was satisfied
that constant progress by blacks meant that "segregation is gradually disappearing." He regarded desegregation as a problem the
states should work out for themselves.

And so the conference continued. Justice William O. Douglas
later wrote in his autobiography that only three Justices in addition
to himself considered school segregation to be unconstitutional.

Douglas was a brilliant eccentric from Washington state who had worked his way through Columbia Law School. He had been a Yale law professor and then head of the newly formed Securities and Exchange Commission before being appointed to the Court by Roosevelt at age forty-one. Douglas recognized difficulties, but thought that the Court should act swiftly to end segregation. Justices Sherman Minton and Harold Burton, former midwestern senators appointed to the Court by Truman, shared Douglas' opinion.

Justice Tom Clark, a close friend of Chief Justice Vinson who voted with him 90 percent of the time, had been Harry Truman's attorney general. While in his own mind he wanted *Plessy* to be overturned, he was concerned that Court precedent had led the states to believe that "separate but equal" was "okay." He did not want to rush to go back on the law.

Although most of the questions from the bench during oral arguments had come from Felix Frankfurter, Frankfurter did not show his cards. As a law professor, Frankfurter had been an exponent of judicial restraint. His problem now was to figure out how to move the Court to abandon restraint and to strike down the segregation that he abhorred. He knew the decision would have to be unanimous because of the absence of a strong legal argument. To give himself time, Frankfurter urged that the case should be reargued.

The man whose comments made things most difficult for Frankfurter and the other Justices who were trying to dispose of segregation was Justice Robert H. Jackson. To Jackson, such a ruling would constitute a blatantly political act. Jackson, the former chief prosecutor of Nazi war criminals at Nuremberg, said that instead of thinking like a policymaker, he approached the issue "as a lawyer." Jackson was a former general counsel to the Bureau of Internal Revenue and had won a $750,000 judgment against former Treasury Secretary Andrew Mellon. On this victory his career soared, and he became a close Roosevelt advisor as

solicitor general and attorney general. It was clear to Jackson
that nothing in the text, court opinions, or history of the
Fourteenth Amendment warranted the conclusion that segregation was unconstitutional. Jackson feared the "ruthless use of federal judicial power" that would follow if segregation were abolished by decree. Jackson also opposed taking such an extraordinary course based on nonlegal opinion. He noted that Thurgood
Marshall's brief "starts and ends with sociology."

Jackson's clerk, William H. Rehnquist, who had graduated at
the top of his class at Stanford Law School and would someday sit
on the Court himself as a Justice and then Chief Justice, summed
up this position in a memo Jackson asked him to prepare about
Brown. Echoing a famous dissent by Oliver Wendell Holmes—that
the Constitution did not enact Herbert Spencer's book, *Social
Statics*—Rehnquist wrote that the Fourteenth Amendment "sure-
ly did not enact Myrdal's *American Dilemma*." Despite Jackson's
disdain for segregation, he thought it should be ended legislative-
ly, not judicially.

Thurgood Marshall's eventual victory in the *Brown* decision
could not have occurred without Justice Felix Frankfurter.
Recognizing the strength of the arguments against ending segregation by judicial fiat, Frankfurter designed a strategy to ease the
Court around the obstacles. He knew that a decision striking down
segregation had to be unanimous to have the sheen of legitimacy.
To achieve this outcome, Justice Frankfurter had to figure out
some way to neutralize the decades of precedent stemming from
Plessy, and he had to divert the NAACP from the implausible argument that the original intent of the Fourteenth Amendment was to
abolish segregation. The former law professor had to persuade
old-fashioned lawyers to give sociology priority over law.

Initially, Frankfurter was not sure how he was going to re-
educate the Court. So he orchestrated a two-year delay and subsequent reargument of the case to overcome Marshall's initial failure

before the Court in 1952. During the time gained, he conspired with the solicitor general's office to shape the Justice Department's briefs and oral argument in a manner designed to sway his colleagues on the Court. It took him almost two years and required the help of his clerk, Alexander Bickel, and former clerk, Philip Elman, a Justice Department official, to overcome the legal scruples of his fellow Supreme Court Justices. Thus, the *Brown* decision was won not only at the expense of the democratic process, but also at the expense of judicial impartiality.

The change in administration from Truman to Eisenhower early in 1953 gave Frankfurter an opportunity. As the Court's term progressed, Frankfurter reiterated his position that the case should be reargued to give the new administration a chance to submit a brief and to participate in oral argument.

Toward the end of May 1953, after the Justices had heard the last arguments for the term, they met to divide up their remaining writing assignments so that they could leave for their summer recess. Frankfurter returned from this conference to his chambers in a "euphoric" mood. He told his clerk, Alexander Bickel, who would later become a Yale law professor, that he had convinced his colleagues to order a reargument the next autumn.

Unbeknownst to his fellow colleagues, Frankfurter had assigned Bickel to do research on the history of the Fourteenth Amendment and the Reconstruction Congress and state legislatures that had enacted it. Frankfurter was hoping that language might be found that would either strengthen Marshall's or weaken Davis' position on original intent. But the chance was slight. Jack Greenberg, a member of the NAACP's legal team, reports in his autobiography that no less a foe of segregation than historian Henry Steele Commager told the NAACP that the framers of the Fourteenth Amendment did not "intend that it should be used to end segregation in schools." Commager urged the NAACP not to base its case on the intent of the Fourteenth Amendment.

Bickel found that it was impossible to conclude that the thirty-ninth Congress foresaw that segregation might be abolished, because public education was in its infancy. Moreover, where it existed it was often segregated, even in the North. Indeed, it was only after the Civil War that public education was widely established in the South. A prominent Virginia Episcopal clergyman, the Reverend Kinloch Nelson, had fought public education and labeled it "essentially communistic." For former slaves, public education, even though segregated, was a step forward. Had segregation not existed in the schools, public education would have lost what weak support it had.

Bickel urged a different approach. He argued that the language used by the Constitution's framers was so elastic that the Court could reinterpret it according to the needs of the times. From this perspective, Bickel argued that the legislative history of the Fourteenth Amendment was "inconclusive."

On June 8, 1953, the Supreme Court unanimously restored *Brown* to the docket for reargument on October 12. To be discussed were questions about original intent and the implementation of a possible decree ending segregation that Bickel and Frankfurter had drafted. The last sentence of the two-page order's list of questions invited the attorney general of the United States to take part in the oral argument and file an additional brief "if he so desires."

This seemingly innocuous sentence was in reality a lateral pass from Frankfurter to Philip Elman who, after a stint as Frankfurter's clerk in the 1940s, had been serving on the solicitor general's staff. At the solicitor general's office, Elman handled all civil rights cases before the Supreme Court in which the United States was involved as either a party or amicus curiae.

In the judicial equivalent of insider trading, Frankfurter and Elman frequently discussed *Brown* by telephone and in person. Elman had used confidential information from Frankfurter to shape the Truman administration's *Brown* brief to influence the

Justices' views more effectively. Frankfurter and Elman used code names for the various Justices. Justice Douglas was "Yak" because he came from Yakima, Washington. Hugo Black was "Lafayette," his middle name. Justice Minton was "Shay." Stanley Reed was "Chamer," meaning fool, dolt, or mule in Hebrew. And "Jamestown" was the code name for Justice Jackson, referring to Jackson's hometown in upstate New York.

Frankfurter counted on Elman collaborating again. In fact, the idea that the cases should be reargued was hatched during one of Frankfurter and Elman's strategy sessions. The coconspirators believed that if the government's "independent" examination of original intent would mirror the conclusion of Bickel's internal court memo, Davis' legal argument could be neutralized.

Elman's first hurdle at the Justice Department was to overcome the fact that the new administration would have been happier if the Supreme Court's special invitation to the attorney general had been lost in the mail. Attorney General Herbert Brownell called a meeting of top Justice Department officials. Included were Assistant Attorney General Warren Burger, who would be appointed Chief Justice by President Nixon, and Deputy Attorney General William Rogers, who would later become attorney general and President Nixon's secretary of state. Rogers expressed the prevailing attitude: "Jesus, do we really *have* to file a brief? Aren't we better off staying out of it?" Elman, one of the two Truman holdovers to attend the meeting, said, "When the Supreme Court invites you, that's the equivalent of a royal command. An invitation from the Supreme Court just can't be rejected. Besides, if you turn it down, how are you going to explain it to the press?"

Elman won his point. At the beginning of August, Assistant Attorney General J. Lee Rankin called Elman into his office and assigned him the task of leading the Justice Department's research effort and drafting its brief.

The first thing Elman did was to convince Attorney General

Brownell to ask the Supreme Court to delay the reargument. Chief Justice Fred Vinson complied with Brownell's request and postponed the reargument from October until December. Unsurprisingly, when the government's six-hundred-page brief was hand-delivered to the Supreme Court in November, it contained the same conclusion that Bickel had provided for Frankfurter: The elasticity of the Fourteenth Amendment's language, read in the light of changing times, rendered its original intent ambiguous.

Frankfurter and Elman were aided and abetted in their endeavor by the death of Chief Justice Vinson in September. To fill the vacancy, President Eisenhower appointed California Governor Earl Warren. As a governor, Warren was accustomed to the exercise of power. Unlike Vinson, Warren was prepared to exercise as much judicial power as he could get away with. He would not be deterred by arguments resting on the separation of powers and federalism. Warren saw his Court appointment as a more prestigious and powerful executive office.

Except for the new occupant of the Chief Justice's chair, the reargument was essentially a repeat performance from the year before. Justice Jackson, whose experience at Nuremberg had burned into him a deep appreciation of the separation of powers, asked Thurgood Marshall whether it was right for the Supreme Court to do what Congress had not done after the passage of so many years, namely to abolish segregation. Spottswood Robinson, another NAACP attorney, had just skirted a similar question from Justice Reed. Reed noted that section five of the Fourteenth Amendment states that "Congress shall have power to enforce, by appropriate legislation, the provisions of this article." John Davis, making his last of 140 appearances before the Court, reminded the Justices that under the Constitution's allocation of powers, "Your Honors do not sit, and cannot sit, as a glorified Board of Education for the State of South Carolina or any other state. Neither can the District Court."

Just before the reargument, Frankfurter had copies of Bickel's research memo, specially typeset in the Court's printing office, distributed to his colleagues. Frankfurter's cover memo endorsed Bickel's conclusion that the Fourteenth Amendment's elasticity of language made its original intent inconclusive. With Elman's Justice Department brief taking the same line, Davis' victory over Marshall's legal argument was neutralized. The question was pushed outside the realm of law into one where sociological arguments could carry the day.

This ploy would have failed under Chief Justice Vinson, who did not believe that the judiciary should remake the law, but Earl Warren had no such inhibitions. Warren and Frankfurter worked together to persuade their colleagues to speak with a unanimous voice to end segregation. As a politician, Warren had the interpersonal skills to promote the goal that Frankfurter's pedantic manner impeded. Frankfurter wrote his colleagues long memos rationalizing the result he wanted. He urged that law must respond to the "transformation of views" and the "changes in men's feelings for what is right and just." Yet, as spring approached, and Warren's recess appointment was finally confirmed by the Senate, Justices Reed and Jackson still held out.

Jackson continued to view segregation as a question of politics and, therefore, believed that it could not be abolished as a judicial act. Reed asked his clerk to draft a dissent. When his clerk, John Fasset, balked and said that he thought the other side had reached the right decision, Reed asked him whether he favored a "kritarchy." His crack legal assistant did not know what the word meant, so Reed pointed to the *Oxford English Dictionary*. Fasset soon learned the definition of the phenomenon whose inception he was witnessing—government by judges.

At the end of March 1954, Jackson suffered a nonfatal heart attack. Warren seized the opportunity and rushed to the hospital. Taking advantage of Jackson's weakened state, Warren successfully pressured him to join the opinion that he had drafted. With Jackson's vote in his pocket, Warren told Reed, "Stan, you're all by yourself in this now. You've got to decide whether it's really the best thing for the country." Isolated, Reed caved in to Warren's pressure, but reportedly never agreed with the decision.

On May 17, 1954, Frankfurter's strategy triumphed when Warren read the unanimous opinion from the bench. Chief Justice Earl Warren kept the opinion brief so that it would fit into newspapers without having to be excerpted. As legal reasoning played no role, brevity was not a problem. The gist of the opinion was captured by a *New York Times* headline on May 18, 1954: "A Sociological Decision: Court Founded Its Segregation Ruling On Hearts and Minds Rather Than Laws." James Reston commented that "the Court's opinion reads more like an expert paper on sociology."

It is easy to understand the Court's preference for sociology. Segregation was supported by more than a half century of precedent based on the 1896 *Plessy v. Ferguson* separate-but-equal doctrine. Moreover, the Court's reargument and reexamination of the intent of the Fourteenth Amendment was, at best, inconclusive. Chief Justice Warren shrugged off the legal issues with the statement that "we cannot turn the clock back to 1868 when the Amendment was adopted, or even to 1896 when *Plessy v. Ferguson* was written." The relevant question, he said, is whether "segregation of children in public schools solely on the basis of race, even though the physical facilities and other 'tangible' factors may be equal, deprive the children of the minority group of equal educational opportunities?" The Court's answer was, "We believe that it does."

The *Plessy* decision, he reasoned, was based on inadequate psychological knowledge, and its continued use as precedent was inconsistent with modern authority. At this point he attached a paragraph-long footnote listing social science references beginning with Kenneth Clark's doll experiments and ending: "And see generally Myrdal, *An American Dilemma* (1944)." Warren concluded, "Separate educational facilities are inherently unequal." He limited this ruling to "the field of public education."

Minutes after the Chief Justice read the opinion from the Supreme Court bench, the Voice of America flashed news of it around the globe in thirty-four languages. The *New York Times* editorial board declared that the Warren Court was "the guardian of our national conscience" and congratulated the Court for reaffirming faith "in the equality of all men and all children before the law." The *Nation* editorialized that the Supreme Court's decision replaced the *Plessy* precedent and made Justice John Marshall Harlan's original dissent in that case the law of the land. A subsequent *New York Times* editorial repeated the *Nation's* interpretation that Harlan's "voice crying in the wilderness" in 1896 finally became "the expression of a people's will."

The *Washington Post*, for its part, editorialized that the decision "affords all Americans an occasion for pride and gratification" and said that the decision "will bring to an end a painful disparity between American principles and American practices." The *Post* expressed "to the Court a warm sense of gratitude for a great service nobly discharged." An expanded editorial the next day said that "the manner in which this decision was rendered reflects judicial statesmanship of the highest order" and that the decision represents "a new birth of freedom.... Abroad as well as at home, this decision will engender a renewal of faith in democratic institutions and ideals."

The *Boston Herald* also rejoiced that the "frankly expedient" decision proves that "the Constitution is still a live and growing document.... It recognizes the growing national feeling that the separation of Negroes (or other minority) children from the majority race at school age is an abuse of the democratic process and the democratic principle."

Harvard Law School Dean Erwin N. Griswold justified the

ruling not on its legal merit but for "carrying out the spirit which lies behind" the equal protection clause. And Yale Law School Dean Wesley A. Sturges said frankly that "the Court had to make the law."

Former Secretary of State Dean Acheson, who witnessed Warren deliver the opinion, gave his opinion that the decision was "great and statesmanlike." Harvard historian Arthur M. Schlesinger declared that "this is wonderful" and that "the Supreme Court has finally reconciled the Constitution with the preamble of the Declaration of Independence." Schlesinger predicted that the decision "will be a very great aid in clarifying to the world our conception of democracy."

There was, of course, dissent from these accolades. Some felt that democratic processes had taken a hit, but these forebodings seemed unimportant. The implications of Myrdal's argument—that democratic processes could not be relied upon to produce the morally correct result—passed unnoticed in the jubilation over the fall of segregation.

There were other pitfalls in the judicial resolution of segregation. In the *Federalist Papers* James Madison had foreseen that the American experiment would be tested by its ability to protect the liberty of minorities without employing favoritism or extrademocratic measures. He reasoned that there are two alternative methods of preventing majorities from oppressing minorities. One is consistent with democracy and a rule of law; the other leads back to privilege and feudalism.

The wrong approach, Madison said, is to create "a will in the community independent of the majority—that is, of the society itself." He noted that this approach "prevails in all governments possessing an hereditary or self-appointed authority." This option provided a "precarious security" because "a power independent of the society may as well espouse the unjust views of the major as the rightful interests of the minor party, and may possibly be turned against both parties." Madison thought that the greatest danger would be the emergence of a "will independent of the society itself." A will not dependent on majority opinion would inevitably come to resemble the tyranny that the colonists had repelled in the American Revolution.

Madison believed that the new American society embraced a more promising method of protecting against the tyranny of the majority. The many different factions and opinions "will render an unjust combination of a majority of the whole very improbable, if not impracticable." He compared security for civil rights in a free society to religious freedom: "It consists in the one case in the multiplicity of interests, and in the other in the multiplicity of sects." The multiplicity of interests would require compromise on shared values. Minorities would be protected by free debate to influence public opinion and, thereby, the democratic process.

Madison clearly believed that in a democratic society appeals to goodwill would produce tolerable enough results to keep society liveable for all. Indeed, it is precisely on this confidence in democratic outcomes that the American experiment is based. This confidence was shaken by Myrdal's depiction of the permanence of segregation in American democracy without the intervention of an extrademocratic power.

In *Brown*, the Supreme Court elevated Myrdal's doubts about American democracy above Madison's confidence in it and made itself a "will independent of the society." In the eyes of the Justices and their peers, desegregation had become the hallmark of moral society. This pressing goal overshadowed in importance the respect for democratic processes that had kept the antisegregation Vinson Court from overturning *Plessy*.

It was left to Columbia Law Professor Herbert Wechsler, who had assisted the NAACP as a consultant in cases leading up to and including *Brown*, to worry about the absence of any legal justification for Chief Justice Warren's central premise that segregated schools were "inherently unequal" and therefore illegal. At a speech at Harvard Law School, Wechsler suggested that Warren's premise be accepted on faith. "I should like to think there is" some neutral constitutional principle that justifies the ruling, Wechsler stated, "but I confess that I have not yet written the opinion." Perhaps the most persuasive evidence that no such principle exists is the alacrity with which legal scholars abandoned the search.

After ruling in the plaintiffs' favor, the Court delayed its implementation for a year. The Court was aware that it had intruded into social life and wanted the decision to sit rather than ruffle society too suddenly. Elman and Frankfurter had previously decided that any decree abolishing segregation had to be implemented slowly.

Finally, on May 31, 1955, the Court ruled that the nation's school districts must "make a prompt and reasonable start" of complying with the Court's ruling a year earlier. Using an oxymoron that Frankfurter had inserted into the opinion, Warren said that compliance had to be accomplished "with all deliberate speed." The federal district courts were directed to enforce this decision in what has become known as *Brown II*. As Justice Black had predicted, law by injunction was unleashed on the land.

The *Brown* decision was the product of an ex parte dialogue between a sitting judge (Frankfurter) and a litigant (Elman), which transgressed the fundamental ethical norms for judges that have changed little since English King Alfred the Great's legal reforms after his triumph over the Danes in the year 878. The bedrock of the system of justice that we have inherited is the impartiality of judges. Judges are required to conduct themselves in a manner that promotes public confidence in the integrity and the objectivity of the judiciary and must avoid even the appearance of impropriety. But in *Brown*, Frankfurter, in effect, received an ongoing brief from the government, to which neither Thurgood Marshall nor John Davis had a chance to reply.

Elman thought that this "ordinary rule" did not apply because, he wrote, "*Brown v. Board of Education*, which we fully discussed, was an extraordinary case.... In that case I knew everything, or at least [Frankfurter] gave me the impression that I knew everything, that was going on at the Court. He told me about what was said at conference and who said it."

In the February 1987 *Harvard Law Review*, Elman revealed his conspiracy with Frankfurter, not in contrition over his unethical behavior that has riven judges from the law, but to claim credit for himself and Frankfurter for "this enormous contribution to American constitutional law of the 20th century." Defending himself from impropriety, Elman said, "In *Brown* I didn't consider myself a lawyer for a litigant. I considered it a cause that transcended ordinary notions about propriety in litigation." Frankfurter had been the "Kochleffel," the "man stirring everything up inside the Court." Marshall and the NAACP's briefs were not even good foils for Frankfurter, *Brown*'s "grand strategist." "Thurgood Marshall," said Elman, "could have stood up there and recited 'Mary had a little lamb,' and the result would have been exactly the same."

When Elman spilled the beans about the conspiracy, liberals who had welcomed the *Brown* decision roundly condemned the means by which it was obtained. In a rare attack on two Harvard liberals, the March 24, 1987, *New York Times* said that Frankfurter and Elman's acts were "deeply disturbing" and "crossed a clear ethical line." The editorial, "With All Deliberate Impropriety," noted that if a Justice had similarly collaborated with the Reagan Justice Department over abortion, "there'd be instant demands for resignation and threats of impeachment for impropriety. Loftiness of purpose or concern for national interest would be no defense." Dismayed that the means had sullied the ends, the *Times* acknowledged: "It has always been improper for one side to have this kind of intimacy with a judge. It's no answer that the *Brown* case was special. Special cases bubble up in every era." Even the "hateful" segregationist states "deserved a tribunal unsullied by acts of partisanship."

Erwin N. Griswold, a former solicitor general and dean of Harvard Law School, was "startled" at the impropriety, as were many others. Griswold said the behavior of Frankfurter and Elman was "clearly regarded as improper at the time and would clearly be improper now."

Swept up by a cause, Frankfurter and Elman had forgotten that the road to tyranny is paved with noble ends. In pursuit of a just cause, they shattered the bedrock of jurisprudence—the impartiality of judges, subordinated the law to sociology, and replaced the democratic process and its appeal to goodwill with the rule of judges. The end, they thought, justified the means, and they led the Court in a new direction at odds with the American political tradition.

Despicable means cannot produce good outcomes. The *New York Times* and Griswold have kept *Brown*'s desegregation decree clutched to their breasts while denouncing the means by which it was obtained. But the most important result of *Brown* was not desegregation but the rise of kritarchy: the rule of judges. From Prince Edward County to Yonkers to Kansas City, cities, counties, and states have lost their sovereignty to federal judges who overturn democratic outcomes and usurp the power of the purse. *Brown* has led a generation of judges to believe that they are the ultimate power because the Constitution has no meaning to them other than their subjective feelings about social policy.

Rule by Judges

It is difficult to speak of the United States today as a democratic country when even the most basic functions of local governance have been taken away from towns and cities by federal judges. Yonkers is a case in point.

During World War II, the city fathers of Yonkers, New York, decided to build low cost housing for Yonkers' poorer citizens. The city followed the traditional principle of minimizing the burden of public support on the taxpayers. Consequently, the housing projects were built in low-cost areas. Decades later, this act of charity would cause Yonkers to lose its sovereignty to a federal judge.

In the late 1970s, the NAACP and the Justice Department, in a policy initiated by the Carter administration and continued by the Reagan administration, sued Yonkers for alleged racial discrimination because of its choice of site for its public housing projects. The lawsuit was absurd on its face because the original occupants of the public housing, allegedly located for segregationist reasons, were white. Yet, as Federal Judge Leonard Sand knew, once the city was branded as racist, he could use levers crafted by the judiciary in the days following *Brown* to impose his dictates as a "remedy" for the "intentional" "constitutional violation" of locating public housing in areas where property values were lowest.

Judge Sand, a wealthy Carter appointee whose wife Ann is a cousin of the publisher of the *New York Times*, lives on a thirty-two-acre estate in the picturesque Pound Ridge region of northern Westchester County, which has no public housing. But segregation is in the eye of the beholder, and he saw it in Yonkers. He ordered the elected city government to authorize four thousand new public housing units, of which one thousand would be subsidized public housing. He further ordered that these one thousand units be distributed in city neighborhoods not previously impacted by public housing.

To implement the judge's order, the democratically elected city government was required to ignore the city's zoning laws, property tax, and wishes of its citizens. Public housing projects have acquired the reputation of being hubs from which crime radiates outward to the surrounding environs. Black as well as white homeowners in Yonkers were incensed at the judge's plan to riddle their city with housing projects. Fearing the impact on their safety and property values and infuriated over the estimated 30 percent tax increase necessary to carry out the judge's plans, the citizens forced the elected city government to resist the judge's dictates. Relying on the long-standing constitutional doctrines of federalism and the separation of powers, a majority on the city council argued that a federal court does not have the authority to order them to enact specific laws, much less in direct violation of their constituents' wishes.

In the face of such resistance, Judge Sand resorted to the application of naked power in order to force the city to acquiesce quickly. He imposed $500 daily fines on the city's public officials and threatened them with an indeterminate stay in jail until they voted as he instructed. He then capped tyranny with absurdity by imposing a geometric fine on the city itself that would have reached $29 trillion after thirty-eight days, a sum equal to 1.5 times the gross national product of the entire world. This latter action sealed the city's fate.

A New York State law, dating back to the bankruptcy of New York City in the 1970s, permits an unelected state Emergency Financial Control Board, which is unaccountable to the electorate, to take control of a city's finances if it is threatened with bankruptcy. Since the fines meant bankruptcy for Yonkers, the control board asserted authority over the city. Its chairwoman, an ally of the judge, made the city's choice clear: "No municipal services whatsoever. No policeman when you call for help, no fire fighter when your house is burning, no garbage pickup as the trash piles up on your curb, no senior citizen services, no water as the tap runs dry." When the layoffs began, the city officials succumbed and voted as the judge had instructed.

Judge Sand's gamble paid off because he moved the situation too fast for anyone to understand what was at stake. Reagan Justice Department officials William Bradford Reynolds and Mark R. Disler covered for the judge by declaring the matter to be one of "bigotry and racism" on the part of "recalcitrant, lawless city officials." *Time* magazine and the *New York Times* led the rest of the media into erroneously characterizing the episode as "white resistance to integration." Smearing the city for resistance to racial goals covered up the destruction of its self-governance and the democratic process.

The decades of precedent rooted in *Brown* of rule by judges meant that the conservative Reagan Court ultimately saw nothing wrong with Judge Sand's assertion of power to rule Yonkers. In a five-to-four opinion, the Court did strike down the individual fines on the city council members on the grounds that the fines perverted the legislative process by encouraging the legislators "to

declare that they favor an ordinance not in order to avoid bankrupting the city for which they legislate, but in order to avoid
bankrupting themselves." Justice Brennan's dissent lamented any
limits to the discretion of federal district judges.

The rallying cry of the American Revolution was "no taxation
without representation." When the English Parliament raised
taxes on tea in 1773, the American colonists were furious. In
Philadelphia and New York, protesters prevented newly arrived
tea from leaving British ships. On the evening of December 16,
1773, Boston colonist Samuel Adams orchestrated a drama in
which three fifty-man companies masquerading as Mohawk
Indians stormed three British ships containing tea, broke open the
tea chests, and heaved them into Boston harbor to the cheers of a
multitude of spectators. The tea tax was just one of the taxes
Jefferson and his fellow members of the Continental Congress had
in mind when the Declaration of Independence attacked King
George III for "imposing Taxes on us without our Consent."

The power of taxation was limited by the founding fathers to
legislatures. As James Madison wrote in the *Federalist Papers*,
"the legislative department alone has access to the pockets of the
people." The federal judiciary's inability to wage war and impose
taxes led Alexander Hamilton to write in the *Federalist Papers*
that the federal judiciary was the "least dangerous" branch of government "to the political rights of the Constitution" because it "has
no influence over either the sword or the purse."

On April 18, 1990, the two hundred fifteenth anniversary of
Paul Revere's famous horseback ride alerting Massachusetts
colonists to the approaching British, the Supreme Court in
Missouri v. Jenkins struck a devastating blow to American democracy by grabbing the power of the purse for the judiciary. Three
years previously, U.S. District Judge Russell Clark had ordered
that property taxes be doubled in Kansas City, Missouri. The citizens of that city had spent the intervening years shouting, "No

taxation without representation!" and dumping teabags on the courthouse steps.

In 1984 Judge Clark ruled that the Kansas City, Missouri, School District operated an unconstitutional school system. Clark reached this conclusion not because the school district had discriminated against blacks or had any racially motivated animus against minorities, but because sociological testimony alleged that the school district had not done enough to achieve the proper "mathematical racial balance" in its schools.

With this "finding of fact," the judge ordered Kansas City to build a luxurious $700 million school system to draw whites back into inner city public schools. The judge required that the school have a planetarium, a vivarium, greenhouses, a model United Nations wired for language translation, radio and television studios, movie editing and screening rooms, swimming pools, a zoo, a farm, a wildland area, and a temperature-controlled art gallery. The decree also specified aesthetically pleasing carpets and fifteen computers per classroom. The judge even ordered the hiring of public relations specialists to persuade the public to embrace his edict. Besides decreeing that buildings should be built, the judge also decreed, over the objections of citizens and historic preservationists, that other buildings be demolished, including Kansas City's historic Paseo High School, which was made of a unique type of limestone.

All of this, and nothing less, the judge insisted, was required by the U.S. Constitution. When the citizens of Kansas City balked at his decree and voted not to finance his social experiment, he struck down as unconstitutional a supermajority requirement in Missouri's Constitution for property tax levies over $3.25 per $100 assessed value and raised the taxes himself. In *Missouri v. Jenkins*, the Supreme Court let stand the Kansas City plan and laid down a precedent establishing the procedures for taxation by a local federal district judge whenever he or she is moved with the spirit of social engineering. This extraordinary destruction of American democracy is the true legacy of *Brown*.

In the *Jenkins* case, Justices Kennedy, Rehnquist, O'Connor, and Scalia said that the Court's "casual embrace of taxation imposed by the unelected, life-tenured federal judiciary disregards fundamental precepts for the democratic control of public institutions." The four Justices reminded their colleagues that under the Constitution, "the power of taxation is one that the federal judiciary does not possess" and that the taxing power is reserved for the legislature, which reflects "our ideal that the power of taxation must be under the control of those who are taxed."

Brown has proved to be a slippery slope. Once the end justifies the means, the fundamental principles that undergird the Constitution—democratic process, the separation of powers, and federalism—are all expendable. Today we are ruled by the anti-American ideas of Gunnar Myrdal operating through the federal judiciary. In chasing after the devil of segregation, we have cut a swath through democracy.

Even the *Washington Post*, which worships at the shrine of *Brown*, was stunned by the decision. The newspaper editorialized that "the taxpayers of Kansas City, Missouri, must be wondering if they have for years completely misunderstood all the civics courses they took in high school." Yet the Missouri result was nothing but the logical outcome of *Brown*. If people are stunned by the falling pillars of our constitutional order, it is because they did not realize the antidemocratic blows struck by *Brown*.

Just as Madison feared, as the result of favoring one faction in the political process, the American Revolution has been subverted by an unchecked "will independent of society." Judge Clark did exactly what the Declaration of Independence condemned King George III for doing: "imposing taxes on us without our Consent... taking away our Charters, abolishing our most valuable Laws, and altering fundamentally the forms of our Governments."

After the Supreme Court gave its blessing to judicial taxation, the *New York Times* mocked the critics of Judges Clark and Sand in an April 20, 1990, editorial, "Oh, Those Imperial Judges!" "With remarkable generosity," the Supreme Court "has upheld the broad powers of Federal judges to devise creative remedies for constitutional violations," the paper said. "Vindicating those rights against recalcitrant officials often forces judges to step down from their judicial thrones into gritty local reality." By referring to the judicial benches as thrones, the *Times* at least recognized that American democracy had been supplanted by a new form of royalty. Missing from the editorial was any recognition of the constitutional violations resulting from the judges' remedies. Racial integration had become a more important constitutional principle than any other. One supreme end has mowed down the unique achievement known as American constitutional democracy.

Granted, this outcome was not apparent to very many when the *Brown* decision was handed down. Moreover, any second thoughts about the democratic process and the separation of powers were quickly lost in the uproar over Southern resistance to the federal judiciary's implementation of the decision. Judges were believed to need all the power they could assume to stand up to such uncouth products of the democratic process as Arkansas Governor Orval Faubus, Georgia Governor Lester Maddox, and Alabama Governor George Wallace. The Southern resistance was seen as confirmation of Myrdal's premise that democracy would not produce moral outcomes. Many saw no alternative to judicial coercion of a recalcitrant populace.

Yonkers and Kansas City were presaged by what happened in a Virginia county. Rather than submit to the governance of distant judges, Prince Edward County, Virginia, decided to get out of the business of running public schools altogether. Neither Virginia nor federal law required Prince Edward County to maintain public schools, and the action the county took in closing the public schools was perfectly legal. But it was seen by the Supreme Court and the NAACP as an act of white defiance that would undercut *Brown* throughout the South. In 1964 the Court produced a ruling that the county had transgressed *Brown*'s new interpretation of the Fourteenth Amendment because it had closed its schools for impermissible reasons of race. The Court did not have to prove the county's motives but merely assert them, and it issued its own law to fill the statutory void by requiring the county to provide a public school system.

This time the Court lost the unanimity that had been carefully crafted for *Brown*. Justices Tom Clark and John Marshall Harlan (grandson of the *Plessy* dissenter) dissented from the view that the federal judiciary had the power to order governments to provide public schooling. But in an editorial typical of the reaction to the ruling, the *New Republic* dismissed the eyebrows that were raised, and gave its opinion that the "holding presented no doctrinal difficulties." After all, schools were being integrated, and the end justified the means.

The judiciary soon asserted new powers over local affairs. Fully integrated schools in the sense of reflecting black/white population ratios were still blocked by the tradition of neighborhood school districts. If the neighborhoods were not thoroughly integrated, neither would be the schools. This required remedial action.

It came from a judge on the Fifth Circuit Court of Appeals named Minor Wisdom. He decreed that *Brown* meant schools had a positive duty to integrate, not merely to cease segregating. In making this decree the judge ignored the clear statutory language of the 1964 Civil Rights Act that "desegregation" is "the assignment of students to public schools and within such schools without regard to their race, color, religion, or national origin" and that "'desegregation' shall not mean the assignment of students to public schools in order to overcome racial imbalance." Judge

Wisdom, however, recognized that the judiciary could bypass any statute that Congress passed because *Brown* had given the judiciary the power to rewrite the Constitution.

The Supreme Court embraced Wisdom's ruling and gave it the imprimatur of constitutional obligation. By the early 1970s, the Supreme Court had enunciated a national policy of massive busing schemes that transported students daily many miles from their neighborhoods to distant schools where they were assigned on the basis of race for the sole purpose of achieving what judges considered to be the proper statistical mix of black and white students.

The irony of his decision was lost on Judge Wisdom. In the cases leading up to *Brown*, the NAACP's expert witnesses had cited the injury experienced by the black plaintiffs from being bused nine miles across town to segregated black schools. The "bus travel increased fatigue and irritability, thereby impairing the learning process." In his own argument of the case before the Court, Thurgood Marshall had said that the Constitution does not require integration, but merely forbids the use of government power to enforce segregation. These arguments had been important in producing the *Brown* decision, but with *Brown* decided, the Justices found that there was no longer any constraint on their interpretative powers, and these arguments could be stood on their head.

The extraordinary accumulation and exercise of power by the judiciary shows the extent to which federal judges have become a "will independent of society itself." As time goes by, the malevolent implications of Myrdal's thesis that democracy cannot produce the correct moral results becomes more apparent.

With each passing year judges deliver more blows to the principle of popular sovereignty that culminated in the American Revolution, the Declaration of Independence, and the Constitution. "We the People" are deemed unable to rise above prejudices and, therefore, unable to serve society's true interests. Judges and regulatory bureaucrats have assumed the functions of legislators.

In their Kansas City dissent, Justice Anthony Kennedy and his three colleagues pointed out that "there is no obvious limit to [the ruling] that would prevent judicial taxation in cases involving prisons, hospitals or other public institutions, or indeed to pay a large damages award levied against a municipality."

In other words, all U.S. property owners now have unpredictable and open-ended financial obligations for which there is no recourse. Any federal judge can decree that anything less than a country club life for prisoners is "cruel and unusual punishment" and mandate taxes to accommodate and educate prisoners according to the standards that prevail in civil society. Federal judges can now redesign the physical plant of every school system to match the fabulously luxurious one that Judge Clark ordered in Kansas City. Edicts can now be issued mandating the location, amenities, and square-footage per resident of public housing, along with an enforceable judicial order to raise taxes to pay for it. Similarly for all public hospitals. Taxpayers can now be saddled with the costs of equipping them to the standards, or for that matter above the standards, of the most expensive private hospitals. Federal judges can now destroy legislative resistance by levying massive damage awards against municipalities and states and ordering them to raise taxes to pay up.

In Prince Edward County, Yonkers, and Kansas City, fundamental precepts of representative democracy fell into the constitutional sinkhole inaugurated by *Brown*. Judges are free to use any means in the pursuit of their view of social morality. Clear, unambiguous language and original intent carry no weight. *Brown*, based as it was on doll experiments and sociological speculation, let all future litigants know that courts of law no longer rule on the basis of law.

Brown's assault on democracy shows no sign of abating. In our nation's law schools, Myrdalian sociology is supplanting the study of law. Statute and legal precedent are diminishing in importance as *Brown*'s precedential example of sociological sentiment coerced through judicial decree is hailed as the answer to every perceived social ill.

The Assault on Freedom
of Conscience

The transformation of a government of elites into a democracy rested upon faith in the ability of ordinary people to recognize right from wrong. Liberals were confident that within each human heart there existed a moral gyroscope. Injustice would diminish, they believed, as freedom of conscience replaced self-serving dogmas.

In colonial America, respect for freedom of conscience was bolstered by the multiplicity of religious sects. Sects which had persecuted one another in different parts of the Old World found themselves together in the New World. In the face of hostility from the elements, Indians, and English oppression, the colonists found that they needed one another in order to survive and, therefore, had to respect one another's right to view their Creator differently.

Freedom of conscience became a bedrock value of liberalism. Ralph Waldo Emerson said that "the great man is he who in the midst of the crowd keeps with perfect sweetness the independence of solitude." Henry David Thoreau wrote from the solitude of Walden Pond, "If a man does not keep pace with his companions, perhaps it is because he hears a different drummer. Let him step to the music which he hears, however measured or far away."

Freedom of conscience lets individuals sort out their affairs on their own. It also recognizes that individuals have the right to be wrong. Instead of coercing people to change their minds, liberalism favors patience and persuasion. Ultimately, society is transformed as persuaded individuals vote their conscience.

Liberals respect freedom of conscience also for the pragmatic reason that suppression of dissent from widely held opinions robs everyone, especially those holding prevailing opinions. John Stuart Mill wrote that if people with prevailing opinions stifle dissent and "the [dissenting] opinion is right, they are deprived of the opportunity of exchanging error for truth: if wrong, they lose, what is almost as great a benefit, the clearer perception and livelier impression of truth, produced by its collision with error."

Freedom of conscience thus enhances the quest for truth. "There is the greatest difference between presuming an opinion to be true," wrote Mill, "because, with every opportunity for contesting it, it has not been refuted, and assuming its truth for the purpose of not permitting its refutation. Complete liberty of contradicting and disproving our opinion is the very condition which justifies us in assuming its truth for purposes of action; and on no other terms can a being with human faculties have any rational assurance of being right."

Although the will of the people—vox populi—did not begin with liberalism, liberalism created the modern notion of public opinion. Before liberalism, public opinion lived a restricted life, only rarely coming into play when monarchs provoked rebellious outbursts by overriding traditional practices or engaging in unusual conduct. With the advent of liberalism, the elite found their opinions on an equal footing with those of the common people, whose votes counted the same, but the solitary opinions of single persons now added up to something more significant than had ever existed before: public opinion. Brown University historian Gordon S. Wood has compared liberalism's notion of public opinion with Adam Smith's invisible hand: "Just as numerous economic competitors, buyers and sellers in the market, were led by an invisible hand to promote an end that was no part of their intent, so too could men now conceive of numerous individual thinkers, makers, and users of ideas, being led to create a result, a public opinion, that none of them anticipated or consciously brought about."

It is ironic that the Civil Rights Act of 1964, itself the result of an appeal to conscience, ripped freedom of conscience from the body politic and replaced it with regulatory coercion. Today few, if any, of the regulated view civil rights compliance as a moral issue. It is a pocketbook matter pure and simple. The goals are to escape from impoverishing lawsuits and to hold on to government contracts or, for beneficiaries of the law, to obtain favor unrelated to merit. Doing the right thing has been disconnected from moral consciousness. Indeed, the quotas required to prove that one is upright offend morality by requiring that decisions be made on the basis of the color of a person's skin.

Intent itself has become irrelevant. Employers navigating through the mine field of civil rights compliance have found that race and gender statistics are the only things that matter. Today we all march in forced lockstep to the beat of the regulator. Gunnar Myrdal's "Negro Problem" has been reduced to a litigation problem, and we don't look to lawyers for morality. As Karl Marx would have said, the lawsuits that followed from the 1964 Civil Rights Act turned moral conscience into a commodity that is bought and sold.

It is also ironic that during the 1950s and 1960s a public deemed to be racist sided with the black protestors against the white sheriffs. The coming of age of television news coincided with the civil rights movement, and public opinion was informed for the first time by television. TV coverage, of course, is sensational, and the sight of police dogs snapping at civil rights protestors fueled impatience with segregation.[1] The Court's policy stemming from *Brown* had steadily eradicated segregation in government-funded facilities but had not addressed segregation in private life. Congress took up this task with the 1964 Civil Rights Act.

The civil rights debate was a debate about racial quotas. The Civil Rights Act never would have passed without the statutory language and amendments expressly prohibiting quotas. The turning point was when Senate Minority Leader Everett Dirksen (R-Ill.) inserted what is probably the longest sentence in the English language as an amendment to the act. It expressly and unambiguously forbade quotas. The 170-word sentence is worth reading in full. Entitled "Preferential treatment not to be granted on account of existing number or percentage imbalance," the provision said:

> Nothing contained in this title shall be interpreted to require any employer, employment agency, labor organization, or joint labor-management committee subject to this title to grant preferential treatment to any individual or to any group because of the race, color, religion, sex, or national origin of such individual or group on account of an imbalance which may exist with respect to the total number or percentage of persons of any race, color, religion, sex, or national origin employed by any employer, referred or classified for employment by any employment agency or labor organization, admitted to membership or classified by any labor organization, or admitted to, or employed in, any apprenticeship or other training program, in comparison with the total number

---

[1] Noticing the impact of television coverage of civil rights demonstrations in Birmingham, Alabama, in May 1963, President Kennedy remarked at one White House strategy session that "Bull Connor has done more for civil rights than anyone in this room."

or percentage of persons of such race, color, religion, sex, or national origin in any community, State, section, or other area, or in the available work force in any community, State, section, or other area.

The Civil Rights Act did what Myrdal said American democracy could not do. It dealt with race not only in public life but also in private life. The legislation codified *Brown* by prohibiting segregation by government entities and recipients of federal funds. It also outlawed segregation in privately owned public accommodations, such as restaurants and hotels, and forbade discrimination in private employment. The legislation was based in the moral conscience of the American people and in their commitment to equal treatment. The racial quotas that we experience today are blatant perversions that are illegal under the statutory language of the Civil Rights Act.

President John F. Kennedy proposed the Civil Rights Bill in June 1963. Fearing a Senate filibuster, Kennedy's civil rights strategists decided first to seek House passage of the bill. Kennedy's original proposal did not include a provision forbidding discrimination in employment. Such an intrusion, Kennedy feared, would sink the entire package, as opponents of the bill would claim the government intended to supervise the affairs of private employers and perhaps even impose racial quotas for hiring. Kennedy's proposed expansion of regulation into the private sphere by outlawing discrimination in public accommodations such as restaurants and hotels was controversial enough.

Many liberals were dissatisfied with Kennedy's proposal, however. When leaders of the two hundred thousand–person August 28, 1963, march on Washington, at which Martin Luther King, Jr., gave his famous "I Have a Dream" speech, met with Kennedy at the White House at 5:00 P.M., King, Walter Reuther, A. Philip Randolph, Whitney Young, and Roy Wilkins urged

Kennedy to beef up his bill with an employment provision. Kennedy, whose skills at counting votes exceeded even those of Lyndon Johnson, replied by giving an alphabetical state-by-state analysis of House members starting with Alabama. After working his way to Wyoming, Kennedy counted 158 to 160 Democratic supporters. He pointed out that the other sixty votes, which would have to come from Republicans, "are hard to get." Before the civil rights leaders could respond, Kennedy said, "If I wanted to beat your bill, I would put FEPC [Fair Employment Practices Commission] in. And I would vote for it, and we would never pass it in the House. I don't want the whole thing lost in the House." When the leaders then urged the president to push publicly for the provision, Vice President Lyndon Johnson, who had been silent from the start of the meeting, chimed in: "He can plead and lead and persuade and even threaten Congress, but he can't run the Congress. This president can't get those sixty votes if he turns the White House upside down and he pleads on television an hour every day."

The employment provision, which would eventually give rise to racial quotas, came from the House Judiciary Committee, where it was inserted by Rep. Peter Rodino (D-N.J.). Within the Judiciary Committee, contradictory dynamics ultimately converged for its inclusion. Liberals insisted upon it because of pressure from civil rights groups and a resurgence of racial tension in Birmingham, Alabama. Southern opponents hoped that its inclusion would sink the bill in the House. The Kennedy administration initially balked and Attorney General Bobby Kennedy testified against such a provision in executive session: "What I want is a bill not an issue." But in the face of criticism from NAACP's Clarence Mitchell accusing the administration of a "sellout," the Kennedys accepted it on the grounds that it could be dropped in the Senate to break a filibuster.

The bill was conveyed to the clerk of the House and then to the House Rules Committee on November 21, 1963. The Rules

Committee was the bottleneck through which all bills had to pass before making it to the House floor. The committee set timing and other parameters of debate. Octogenarian Virginia Democrat and former Virginia state judge Howard W. "Judge" Smith, a vocal opponent of civil rights legislation, ruled the committee. As Rules Committee chairman, many considered the tall, slender, white-haired Smith, who had represented Virginia's apple country for thirty-three years, the most powerful man in Congress. Although Smith could not always stop bills, he could delay them. Smith had delayed the 1957 civil rights bill simply by leaving Washington. When he returned, he said that a barn on his 170-acre Fauquier County, Virginia, dairy farm had burned down. House Speaker Sam Rayburn (D-Tex.) said that he knew Smith was opposed to the bill, but never suspected that he would resort to arson to stop it. When another bill he did not like made it to the Rules Committee in 1959, Smith again returned to his farm, claiming that his cows were ill. The day the Rules Committee received H.R. 7152, a reporter asked Judge Smith about its prospects. He puffed on his ever-present cigar and said simply that no hearings were planned.

The next day, President John F. Kennedy was assassinated. Historians still debate whether the civil rights bill would have become law if Kennedy had lived, but the political dynamic changed after Kennedy's death. Upon his return to Washington from Dallas, where Kennedy had been shot, Lyndon Baines Johnson, the brand-new president, told his advisers Jack Valenti and Bill Moyers that passage of the Civil Rights Act was "the first priority." The night before Thanksgiving, President Johnson addressed the grieving nation from a joint session of Congress and said that "no memorial oration or eulogy could more eloquently honor President Kennedy's memory than the earliest possible passage of the civil rights bill for which he fought so long."

A Southerner who had always been distrusted by Kennedy's

circle of New England elites, Johnson seized on the civil rights bill as an instrument to establish his liberal credentials.[2] M.I.T. economist Paul Samuelson wrote in the *Washington Post* that "we should scrutinize each act of President Johnson to see whether it is along the main road of the New Frontier." In putting his prestige on the line for Kennedy's civil rights bill, Johnson changed his position. In his 1948 campaign for the Senate, he had told Texas audiences that President Truman's civil rights program was "a farce and a sham—an effort to set up a police state in the guise of liberty." Sixteen years later, Johnson said in his State of the Union address on January 8, 1964, that, "as far as the writ of federal law will run, we must abolish not some, but all racial discrimination. For this is not merely an economic issue, or a social, political, or international issue. It is a moral issue, and it must be met by the passage this session of the bill now pending in the House."

Even before former First Lady Jacqueline Kennedy had moved out of the White House, Johnson began his daily campaign for the civil rights bill in the limousine that picked him up at his mansion, The Elms. He had a daily "taxi service" in which he would pick up someone who would be crucial to passage of the civil rights act. On the service's first day, Johnson met with the AFL-CIO chief George Meany. Once at the White House, Johnson breakfasted with Everett Dirksen. The second day, Johnson picked up House Minority Leader Charles Halleck (R-Ind.), whose support was critical to the bill's success in the House Judiciary Committee.

---

[2] Attorney General Robert Kennedy later told Anthony Lewis of the *New York Times* that in early 1964 Johnson shrewdly said to Robert Kennedy, "I'll do on the bill just what you think is best to do on the bill. We'll follow what you say we should do on the bill. We won't do anything that you don't want to do on the legislation. And I'll do everything you want me to do in order to obtain the passage of the legislation." Johnson thus preempted attacks from the Democratic party's left flank if the legislation failed.

In mid-December, Judge Smith announced that the Rules Committee would hold hearings on the bill "reasonably soon in January." Overcoming several attempts to get the bill discharged from the committee, Smith began hearings on January 9 on what he called "this nefarious bill," which is "as full of booby traps as a dog is full of fleas." After hearing testimony from forty members of Congress, however, Smith succumbed to pressure from the House leadership and members of his own committee to move the bill along. "I know the facts of life around here," he said. On January 30, the committee voted to send the bill to the House floor.

The House debate on H.R. 7152 was dominated by Judge Smith and Judiciary Committee Chairman Emanuel Celler (D-N.Y.) who introduced the bill. Bald and bespectacled, Celler was in his forty-first year as a congressman from Brooklyn and had the second longest seniority in the House. Celler's introduction responded to the grilling he and other bill supporters had just received in Judge Smith's committee. As expected, the public's chief concern, expressed by former President Eisenhower, among others, was that the employment provision would lead to racial quotas. Rep. Armistead I. Selden, Jr. (D-Ala.), charged that Title VII, the employment section, "would establish a veritable 'Star chamber employment bureau'—a Federal commission empowered to regulate American business and economic relationships and rights hitherto reserved to individual Americans." So much did the public's fear and the bill's opponents focus on the possibility of quotas, that advocates of the bill made reassurances that there would be no quotas a top priority.

Celler summarized the "unfair and unreasonable" criticism leveled at the bill in which opponents "cry with alarm about what they claim are infringements of the rights of nonminority American citizens. They invoke the baleful specter of Federal inspectors wielding unlimited power over innocent victims of governmental tyranny.... The charge has been made that the Equal

Employment Opportunity Commission to be established by Title VII of the bill would have the power to prevent a business from employing and promoting the people it wished, and that a 'Federal inspector' could then order the hiring and promotion only of employees of certain races or religious groups." Celler said this charge was "entirely wrong."

He assured the House that even after a discrimination suit reached a court, "the court could not order that any preference be given to any particular race, religion or other group, but would be limited to ordering an end to discrimination. The statement that a Federal inspector could order the employment and promotion only of members of a specific racial or religious group is therefore patently erroneous." Celler said also that "it is likewise not true" that the EEOC "would have power to rectify existing 'racial or religious imbalance' in employment by requiring the hiring of certain people without regard to their qualifications simply because they are of a given race or religion. Only actual discrimination could be stopped."

Other supporters of the bill took up Celler's theme. New York Republican and Judiciary Committee member John Lindsay reiterated that the bill "does not, as has been suggested heretofore both on and off the floor, force acceptance of people in schools, jobs, housing, or public accommodations because they are Negro. It does not impose quotas or any special privileges of seniority or acceptance. There is nothing whatever in this bill about racial balance."

To counter lingering concerns that the EEOC might define discrimination as statistical disparities, which would lead to racial quotas, Judiciary Committee Chairman Celler proposed an amendment restricting the EEOC from making "substantive regulations." In 1946 Congress had passed, and President Truman signed, the Administrative Procedure Act, which put checks on regulatory agencies that had mushroomed during the New Deal and carefully delineated their powers. Celler's proposed amendment limited the EEOC's authority by allowing it to promulgate only internal procedural regulations, but not substantive interpretative regulations. The amendment was immediately adopted by a voice vote. This amendment was one of ten "perfecting amendments" Celler proposed.

Judge Smith then rose and chided his fellow committee chairman: "We were told yesterday that this legislation was perfect and it did not need any amendments." Smith said that once Celler was finished, he had a "meritorious" amendment of his own. After the rest of Celler's amendments were approved by voice vote, Smith said, "Mr. Chairman, I offer an amendment."

When the clerk finished reading Smith's amendment, the House was shocked. Smith proposed making the three-letter word "sex" a prohibited form of discrimination. "Now, what harm can you do this bill that was so perfect yesterday and is so imperfect today?" Smith asked. As soon as the judge finished, a flustered Representative Celler stood up and said, "Mr. Chairman, I rise in opposition to the amendment." As the seventy-five-year-old Celler and the eighty-year-old Smith bantered back and forth, people in the galleries could not help snickering.

Celler went on to say that having been married to a woman for forty-nine years, women "are not in the minority in my house.... At first blush it seems fair, just, and equitable to grant these equal rights. But when you examine carefully what the import and repercussions are concerning equal rights throughout American life, and all facets of American life you run into a considerable amount of difficulty." Celler continued: "You know, the French have a phrase for it when they speak of women and men. When they speak of the difference, they say, '*Vive la différence.*' I think the French are right." Celler, in effect, found himself giving arguments against the regulation of relations between the sexes that paralleled arguments the bill's opponents made against the regulation of race relations:

Imagine the upheaval that would result from adoption of blanket language requiring total equality. Would male citizens be justified in insisting that women share with them the burdens of compulsory military service? What would become of traditional family relationships? What about alimony? Who would have the obligation of supporting whom? Would fathers rank equally with mothers in the right of custody to children? What would become of the crimes of rape and statutory rape?

"You know the biological differences between the sexes," Celler said to Smith. "It is rather anomalous that two men of our age should be on the opposite sides of this question." Celler ended his speech by saying that he was surprised by Smith's amendment, because it was "illogical, ill-timed, ill-placed, and improper." Smith replied, "Your surprise" does not "nearly approach my surprise, amazement, and sorrow at your opposition to it." And so it went.

Despite the opposition of the Johnson administration and the bill's leading supporters, a group of women representatives united with Southern opponents of the bill and approved Judge Smith's amendment after only two hours of debate. "We've won, we've won," a woman jubilantly shouted from the gallery. Years later Smith admitted to Rep. Martha Griffiths (D-Mich.), who had supported his amendment, that he had offered it "as a joke."

With the assurances of Congressman Celler and many others that the proposed law would not cause racial quotas, the House overwhelmingly agreed to the bill at 7:00 P.M. on February 10, 1964, with a vote of 290-130. Supporting the bill were 152 Democrats and 138 Republicans; voting against were 96 Democrats and 34 Republicans. Celler said it was his life's greatest accomplishment: "I sort of feel like I climbed Mount Everest, and I'm just pausing up there and looking around."

For advocates of the bill, the certain Senate filibuster seemed a bigger obstacle than Mount Everest. Once again quotas were the chief issue. So, repeating the pattern set by Congressman Celler in the House, Senator Hubert H. Humphrey (D-Minn.) repeatedly renounced quotas when he introduced the bill to the Senate.

When Humphrey reached the employment provision in his three and one-half-hour long introductory speech, he said that the "simple and complete truth about Title VII" is that it "forbids discriminating against anyone on account of race." Humphrey said that racial preferences for minorities would therefore violate Title VII:

> Contrary to the allegations of some opponents of this title, there is nothing in it that will give any power to the Commission or to any court to require hiring, firing, or promotion of employees in order to meet a racial "quota" or to achieve a certain racial balance.

> That bugaboo has been brought up a dozen times; but it is nonexistent. In fact, the very opposite is true. Title VII prohibits discrimination. In effect, it says that race, religion, and national origin are not to be used as the basis for hiring and firing. Title VII is designed to encourage hiring on the basis of ability and qualifications, not race or religion.

Humphrey argued that because the "bill cannot be attacked on its merits," opponents of the bill were raising "bogeymen and hobgoblins" to "frighten well-meaning Americans" by claiming that the bill would lead to racial quotas:

> It is claimed that the bill would require racial quotas for all hiring, when in fact it provides that race shall not be a basis for making personnel decisions.

> As I have said, the bill has a simple purpose. That purpose is to give fellow citizens—Negroes—the same rights and opportunities that white people take for granted. This is no more

than what was preached by the prophets, and by Christ Himself. It is no more than what our Constitution guarantees.

Humphrey's Republican counterpart in support of the bill, Thomas H. Kuchel, was a protégé of Earl Warren. In 1952 Kuchel had been appointed by California Governor Earl Warren to the Senate to fill Richard Nixon's Senate seat after Nixon was elected vice president in 1952. Following Humphrey, Kuchel said that Title VII:

> is pictured by its opponents and detractors as an intrusion of numerous federal inspectors into our economic life. These inspectors would presumably dictate to labor unions and their members with regard to job seniority, seniority in apprenticeship programs, racial balance in job classifications, racial balance in membership, and preferential advancement for members of so-called minority groups. Nothing could be further from the truth.

Kuchel maintained that even should a court conclude that racial discrimination had taken place, it "cannot order preferential hiring or promotion consideration for any particular race, religion, or other group. Its power is solely limited to ordering an end to the discrimination which is in fact occurring."

The senators charged with defending Title VII, Senator Joseph Clark (D-Penn.) and Senator Clifford Case (R-N.J.), distributed a memo disavowing quotas:

> There is no requirement in Title VII that an employer maintain a racial balance in his work force. On the contrary, any deliberate attempt to maintain a racial balance, whatever such a balance may be, would involve a violation of Title VII because maintaining such a balance would require an employer to hire or to refuse to hire on the basis of race. It must be emphasized that discrimination is prohibited as to any individual.

At another point Senator Clark assured the Senate that "quotas are themselves discriminatory."

In response to charges that employers might be coerced by federal agencies into giving racial preferences for minorities, Senator Harrison Williams (R-N.J.) insisted that:

> to hire a Negro solely because he is a Negro is racial discrimination, just as much as a 'white only' employment policy. Both forms of discrimination are prohibited by Title VII of this bill. The language of that title simply states that race is not a qualification for employment.... Some people charge that H.R. 7152 favors the Negro, at the expense of the white majority. But how can the language of equality favor one race or one religion over another? Equality can have only one meaning, and that meaning is self-evident to reasonable men. Those who say that equality means favoritism do violence to common sense.

With his wife and brother sitting in the Senate gallery's front row, Edward Kennedy (D-Mass.) in his maiden speech labeled as "groundless" the argument that "Title VII can only make jobs for Negroes by taking them away from whites." Senator Edmund Muskie (D-Maine) similarly declared, "It has been said that the bill discriminates in favor of the Negro at the expense of the rest of us. It seeks to do nothing more than to lift the Negro from the status of inequality to one of equality of treatment." And Senator John Williams (R-Del.) promised that the bill would allow an employer to hire "only the best-qualified persons even if they were all white."

Proponents of the bill off the Senate floor argued with equal conviction that its nondiscrimination language precluded the possibility of quotas. A notice distributed to senators by the Leadership Conference on Civil Rights was inserted into the *Congressional Record*. It said that the bill "contains no provision requiring an employer to set up a quota system or to maintain any kind of racial or religious balance. Indeed, preferential treatment of Negroes or any minority group would violate this section. Its whole point is that all workers should be treated equally." A *New York Times* editorial endorsing Title VII charged that "misrepresentations by opponents of the civil rights legislation are at their wildest in discussion of this title." The editorial went on to say that the bill would not "require anyone to establish racial quotas; to the contrary, such quotas would be forbidden as a racial test. The bill does not require employers or unions to drop any standard for hiring or promotion or membership—except the discriminatory standard of race or religion."

The most dramatic assurance that quotas would not result from Title VII came from Senator Humphrey. In response to a charge that federal bureaucrats could force companies to establish hiring quotas, Humphrey said, "If the senator can find in Title VII... any language which provides that an employer will have to hire on the basis of percentage or quota related to color, race, religion, or national origin, I will start eating the pages one after another, because it is not in there."

For all their reassurances, however, advocates of the bill were still far short of the two-thirds majority they would need to break a filibuster, close debate, and come to a vote on the bill. The only way to get the votes would be to persuade one man, the Senate's leading Republican, Minority Leader Everett Dirksen of Illinois, to change sides.

Dirksen, a legend in the Senate, was a master at taking advantage of fratricidal battles among his Democratic opponents. The object of deep loyalty from Senate Republicans (he twice gave up choice committee assignments to move up younger Republican colleagues), Dirksen could charge in like the cavalry at the last moment with Republican votes to break Senate deadlocks between Democrats. Unlike many of his colleagues, Dirksen loved applying his legal skills to mastering the details of legislation and drafting amendments. His fellow senators were often willing to let him cross the final 't's and dot the final 'i's of bills.

Dirksen was at his best when the Senate was caught in controversy. He had an unruly thatch of gray hair, heavy-lidded eyes, and often wore seedy clothes, but he was best known for his deep voice. Every day he gargled and swallowed a mixture of Pond's cold cream and water to keep "my pipes lubricated." One reporter described Dirksen as "the last of the Fourth of July picnic orators." His patriotic speeches would often remind audiences that before being elected to the Senate, he had held the Illinois congressional seat of the Republican party's first president, Abraham Lincoln. To his supporters he was the "Wizard of Ooze," to his detractors, "Old Doctor Snake Oil." Both labels attested to his skills.

Dirksen's power was greater whenever the issue before the Senate required two-thirds approval, such as treaties. With Southern Democrats filibustering the civil rights bill (it required a two-thirds vote to break a filibuster in those days), he found himself in just such a commanding position.

Jimmy Stewart made the filibuster famous in the movie *Mr. Smith Goes to Washington* when he delayed a Senate vote on his expulsion by speaking around the clock, reading from the Declaration of Independence, the Constitution, and the Bible. In 1957 Strom Thurmond, then a South Carolina Democrat and today a Senate Republican in his nineties, turned Stewart's fictional character into reality by speaking for twenty-four hours in opposition to civil rights legislation. By 1964 filibusters had buried eleven civil rights bills in which cloture votes failed to break the deadlock.

With twenty-one of the Senate's sixty-seven Democrats being Southerners, President Johnson, a former Senate majority leader himself, knew that Everett Dirksen was the key to getting at least twenty-two of the Senate's thirty-three Republicans on a cloture vote. Johnson and his Senate floor leader for the bill, Hubert Humphrey, whose civil rights plank at the 1948

Democratic convention had split the Democratic party and led to Strom Thurmond's Dixiecrat ticket, agreed to do everything they could to get Dirksen's support. Johnson told Humphrey, "The bill can't pass unless you get Ev Dirksen. You and I are going to get Ev. It's going to take time. We're going to get him. You make up your mind now that you've got to spend time with Ev Dirksen. You've got to let him have a piece of the action. He's got to look good all the time. Don't let those bomb throwers, now, talk you out of seeing Dirksen. You get in there to see Dirksen. You drink with Dirksen! You talk with Dirksen! You listen to Dirksen!"

Humphrey was a consummate talker with boundless energy and optimism. His Chevy Chase, Maryland, neighbor, South Dakota Senator George McGovern, who would defeat Humphrey in his bid for the 1972 Democratic nomination, said that Humphrey often swept his garage after midnight and washed kitchen walls at 2:00 A.M. One day when Humphrey had the flu and was running a temperature of 102 degrees, he planned to stop by a convention meeting at a Washington hotel and, rather than give a speech, simply wave to the crowd for a minute and leave. Instead, he spoke for over forty-five minutes and said that he was feeling "just great." Humphrey managed to give more speeches than anyone else during the civil rights debate—a total of 153.

Humphrey recalled that "I courted Dirksen almost as persistently as I did Muriel," his wife. Humphrey made a daily point of telling Dirksen, "Everett, we can't pass this bill without you," "We need your leadership in this fight, Everett," or "This will go down in history, Everett." President Johnson often invited Dirksen to the White House for drinks and told Dirksen that he would become a "hero in history" if he rescued the legislation. Even though Johnson preferred drinking scotch, Johnson matched Dirksen's fondness for Jack Daniel's drink for drink. "But," according to Johnson aide Joseph Califano, "the President's drinks had only half an ounce of liquor in them; Dirksen's had an ounce-and-a-half."

After discussing the bill with other Republicans, Dirksen finally decided to begin behind-the-scenes negotiations to break the filibuster in early May. One Humphrey staffer recalled that although debate continued on the Senate floor, "the battle for the Civil Rights Act of 1964 shifted into the rear of Dirksen's chambers on the second floor of the Capitol." During the first two weeks of May, Senator Dirksen held court five times with the three major Senate advocates of the bill, Senator Humphrey, Senate Majority Leader Mike Mansfield of Montana, and California Republican Thomas H. Kuchel, and key administration figures, Attorney General Robert Kennedy, Deputy Attorney General Nicholas Katzenbach, and a group of Justice Department lawyers. They sat with Dirksen around his large mahogany table to work out amendments and compromise language acceptable to the Republican leader. Dirksen's price was an antiquota amendment, a related amendment defining discrimination as an intentional rather than an accidental or statistical act, protections of bona fide seniority and merit systems, and limitations on EEOC enforcement powers. In exchange Dirksen would break the longest filibuster in the history of the Senate.

At last on May 13, 1964, the parties reached an agreement. Dirksen called a news conference to announce his support for the bill. Roger Mudd of CBS News and the NAACP's Clarence Mitchell were shocked. Most reporters and civil rights activists had viewed Dirksen as an opponent of the legislation. Dirksen compared the civil rights bill to other events in American history—civil service reform, the popular election of senators, women's suffrage, the Pure Food and Drug Act, child labor laws—and then quoted Victor Hugo's line that "no army is stronger than an idea whose time has come." He pointed toward the Senate chamber and finished with a dramatic flourish: "No one on that floor is going to stop this. It is going to happen!"

However, Dirksen made certain that it didn't happen until

racial quotas were bottled up tightly with statutory language. To
his amendment prohibiting quotas, he added another defining discrimination as an intentional act, rather than mere statistical disparities. As Senator Humphrey explained it:

> Section 706(g) is amended to require a showing of intentional
> violation of the title in order to obtain relief. This is a clarify-
> ing change. Since the title bars only discrimination because of
> race, color, religion, sex, or natural origin it would seem
> already to require intent, and, thus, the proposed change does
> not involve any substantive change in the title. The express
> requirement of intent is designed to make it wholly clear that
> inadvertent or accidental discriminations will not violate the
> title or result in entry of court orders. It means simply that the
> respondent must have intended to discriminate.

Concerns that discrimination could be defined as uninten-
tional statistical disparities were not imaginary. In March 1964,
New York Times Washington Bureau Chief Arthur Krock suggested in a column that Title VII might outlaw employment tests if their
use disproportionately impacted racial minorities. Krock
described how the Illinois Fair Employment Practice Commission
had recently ordered Motorola Corporation to cease giving a standard multiple choice general ability test for that reason. Krock
warned that Title VII threatened "to project the rationale of the
Illinois FEPC ruling throughout the free enterprise system of the
United States.... Then a Federal bureaucracy would be legislated
into senior partnership with private business," Krock predicted,
"with the power to dictate the standards by which employers
reach their judgments of the capabilities of applicants for jobs, and
the quality of performance after employment, whenever the issue
of 'discrimination' is raised."

After Krock's column was published, Senator John Tower (R-
Tex.)—the first Southern Republican senator since Reconstruction—

who was elected to Lyndon Johnson's seat in 1961, took up the cause of protecting the use of professionally developed employment tests from Title VII attack. Senators Clark and Case immediately distributed a memo stating that Title VII would not have the effect that Krock predicted:

> There is no requirement in Title VII that employers abandon bona fide qualification tests where, because of differences in background and education, members of some groups are able to perform better on these tests than members of other groups. An employer may set his qualifications as high as he likes, he may test to determine which applicants have these qualifications, and he may hire, assign, and promote on the basis of test performance.

Senator Case thought that the *Motorola* case was a red herring and said:

> It would be ridiculous, indeed, in addition to being contrary to Title VII, for a court to order an employer who wanted to hire electronics engineers with Ph.Ds to lower his requirements because there were very few Negroes with such degrees or because prior cultural or educational deprivation of Negroes prevented them from qualifying.... Title VII would in no way interfere with the right of an employer to fix job qualifications, and any citation of the Motorola case to the contrary as precedent for Title VII is wholly wrong and misleading.

Humphrey and his fellow supporters accepted Senator Tower's amendment because they thought that, like Dirksen's several amendments, it was "in accord with the intent and purpose" of Title VII.

Perceiving that the danger in the Civil Rights Act was quotas and restrictions on hiring on the basis of merit, and having tied down this hydra with amendments and statutory language, the Senate broke the filibuster and passed the bill on June 19 by a vote of 76–18. The regulatory intrusions into freedom of conscience and the implicit rejection of one of democracy's basic premises did not feature in the debate. As often happens, a big change occurred in the way people would be governed without much recognition of what was happening.

It was in the context of public accommodations that the bill's regulatory provisions were noticed. Senator George D. Aiken (R-Vt.), who supported the bill, commented to reporters after a White House briefing: "Let them integrate the Waldorf and other large hotels, but permit the 'Mrs. Murphys,' who run small rooming houses all over the country, to rent their rooms to those they choose." Recognizing that "Mrs. Murphy" was a sympathetic figure, Hubert Humphrey quipped that in heavily Swedish and Norwegian Minnesota, it is not "Mrs. Murphy's boarding house," but "Mrs. Olsen's." Because the discussion about "Mrs. Murphy" struck a popular chord, the final bill had a "Mrs. Murphy's exemption" for small owner-occupied boarding houses, but it was the only limit to the statute's general intrusion into private life.

When the bill had first been introduced in 1963, Senator Strom Thurmond complained that "even many who favor integration indicate in correspondence to me that they oppose this legislation because it would give unprecedented power to Washington bureaucrats to try to force changes in human attitudes on the selection of associates, both in private as well as in public life." But the Dixiecrat lacked the credibility to address issues of this kind. It was Arizona Senator Barry Goldwater who noted that Dirksen's amendments did not address the bill's real problem. Goldwater said that the bill commingled public and private life in a manner that permitted the tentacles of government regulation to enter the inner sanctum of individual conscience.

Goldwater was an integrationist, but he appreciated the distinction between public and private that the preoccupation with quotas had obscured. He did not think government could treat its citizens differently on the basis of race, but how people treated each other was "fundamentally a matter of the heart." When he organized the Arizona Air National Guard in 1946, he insisted that the unit be desegregated—this was two years before President Truman's 1948 military desegregation order. However, the campaign Goldwater led in the early 1950s to integrate Phoenix lunch counters was based on persuasion and appeals to goodwill.

Goldwater supported those parts of the civil rights bill that codified *Brown* by ending discrimination by government. He had supported similar legislative efforts in 1957 and in 1960, but he was opposed to the government's regulation of individual conscience. He thought the bill's employment and public accommodation titles took us across a watershed that "could ultimately destroy the freedom of all American citizens."

Goldwater's intervention came too late to have any effect. He had spent 1964 on the campaign trail, where he had finally wrested the Republican presidential nomination from New York Governor Nelson Rockefeller in the California primary the first week of June. By then the die was cast, and too many deals had been made to be undone by an argument that civilized society depended on people's hearts and souls, and not on the government's coercive powers.

Both Milton Friedman in *Capitalism and Freedom* and Robert Bork in the *New Republic* had cautioned against using up freedom by relying on regulation to do the work of moral conscience. But in the aftermath of Myrdal and *Brown*, these arguments must have seemed atavistic, harking back to a quaint time before it had been discovered that the individual's conscience was ruled by the immutable self-interest of his race.

After Senate passage, the bill returned to the House, where

members of the Rules Committee outvoted Judge Smith and limited House debate to one hour. On the House floor, Smith said, "The bell has tolled. In a few minutes you will vote this monstrous instrument of oppression upon all of the American people." Celler closed the debate by declaring that the bill's enactment would be like "the voice of Leviticus, 'proclaiming liberty throughout the land to all the inhabitants thereof.'" The House rose in a standing ovation for Celler and a few minutes later approved the bill, 289–126.

At 6:45 P.M. that evening, television lights turned on as President Johnson entered the East Room in the White House, where key supporters of the bill had gathered. Under the gaze of portraits of George and Martha Washington, Johnson sat down at a desk in the center of the room and delivered a short speech in which he said that the Civil Rights Act "does not give special treatment to any citizen." He then picked up his pen and signed the bill into law. After that, Johnson hugged and kissed the first lady. Cameras flashed for the customary signing picture, with the principal supporters of the statute surrounding the president, and Johnson handed out seventy-one souvenir pens that he had used to sign copies of the bill.

As the ceremonies ended, Hubert Humphrey asked Johnson if he could have the manuscript of his speech as a keepsake. Johnson said yes, but when the president and his future vice-president looked for it, the speech was missing. Someone had snitched it. The act itself would disappear just as quickly. All of the legislative history comprised of the promises Humphrey and his House and Senate colleagues had made to secure the act's passage, along with the statutory language and Celler, Dirksen, and Tower amendments, were purloined by courts and EEOC bureaucrats.

Privilege Before the Law

Friedrich A. Hayek warns in *The Constitution of Liberty* that "the greatest danger to liberty today comes from the men who are most needed and most powerful in modern government, namely, the efficient expert administrators exclusively concerned with what they regard as the public good." These bureaucrats, Hayek said, inevitably skirt democratic control and make the administrative state "a self-willed and uncontrollable apparatus before which the individual is helpless."

It took less than a decade after enactment of the 1964 Civil Rights Act for bureaucrats and the federal judiciary to rewrite the law according to their own wishes and use it to force racial quotas on American society. Bureaucrats and judges cast aside Congress' rejection of preferential treatment for minorities and stuffed the pages of the act down Hubert Horatio Humphrey's throat.

The Civil Rights Act of 1964 undertook to put the millions of employer–employee decisions through a government filter. Such a massive intrusion into private life had not previously occurred in a free society. Congress assumed that the Equal Employment Opportunity Commission, the agency created by the act to run the filter, would be like the state Fair Employment Practice (FEP) commissions that had been created in some Northern states after World War II. But these state commissions, many with more power than the EEOC, were being increasingly regarded as ineffective by civil rights activists. There was a sound explanation for this regulatory feebleness, one that years later won a Nobel prize for Chicago economist Gary Becker in 1992: markets don't discriminate because it doesn't pay.

In his 1957 book, *The Economics of Discrimination*, Becker showed that racial discrimination is costly to those who practice it and thereby sets in motion forces that inexorably reduce it. Meritorious employees who are underpaid and underutilized because of their race will work elsewhere, where they get paid according to their contributions to profit. An employer, for example, who hires a less qualified white because of prejudice against blacks will disadvantage himself in competition against those who hone their edge with the best employees that they can find. But this argument did not appeal to those who wished to achieve racial integration through government policy. For activists such as Rutgers law professor Alfred W. Blumrosen, who as compliance chief became the de facto head of the EEOC, racial discrimination was the only or principal explanation of income and employment disparities between blacks and whites. Moreover, the kind of results activists wanted were inconsistent with investigations and corrections of individual acts of discrimination.

Blumrosen was not impressed with the "FEP model." This model required that a discrimination complaint be filed; the commission would then investigate the complaint and the procedures leading up to the employer's decision. If the commission found that an employer had treated a person differently from others because of his race, the commission could order the employer to "cease and desist" from discriminating. This procedure was going nowhere fast. Scholars who studied the cases found that in most instances the complainant's problem was his job qualifications, not his race. Sociologist Leon Mayhew, for example, studied employment discrimination complaints at Massachusetts' FEP commission from 1946 to 1962. He found that most discrimination complaints were based on "mere suspicion" and usually resulted in findings that employers did not discriminate. He concluded that most complainants were poor and without job skills. Thus, normal operations of the job market "regularly produce experiences that could be interpreted as discrimination," but they are not. This phenomenon "permits Negroes to blame discrimination for their troubles. Hence, some complaints represent a projection of one's own deficiencies onto the outside world."

Blumrosen wanted none of this. He wrote in the *Rutgers Law Review* that agencies enforcing antidiscrimination laws should be evaluated by the extent to which complainants *as a general class of victims* got relief. FEPs like New Jersey's focused too much on individual acts of discrimination and "did not remedy the broader social problems" by reducing the disparity between blacks and whites.

It was Blumrosen, as EEOC compliance chief, who shunted aside statutory law and imposed the forbidden quotas. Rejecting what civil rights activists derided as the complaint-based "retail" model of FEP enforcement, Blumrosen envisioned a "wholesale" model attacking what he regarded as the entrenched legacy and effects of discrimination. He thought that the task of combating *intentional* acts of discrimination was not sufficiently broad to permit the use of government power to reshape society. In order to redefine discrimination in terms of statistical disparity, he shoved aside other explanations of economic differences between blacks and whites, such as education and illegitimacy, as harmful "attempt[s] to shift focus" away from racial discrimination.

Blumrosen disdained the Civil Rights Act's definition of discrimination as an intentional action. He favored a definition that Congress had rejected. In his 1971 book, *Black Employment and the Law*, Blumrosen wrote, "If discrimination is narrowly defined, for example, by requiring an evil intent to injure minorities, then it will be difficult to find that it exists.... But if discrimination is broadly defined, as, for example, by including all conduct which adversely affects minority group employment opportunities... then the prospects for rapid improvement in minority employment opportunities are greatly increased." If the broad definition is adopted (contrary to the Civil Rights Act), "the solution lies within our immediate grasp. It is not embedded in the complications of fundamental sociology but can be sharply influenced by intelligent, effective, and aggressive legal action." As he frankly put it, "this view finds discrimination at every turn where minorities are adversely affected by institutional decisions, which are subject to legal regulation."

Blumrosen reasoned that a redefinition of discrimination to include anything and everything that yielded statistical disparities between blacks and whites would force employers to give preferential treatment to blacks in pursuit of proportional representation in order to avert liability in class action suits. He said that he set out to "liberally construe" Title VII to advance "the needs of the minorities for whom the statute had been adopted." By promoting quotas, he could "maximize the effect of the statute on employment discrimination without going back to the Congress for more substantive legislation."

Blumrosen's EEOC colleagues kidded him that he was working on a textbook entitled "Blumrosen on Loopholes." He took pride in his reputation for his "free and easy ways with statutory construction." He later praised the agency for being like "the proverbial bumble bee" that flies "in defiance of the laws governing its operation." Blumrosen's strategy was based on his bet that "most of the problems confronting the EEOC could be solved by creative interpretation of Title VII which would be upheld by the courts, partly out of deference to the administrators." History has proved Blumrosen right.

"Inside-the-beltway" lore says "personnel is policy." Blumrosen had a free hand because Franklin Delano Roosevelt, Jr., who was appointed the EEOC's first chairman, spent most of his time yachting. Staffers jokingly changed the lyrics of the song "Anchors Aweigh" to "Franklin's Away" during his frequent absences. Roosevelt resigned before a year was out, and his successors stayed little longer. The EEOC had four chairmen in its first five years.

Despite Goldwater's fears and Judge Smith's predictions, the Civil Rights Act, if combined with goodwill and moral suasion, might have led to improved race relations and a more open society. But by subverting the law, Blumrosen separated it from its democratic roots and led us back to the Charlemagne model. When faced with the imperfections of democracy, we all dream of Charlemagne, a wise and benevolent ruler, to put things right. But setting up government structures in anticipation of a Charlemagne, much less a succession of Charlemagnes, ultimately results in despotic rule.

The White House Conference on Equal Employment Opportunity in August 1965 indicated what was to come. Speaker after speaker described "deeply rooted patterns of discrimination" and "underrepresentation" of minorities that the EEOC should counter to promote "equal employment opportunity." The conference report, whose cover featured President Johnson with Lady Bird Johnson and Franklin Delano Roosevelt, Jr., stressed on its first page that the "conferees were eager to move beyond the letter of the law to a sympathetic discussion of those affirmative actions required to make the legal requirement of equal opportunity an operating reality."

Blumrosen inserted a paragraph into the report suggesting

that the agency initiate proceedings against employers even without complaints of discrimination. Underutilizers of minority workers could be identified by using "employer reports of the racial composition of the work force as a sociological 'radar net' to determine the existence of patterns of discrimination."

In the end, Blumrosen succeeded in setting up a national reporting system of racial employment statistics despite its prohibition by the Civil Rights Act. One of Dirksen's amendments said that employers did not have to report statistics to the EEOC if they also had to report to local or state FEPs. Blumrosen later admitted that one of the requirements he imposed on employers was "a reading of the statute contrary to the plain meaning." But what was a mere statute? Democracy itself had already been set aside by *Brown*. It was no big deal to set aside the will of a racist people as expressed by a racist Congress. Myrdal had convinced the elite that they must seize the reins of power, and they did.

Columbia Law Professor Michael Sovern predicted that the EEOC would be called on the carpet for exceeding its authority. He wrote in his Twentieth Century Fund study, *Legal Restraints on Racial Discrimination in Employment*, that Title VII "cannot possibly be stretched to permit the commission to insist on the filing of reports" and predicted that Blumrosen would "encounter resistance." But no resistance materialized. As Hugh Davis Graham observed in *The Civil Rights Era,* "In 1965 Congress was distracted by debates over voting rights and Vietnam and Watts and inflation and scores of other issues more pressing than agency records."

Once Blumrosen got his way in forcing employers to submit EEO-1 forms, the agency was confident enough to dispense with other statutory restrictions on its mission just as quickly. Blumrosen knew that "with the aid of a computer," the EEOC could now get "lists of employers who, prima facie, may be underutilizing minority group persons" and eventually force them to engage in preferential hiring of blacks.

In mid-1965 Blumrosen sent EEOC investigators to Newport News, Virginia, to solicit discrimination complaints against the Newport News Shipbuilding & Dry Dock Company, one of the world's largest shipyards, which employed 22,000 workers. Knocking on doors in black neighborhoods, the investigators found forty-one complainants and then narrowed them down to four. Armed with complaints, Blumrosen mobilized the heavy hand of federal power against the company, which received 75 percent of its business from naval contracts. The company buckled under and agreed to promote 3,890 of its five thousand black workers, designate 100 blacks as supervisors, and agreed to a quota system in which the ratio of black to white apprentices in a given year would match the region's ratio of blacks to whites. One shipyard worker told *Barron's* that the EEOC had done its best to "set black against white, labor against management, and disconcert everybody."

Armed with the national reporting system's racial data and the victory at Newport News, Blumrosen and his colleagues decided to build a body of case law to make minority preference schemes like the one at Newport News transferable to employers across the country. But the barrier to this strategy was Title VII itself. An internal EEOC legal memorandum, prepared for EEOC general counsel, concluded: "Under the literal language of Title VII, the only actions required by a covered employer are to post notices, and not to discriminate subsequent to July 2, 1965. By the explicit terms of Section 703(j), an employer is not required to redress an imbalance in his work force which is the result of past discrimination." Fearing another storm over quotas, the EEOC ruled out trying to amend the Civil Rights Act. The memorandum urged the agency to rewrite the statute on its own and influence the courts to embrace the EEOC's "affirmative theory of nondiscrimination" requiring that "Negroes are recruited, hired, transferred, and promoted in line with their ability and numbers."

To get the "affirmative theory of nondiscrimination" under

way, the EEOC decided to assault employment tests that failed blacks at a higher rate than whites. Commissioner Samuel Jackson told members of the NAACP that the EEOC had decided to interpret Title VII as banning not only racial discrimination per se, but also employment practices "which prove to have a demonstrable racial effect."

The EEOC's chief psychologist, William H. Enneis, implemented the agency's assault on testing. Enneis attacked "irrelevant and unreasonable standards for job applicants and upgrading of employees [that] pose serious threats to our social and economic system. The results will be denial of employment to qualified and trainable minorities and women." Enneis insisted that the EEOC would not "stand idle in the face of this challenge. The cult of credentialism is one of our targets," and the agency would fight it "in whatever form it occurs."

The EEOC issued guidelines in 1966 and 1970 designed to abrogate Senator Tower's pro-testing amendment by defining the phrase "professionally developed ability tests" as tests either passing blacks and whites at an equal rate or meeting complex "validation" requirements for "fairness" and "utility." The validation requirements that Enneis designed required employers to prove that the tests measured skills the employer needed. The objective was to make tests so difficult to defend that employers would simply abandon them and hire employees by racial quota to avoid discrimination lawsuits. Enneis testified before Congress in 1974 that he knew of only three or four test validation studies that succeeded in jumping over the hurdles against testing put in place by his guidelines. As a 1971 *Harvard Law Review* survey of developments in employment law deduced, the EEOC guidelines "appear designed to scare employers away from any objective standards which have a differential impact on minority groups because, applied strictly, the testing requirements are impossible for many employers to follow." As a result, the guidelines "encourage many employers to use a quota system of hiring." An EEOC staffer told the *Harvard Law Review* that "the anti-preferential hiring provisions [of Title VII] are a big zero, a nothing, a nullity. They don't mean anything at all to us."

The EEOC's attack on tests not only gutted Senator Tower's amendment, but also the statutory definition of discrimination as an intentional act. The commission was well aware that its bravado trod on thin legal ice. A history of the EEOC during the Johnson administration, prepared by the EEOC itself for the Johnson Library, detailed the EEOC's strategy of redefining discrimination and suggested that it was on a collision course with the text and legislative intent of Title VII. The history said that the commission had rejected the "traditional meaning" of discrimination as "one of intent in the state of mind of the actor" in favor of a "constructive proof of discrimination," which would "disregard intent as crucial to the finding of an unlawful employment practice" and forbid employment criteria that have a "demonstrable racial effect without clear and convincing business motive."

Noting that this redefinition would conflict with Senator Dirksen's insertion of the word "intentional" into the statute, the EEOC said that "courts cannot assume as a matter of statutory construction that Congress meant to accomplish an empty act by the amendment" defining discrimination as intentional. The history predicted that "the Commission and the courts will be in disagreement as to the basis on which they find an unlawful employment practice" and concluded that "eventually this will call for reconsideration of the amendment by Congress or the reconsideration of its interpretation by the Commission."

★   ★   ★

Neither the EEOC nor Congress, as it turned out, had to reconsider the meaning of discrimination because the courts ignored the law as well. In *Griggs v. Duke Power*, the Supreme Court accepted the EEOC's rewrite of the Civil Rights Act. The opinion was written by Chief Justice Warren Burger, President Richard Nixon's first appointee to the Supreme Court. Coveting Earl Warren's fame, Burger told his clerks that he wanted to "confuse his liberal detractors in the press" by writing some "liberal opinions." By 1971 liberalism in Burger's mind had come to be identified with its old enemy—status-based legal privileges.

When Burger declared that "the administrative interpretation of the act by the enforcing agency is entitled to great deference," Professor Blumrosen won his bet that the EEOC's "creative interpretation of Title VII" would be "upheld by the courts, partly out of deference to the administrators." Burger got the acclaim he coveted. Blumrosen cheered the Chief Justice's opinion as a "sensitive, liberal interpretation of Title VII" that "has the imprimatur of permanence."

In *Griggs v. Duke Power,* the Court ignored clear statutory language and unambiguous legislative history. It substituted in their place a new law defining discrimination as unintended statistical disparities between racial groups. There was no basis in law for the Court's decision, especially as *Griggs* paralleled a 1964 Illinois case, *Myart v. Motorola,* which struck down Motorola Corporation's use of an employment test that blacks failed at a higher rate than whites. The EEOC's history for the Johnson Library noted that "many members of Congress were concerned about this issue because the court order against Motorola was handed down during the debates. The record establishes that the use of professionally developed ability tests would not be considered discriminatory." Despite this fact, the Supreme Court ruled that Duke Power Company was discriminating against blacks by requiring employees seeking promotions to have a high school diploma or a passing grade on Wonderlic and Bennett intelligence and mechanical comprehension tests.

The Supreme Court agreed with the lower courts that Duke

Power had not adopted the high school diploma and test requirements with any intention to discriminate against blacks. Burger
admitted that Duke Power's policy of financing two-thirds of the
cost of adult high school education for its employees suggested
good intent.[1] But the lack of a racist motive made no difference to
the Chief Justice. He decreed that the "absence of discriminatory
intent does not redeem employment procedures or testing mecha-
nisms that operate as 'built-in headwinds' for minority groups."
Burger was mistaken when he wrote, "Congress directed the
thrust of the Act to the *consequences* of employment practices, not
simply the motivation." It was precisely this misinterpretation of
the statute that the Dirksen Amendment was crafted to prevent.

Burger viewed the promotion requirements as "built-in
headwinds" against blacks because blacks were less likely than
whites to have completed high school or do as well on aptitude
tests. He cited census statistics showing that in 1960, 34 percent
of white males in North Carolina had completed high school compared to 12 percent of black males, and EEOC findings that 58
percent of whites passed the Wonderlic and Bennett tests compared to 6 percent of blacks. Blaming these disparities on segregation, Burger said that "under the Act, practices, procedures, or
tests neutral on their face, and even neutral in terms of intent,
cannot be maintained if they operate to 'freeze' the status quo of
prior discriminatory employment practices." Burger destroyed
job testing when he declared: "The Act proscribes not only overt
discrimination but also practices that are fair in form, but discriminatory in operation."

Burger's casuistry was to be given a name. In 1976 EEOC
District Counsel Barbara Lindemann Schlei called the change in
emphasis from motivation to consequence "disparate impact" dis-

---

[1] By the time the case reached the Supreme Court, nine of the original thirteen
black plaintiffs had earned promotions, some because of this program.

crimination. One year later, the Supreme Court used this terminology for the first time in the case of *International Brotherhood of Teamsters v. United States*, which dealt with burdens of proof in Title VII cases attacking union seniority systems. "Proof of discriminatory motive," the Court said, "is not required under a disparate-impact theory." In a footnote the Court cited *Griggs*, Schlei, and Blumrosen. Henceforth, any requirement that had a disparate impact on the races, regardless of intent or the reasonableness of the requirement, constituted discrimination. In employment and promotions, unequals had to be treated as equals. The same was soon to follow in university admissions testing. Race-based privileges had found their way into law.

In *Griggs*, Chief Justice Burger said that employers could escape prima facie Title VII liability for discrimination lawsuits only if test requirements were "demonstrably a reasonable measure of job performance." Pulling a phrase out of thin air, Burger wrote that "the touchstone is business necessity. If an employment practice which operates to exclude Negroes cannot be shown to be related to job performance, the practice is prohibited." Employers now had to prove their innocence by race-norming their testing so that blacks could qualify with lower scores. Burger invented a statutory hook for his ruling by asserting, falsely, that "Congress has placed on the employer the burden of showing that any given requirement must have a manifest relationship to the employment in question." It was precisely this heavy-handed intrusion into job requirements that the Tower Amendment was designed to prevent.

Burger's deference to the EEOC made clear that the agency would become the national arbiter of job tests. Following *Griggs*, the agency immediately issued manuals warning employers that unless they "voluntarily" increased their minority statistics, they risked costly liability. Ultimately, it became prohibitively expensive to use job tests unless they were race-normed to eliminate disparate impact. By 1984 it had become illegal to give an IQ test to a black in a public school in the state of California.[2]

In a subsequent case interpreting *Griggs*, Justice Harry Blackmun expressed his concern that the EEOC's guidelines would lead to hiring based on race rather than merit. He warned that "a too-rigid application of the EEOC Guidelines will leave the employer little choice, save an impossibly expensive and complex validation study, but to engage in a subjective quota system of employment selection. This, of course, is far from the intent of Title VII."

But by then it was too late. In *Griggs*, the Court killed four birds with one stone: Senator Tower's amendment on tests, Senator Dirksen's amendment on intent, Senator Humphrey's guarantee that the Civil Rights Act could not be used to induce quotas, and Congressman Celler's amendment preventing the EEOC from issuing substantive regulatory interpretations of Title VII. The EEOC wanted quotas. "At the EEOC we believe in numbers," Chairman Clifford Alexander declared in 1968. In pursuit of its goal, the agency assumed power it did not have. In 1972 Blumrosen went so far as to boast of his usurpation of power. The EEOC's power to issue guidelines, he wrote in the *Michigan Law Review*, "does not flow from any clear congressional grant of authority."

In *Griggs*, Burger created what would come to be known as disparate impact without realizing its quota implications. He thought that he was just attacking what today is called "credentialism." As the holder of a law degree from an obscure night school in St. Paul, Minnesota, Burger may have been thinking of himself when he wrote that "history is filled with examples of men and women who rendered highly effective performance without the conventional badges of accomplishment in terms of certificates, diplomas, or degrees." Surrounded by Court colleagues and

---

[2] *Larry P. by Lucille P. v. Riles*, 793 F.2d 969 (9th Cir. 1984).

clerks with prestigious Ivy League degrees, Burger may have tast-
ed credential discrimination himself. He thought that the Court
could take away the "headwind" of credentialism that blew
against blacks without creating a privileged position for minorities.

Before *Griggs,* any employer so inclined could take the measure of prospective employees and make bets on people with
obscure backgrounds who may not have had the best chances in
life. But after *Griggs*, no employer could risk hiring a white male
from William Mitchell Law School in St. Paul over a black from
Harvard. *Griggs* made race a critical factor in employment decisions. High school diplomas, arrest records, wage garnishments,
dishonorable military discharges, and grade point averages have
all become forbidden considerations in an employer's hiring decisions because they are criteria that could have a disparate impact
on blacks. Farmers have even been sued for asking prospective
farm hands whether they can use a hoe on the grounds that blacks
have a greater propensity to back problems. Disparate impact
does not pertain only to blacks. Perfectly sensible height and
weight requirements for prison guards and police officers have
also been struck down for having a disparate impact on women.
Just as Hubert Humphrey thought that government regulation
could intrude in areas that had always been ruled by freedom of
conscience without leading to any such result as *Griggs*, Burger
thought job requirements could be loosened to boost blacks without creating the privileged estate now known as "protected
minorities."

The EEOC's strategy that led to *Griggs* was not created in a
vacuum. Civil rights activists needed a new cause, and preferences
that would enable blacks to attain equality of result became the
new goal. In January 1965, *Playboy* magazine asked Martin
Luther King, Jr.: "Do you feel it's fair to request a multibillion-dol-
lar program of preferential treatment for the Negro, or for any
other minority group?" King replied, "I do indeed." In 1969 the

Fifth Circuit Court of Appeals—the same court that had initiated
school busing in the name of "racial balance"—cast aside section
703(j) of the Civil Rights Act when it upheld a court order that
every other person admitted to a Louisiana labor union must be
black to attain a one-to-one black/white ratio. Responding to the
argument that this order clearly violated section 703(j), the three-
judge panel simply wrote, "We disagree."

President Johnson was the most prominent proponent of the
shift in philosophy away from the color-blind ideal. At his commencement speech at Howard University on June 4, 1965, Johnson
said that the disappearance of legal segregation was not enough:

> You do not take a person who, for years, has been hobbled by
> chains and liberate him, bring him up to the starting line of a
> race and then say, "You are free to compete with all the oth-
> ers," and still justly believe that you have been completely fair.
>
> Thus it is not enough just to open the gates of opportunity. All
> our citizens must have the ability to walk through those gates.
>
> This is the next and the more profound stage of the battle for
> civil rights. We seek not just freedom but opportunity. We seek
> not just legal equity but human ability, not just equality as a
> right and a theory but equality as a fact and equality as a result.

To back up his speech with action, Johnson issued Executive
Order 11246, which put the phrase "affirmative action" into common parlance.[3] The order itself did not require federal govern-

---

[3] Because of an apparent oversight within the Johnson White House, Executive
Order 11246 did not proscribe discrimination on the basis of sex. When a
reporter asked White House Press Secretary Bill Moyers about the omission when
the order was issued on September 24, 1965, Moyers replied, "Sex also."
However, it took two years before Johnson issued Executive Order 11375 expanding the earlier order with the words: "It is desirable that the equal employment
opportunity programs provided for in Executive Order 11246 expressly embrace
discrimination on account of sex."

ment contractors to hire by the numbers, but Johnson's equality of results rhetoric and his metaphor of helping a hobbled runner provided the primary emotional justification for "affirmative action."

The quotas that now web federal contractors under Executive Order 11246 were implemented by the Nixon administration. Just as Burger thought that *Griggs* was a blow against credentialism that was perfectly compatible with the Civil Rights Act's prohibition of "discriminatory preference for any group," Nixon's Labor Secretary George P. Shultz, a labor economist from the University of Chicago, saw the Philadelphia Plan as a way of making an end run around the Davis-Bacon Act. Davis-Bacon was a pro-union measure enacted in 1931. It inflated the cost of federal construction contracts by setting wages at "prevailing union levels." Chicago economists have always despised Davis-Bacon for the extra burden it placed on taxpayers. The civil rights movement provided them with a way to assault this Democratic sacred cow and open up labor markets. Davis-Bacon meant that nonunion contractors and nonunion labor (many of whom were black) could not get government contract work. Sensitive to charges that he was hostile to civil rights, Richard Nixon wrote in his memoirs that he accepted Shultz's proposal to revive the Philadelphia Plan, which the Johnson administration had shelved, to demonstrate to blacks "that we *do* care."

On June 27, 1969, Assistant Secretary of Labor Arthur A. Fletcher, a former black businessman and Baltimore Colts and Los Angeles Rams football player, announced the Philadelphia Plan in the City of Brotherly Love. He said that while "visible, measurable goals to correct obvious imbalances are essential," the plan did not involve "rigid quotas." The *Congressional Quarterly* disagreed with Fletcher, calling the Philadelphia Plan a "nonnegotiable quota system."

Under the plan, the Labor Department's Office of Federal Contract Compliance (OFCC) would assess conditions in the five-county Philadelphia area and set a target for minorities in several construction trades—ironworkers, plumbers, pipe fitters, steamfitters, sheet metal workers, electrical workers, and elevator construction workers—in order to attain a racially proportionate workforce. Potential federal contractors would then have to submit complex affirmative action plans detailing goals and timetables to hire blacks within each trade to satisfy the OFCC's "utilization" targets as a precondition to having their bids considered. Arthur Fletcher said that the Philadelphia Plan "put economic flesh and bones on Dr. King's dream."

Senator Dirksen recognized a quota when he saw one. He began organizing against the Philadelphia Plan because of its violation of section 703(j) of the 1964 Civil Rights Act. But Dirksen died in September 1969. Senator Sam Ervin (D-N.C.), who would achieve national fame as chairman of the Senate Watergate Committee, tried to carry on the fight after Dirksen's death, but by then the Nixon administration had succeeded in framing the debate in terms of executive power under Executive Order 11246.

When the Philadelphia Plan reached the Third Circuit Court of Appeals in the 1971 case of *Contractors Association of Eastern Pennsylvania v. Secretary of Labor*, the court accepted the Nixon administration's position that "goals and timetables" were not quotas, and even if they were, that the Civil Rights Act's ban on quotas only limited Title VII remedies under the act and did not prohibit the imposition of quotas by other authorities, such as states or federal executive orders.

The Supreme Court avoided the controversial quota issue by refusing to review the case. Although the ruling had no force outside the Third Circuit, the Nixon administration interpreted the Supreme Court's lack of interest as a green light. As Laurence H. Silberman, who was undersecretary of labor at the time, later wrote, the Nixon administration went on to spread Philadelphia Plans "across the country like Johnny Appleseed." The Labor

Department quickly issued Order Number 4, which required all federal contractors to meet "goals and timetables" to "correct any identifiable deficiencies" of minorities in their workforces. Contractors hired minorities to guard against the sin of "underutilization," and racial proportionality became a precondition to government largesse. As Arthur Fletcher estimated at the time, the new quota regime covered "from one-third to one-half of all U.S. workers."

Although the phrase "federal contractor" conjures up images of workers in hard hats busy with construction projects or weapons systems, colleges and universities are also federal contractors, because they receive federal funds for research grants and financial aid to students. Following the Labor Department's lead, Nixon's Department of Health, Education, and Welfare soon required similar "goals and timetables" for faculty hiring—thereby launching the current pervasive quota system in the American academy.

In short, the carrot of government contracts and the stick of disparate impact liability under *Griggs v. Duke Power* quickly established quotas. For many corporate managers, hiring by the numbers was the only protection against discrimination lawsuits and the loss of lucrative government contracts. The section 703(j) prohibition of quotas in the Civil Rights Act remained in the law but meant nothing.

Reverse discrimination was in. When the liberal Justice William O. Douglas, the only remaining member of the *Brown* Court, tried to get his Supreme Court colleagues to review the case of a white who was refused admission to the Arizona bar to make room for blacks with lower bar exam scores, he argued that "racial discrimination against a white was as unconstitutional as racial discrimination against a black." Douglas failed to persuade his fellow Justices. He reports in his autobiography that Thurgood Marshall replied, "You guys have been practicing discrimination for years. Now it is our turn."

Douglas tried again in 1974 to get the Court to address quotas. Marco DeFunis, a Jew, challenged the University of Washington Law School's 20 percent quota for blacks. The school had rejected DeFunis although his GPA and test scores surpassed thirty-six of the thirty-seven admitted blacks. Using his powers as a circuit justice, Douglas stayed the Washington State supreme court's ruling against DeFunis and ordered his admission.

But by the time the DeFunis case came before the Supreme Court, DeFunis was about to receive his degree. This let the Court avoid the quota issue by declaring the DeFunis case moot. Douglas dissented on the mootness ruling and addressed the case's merits. He viewed *DeFunis* just as he had *Brown*: "There is no superior person by constitutional standards. A DeFunis who is white is entitled to no advantage by reason of that fact; nor is he subject to any disability, no matter what his race or color. Whatever his race, he had a constitutional right to have his application considered on its individual merits in a racially neutral manner."

But time had passed Douglas by. In Douglas' mind, discrimination was still connected with merit. DeFunis' scores showed that he met a higher objective standard than those admitted in his place, a clear case of reverse discrimination. By this time, however, any standard that had disparate impact on minorities was ipso facto discriminatory. In the eyes of Douglas' colleagues, DeFunis was simply a beneficiary of a discriminatory standard. Douglas, who had supported the *Griggs* decision, obviously had no comprehension of its implications.

The quota issue reemerged in 1978 when a rejected white male medical school applicant, Allan Bakke, challenged the University of California Medical School's policy of reserving 16 percent of medical school admissions for minorities. Each of the accepted minorities had inferior academic credentials to Bakke. In a 156-page opinion with 167 footnotes, the Justices reached the schizophrenic conclusion that Bakke should be admitted, but that certain skin colors could nevertheless be considered grounds for collegiate admissions if the goal was to enhance "educational diversity."

Bakke destroyed more than equal treatment under the Civil Rights Act. In his book, *The Intelligible Constitution*, Yale law professor Joseph Goldstein argues that the Supreme Court has failed in its role as the interpreter of last resort of the U.S. Constitution because opinions such as *Bakke* are incomprehensible to the public. "We the People" loses its political meaning when people can no longer understand the Court's application of the Constitution to contemporary issues.

A year later the Supreme Court upheld racial quotas. In a case brought by Brian Weber, the Supreme Court ruled that companies could "voluntarily" impose quotas on themselves to avoid liabilities under *Griggs* and the Philadelphia Plan. Pressured by OFCC affirmative action requirements and the need to forestall Title VII liability under *Griggs*, Kaiser Aluminum, like many companies, entered into a quota agreement with its union, the United Steelworkers of America, AFL-CIO, in 1974.[4] The agreement stipulated that "not less than one minority employee will enter" apprentice and craft training programs "for every nonminority employee" until the percentage of minority craft workers approximated the percentage of minorities in the regions surrounding each Kaiser plant. Two seniority lists were drawn up, one white and one black, and training openings were filled alternately from each list.

Brian Weber, a thirty-two-year-old white blue collar worker who had ten years' seniority as an unskilled laboratory technician at Kaiser Aluminum's plant in Gramercy, Louisiana, applied for a training program slot, but was denied in favor of two blacks with

---

[4] In defending its quota system against Weber's suit, Kaiser argued that its plan was justified because it feared black employees would bring suit under Title VII if it did not adopt an affirmative action plan and it would therefore lose government contracts for not complying with the Philadelphia Plan.

less seniority. After his union denied his grievance, Weber wrote the local EEOC office requesting a copy of the 1964 Civil Rights Act. When the Civil Rights Act arrived in the mail, Weber read it through and found that it said "exactly what I thought. Everyone should be treated the same, regardless of race or sex." Encouraged by the statute's words, he filed a class action suit representing his plant's white workers and won before district and appellate courts, but lost before the Supreme Court.

During the Supreme Court oral arguments, Justice Potter Stewart bluntly quipped, "We're here to see if the law lets an employer discriminate against some white people." Justice William Brennan's answer for a 5–2 majority was an emphatic "Yes!" The opinion written by Brennan said that the meaning of the 1964 Civil Rights Act could not be found in its statutory language, but resided in its spirit, which Brennan had divined. Brennan asserted that the act's clear statutory language and the Dirksen, Tower, and Celler amendments conveyed a meaning that was the opposite of what Congress had really intended. A literal reading of Title VII, he said, would "bring about an end completely at variance with the purpose of the statute." In enacting the Civil Rights Act, Brennan said that "Congress' primary concern" was with the plight of the Negro in our economy. Thus, anything that helped minorities was broadly consistent with this purpose. This included racial quotas as long as they were voluntarily adopted by the companies and not required by the federal government under Title VII. Brennan denied that Kaiser's plan would lead to quotas: "The plan is a temporary measure; it is not intended to maintain racial balance, but simply to eliminate a manifest racial imbalance."

Chief Justice Burger had created disparate impact in his *Griggs* opinion without realizing its quota implications. Now that quotas were upon him, he found himself joining in dissent with Justice William Rehnquist. Brennan's *Weber* opinion, they said, was "Orwellian." In *Griggs*, the Court had declared that "discrim-

inatory preference for any group, minority or majority, is precisely and only what Congress has proscribed." But eight years had
passed, and the Civil Rights Act had been fully reconstructed.
Burger and Rehnquist's alarm showed in their dissenting language: "By a tour de force reminiscent not of jurists such as Hale,
Holmes, and Hughes, but of escape artists such as Houdini, the
Court eludes clear statutory language, uncontradicted legislative
history, and uniform precedent in concluding that employers are,
after all, permitted to consider race in making employment decisions." The Court "introduces into Title VII a tolerance for the very
evil that the law was intended to eradicate," Rehnquist said.
Moreover, Brennan's reading of section 703(j) was "outlandish" in
light of Title VII's other "flat prohibitions" against racial discrimination and is "totally belied by the act's legislative history."
Rehnquist cited a congressional interpretative memorandum
making clear that "Title VII *does not permit* the ordering of racial
quotas in businesses or unions and does not permit interferences
with seniority rights of employees or union members." But Burger
had set the stage for *Weber* with *Griggs*, and it was the pot calling
the kettle black when Burger accused Brennan of amending the
Civil Rights Act "to do precisely what both its sponsors and its
opponents agreed the statute was not intended to do."

Having ruled in *Weber* that reverse discrimination was
"benign discrimination," subsequent Supreme Court decisions
upheld other quota schemes. In the 1980 case of *Fullilove v.
Klutznick*, the Court said that a federal spending program setting
aside 10 percent of federal funds for minority businesses on public works projects neither violated the Constitution's guarantee of
equal protection of the laws nor the Civil Rights Act of 1964.

In the 1987 case of *Johnson v. Transportation Agency, Santa
Clara County*, the second-class citizenship of white males became
official. The Court ruled that job discrimination against a white
male in favor of a woman with lower performance ratings was

perfectly legal under Title VII, even though the county's transportation agency had no record of prior discrimination requiring
remedies. Rehnquist, Byron White, and Antonin Scalia didn't like
the decision. Scalia said that "we effectively replace the goal of a
discrimination-free society with the quite incompatible goal of proportionate representation by race and by sex in the workplace."
He noted that civil rights had become a cynical numbers game
played among politicians, lobbyists, corporate executives, lawyers,
and government bureaucrats:

> It is unlikely that today's result will be displeasing to politically
> elected officials, to whom it provides the means of quickly
> accommodating the demands of organized groups to achieve
> concrete, numerical improvement in the economic status of
> particular constituencies. Nor will it displease the world of cor-
> porate and governmental employers (many of whom have filed
> briefs as amici in the present case, all on the side of Santa
> Clara) for whom the cost of hiring less qualified workers is
> often substantially less—and infinitely more predictable—than
> the cost of litigating Title VII cases and of seeking to convince
> federal agencies by nonnumerical means that no discrimina-
> tion exists. In fact, the only losers in the process are the
> Johnsons of the country, for whom Title VII has been not mere-
> ly repealed but actually inverted. The irony is that these indi-
> viduals—predominantly unknown, unaffluent, unorganized—
> suffer this injustice at the hands of a Court fond of thinking
> itself the champion of the politically impotent. I dissent.

Brennan said that the "central meaning" of the *Bakke* decision was that government may take race into account if it acts to
"remedy disadvantages cast on minorities by past racial prejudice" after making appropriate findings by competent judicial, legislative, or administrative bodies. A decade later in *City of
Richmond v. J.A. Croson Company*, the Court established a new
highly paid consulting business preparing "disparity studies" to

justify quota schemes with "proper findings" of past discrimination to "define both the scope of the injury and the extent of the remedy necessary to cure its effects." The disparity studies spawned by *Croson* resulted from the effort of newly appointed Justices O'Connor, Kennedy, and Scalia to bring intent back into the discrimination picture. These appointments produced a new majority somewhat sensitive to the extent to which social engineering had run away with the law.

The August 15, 1994, issue of *Forbes* reports that nationwide, taxpayers have spent $45 million on disparity studies to insulate the hundreds of state and local minority setaside programs from attack. In 1993 University of Maryland scholar George R. LaNoue reported in the *Public Interest* that most of these studies were flawed and were based on contrived anecdotes and statistics. LaNoue noted that "whatever their flaws as social science, the disparity studies have proved a potent weapon in keeping alive racial classifications in public contracting.... No matter how poorly done, a several-hundred-page disparity study 'proving discrimination' will quiet critics in the political and business community just by its existence." At the same time, the studies raised the level of racial tension. LaNoue concluded that "flawed disparity studies have inflated and distorted the presence of discrimination; as a result, they may well worsen racial polarization."

In 1990, in *Metro Broadcasting v. Federal Communications Commission*, the Court used *Croson*'s criterion, "findings of past discrimination," to uphold the FCC's allocation of broadcast licenses by race. In his opinion, Brennan emphasized that Congress and the Federal Communications Commission had made the necessary disparity findings to justify broadcast license quotas.

Six months after *Croson*, the Supreme Court, confronting the brutal quota implications of *Griggs*, balked. In *Wards Cove v. Atonio*, the Court ruled that statistical disparities were insufficient to establish a prima facie case of discrimination. In this case, the

racial minorities who comprised a majority of the unskilled workforce at two Alaskan salmon canneries brought a discrimination
lawsuit based on the fact that whites held a majority of skilled
office positions. The suit claimed that this constituted underutilization of preferred minorities in office positions and was evidence of racial discrimination.

The majority opinion written by Justice White rejected the
discrimination claim. In its opinion, the Court said:

> Any employer who had a segment of his work force that
> was—for some reason—racially imbalanced, could be hauled
> into court and forced to engage in the expensive and time-
> consuming task of defending the "business necessity" of the
> methods used to select the other members of his work force.
> The only practicable option for many employers will be to
> adopt racial quotas, ensuring that no portion of his work
> force deviates in racial composition from the other portions
> thereof; this is a result that Congress expressly rejected in
> drafting Title VII.

The tempo was picking up. A week after *Wards Cove*, the
Court ruled in the case of *Martin v. Wilks* that victims of reverse
discrimination due to consent decrees that imposed quotas had
the right to challenge the decrees in court. The Court noted that
victims of reverse discrimination found their rights affected by
lawsuits to which they were not parties. The majority held that it
was a deep-rooted principle of our jurisprudence that "a person
cannot be deprived of his legal rights in a proceeding to which he
is not a party."

These rulings caused an uproar from civil rights activists
who charged that the new Reagan Court was racist. These cases
in reality were attempts to return to equality under the law and
the statutory language of the Civil Rights Act. Clearly, efforts to
return to law were alarming to a civil rights movement that had

become accustomed to social engineers conveying privileges upon it in pursuit of equal results.

Civil rights activists need not have worried. The illegal privileges that had evolved over eighteen years since *Griggs* had become a squatter's right, and Congress and the Bush administration were bullied into codifying into law the new inequality. The 1991 Civil Rights Act, in effect, repealed the 1964 act by legalizing racial preferences as the core of civil rights law. The 1991 act was designed to overturn the *Wards Cove* and *Wilks* rulings and to codify the statistical disparities standard created by *Griggs*.

The statute also slammed shut the courthouse doors to white male victims of reverse discrimination. If statistical disparities or racial imbalance is proof of discrimination, white males adversely affected by quotas can have no standing in court. To give them standing would necessarily imperil the quota remedies for racial imbalance. You cannot simultaneously declare that anything short of proportional racial representation is discrimination and recognize the adverse impact of the "remedy" on white males. Under the 1991 Civil Rights Act, white males can have no grounds for discrimination lawsuits until they are statistically underrepresented in management and line positions. They have no claims to be statistically represented as hirees, trainees, and promotees until preferred minorities are proportionately represented in management and line positions. If Brennan's interpretation prevails that the Civil Rights Act was enacted because of "the plight of the Negro" and that anything that helps preferred minorities is broadly consistent with the act, the disparate impact standard could one day be ruled inapplicable to whites. The continuing growth of status-based privileges implies a white male underclass.

The 1991 Civil Rights Act added compensatory and punitive damages to the pressure for quotas. In his article, "Understanding the 1991 Civil Rights Act" in *The Practical Lawyer*, Irving M. Geslewitz recommends that corporations apply a cost-benefit analysis to determine whether "they are safer in hiring and promoting by numbers reflecting the percentages in the surrounding community than by risking disparate impact lawsuits they are likely to lose." To counter charges of "hostile work environments," company lawyers want to be able to tell juries that defendants have many minority and women employees at all levels.

The day after the Civil Rights Act of 1991 became law, a *New York Times* article, "Affirmative Action Plans Are Part of Business Life," observed that quota policies are as "familiar to American businesses as tally sheets and bottom lines." A 1991 *Business Week* article, "Race in the Workplace: Is Affirmative Action Working?" reported that affirmative action is "deeply ingrained in American corporate culture.... The machinery hums along, nearly automatically, at the largest U.S. corporations. They have turned affirmative action into a smoothly running assembly line, with phalanxes of lawyers and affirmative-action managers."

The 1964 Civil Rights Act, which undertook to eliminate race and sex from private employment decisions, has instead been used to make race and sex the determining factors. Private decisions that formerly were left to freedom of conscience are now determined by regulation and lawsuit. Reverse discrimination is a fact of life. Indeed, the situation for white males today is, in a strictly legal sense, worse than it was for blacks under *Plessy's* separate but equal doctrine. From a practical standpoint, blacks suffered unequal treatment under *Plessy*, but the constitutional decision required equal treatment under law. In contrast, under today's civil rights regime whites can be legally discriminated against in university admissions, employment, and the allocation of government contracts.

When the Supreme Court permitted racial segregation under Louisiana law regulating public transportation in *Plessy v. Ferguson* in 1896, it did so on the grounds that the state law required equal facilities and that separate accommodation was a social convention, akin to earlier "ladies' cars" on public trains, that did not apply "to nurses attending children of the other race" and did "not necessarily imply the inferiority of either race to the other." In other words, even segregationists had to accept equality before the law as the operative de jure principle.

In his famous dissent, Justice John Marshall Harlan was concerned that the Louisiana law would allow class distinctions to enter the legal system in the form of race distinctions. The Louisiana law was particularly dangerous because blacks and whites were economically as well as racially distinct. Thus, racial distinctions were also class distinctions and a return to status-based law. Harlan was certain that he wanted no status-based distinctions in the law. Our Constitution, Harlan said,

> is color-blind, and neither knows nor tolerates classes among citizens. In respect of civil rights, all citizens are equal before the law. The humblest is the peer of the most powerful.

Harlan's statements that "our constitution is color-blind" and "all citizens are equal before the law" made him a champion of liberal beliefs. Today, Harlan's color-blind views are rejected by civil rights activists. Privilege before the law has replaced equality before the law.

Many federal agencies employ quotas as barriers against the advancement of white men. For example, a Defense Department memo cited by Catherine Crier on ABC-TV's "20/20" program on November 18, 1994, specifies: "In the future special permission will be required for the promotion of all white men without disabilities." A recent court case, *Hopwood v. State of Texas*, indicates that the constitutional rights of whites are being subordinated to the quota privileges of "protected minorities." In his ruling, District Court Judge Sam Sparks found that the constitutional rights of four white law school applicants had been violated by the quota policies of the University of Texas Law School. He awarded them each $1 in damages, but refused to order them admitted ahead of protected minorities with substantially lower scores. In other words, the judge refused to take any steps to enforce the rights of the plaintiffs in whose favor he ruled. The nominal award signals that the constitutional rights of victims of reverse discrimination are not worth protecting.

The Assault on Majority Rule

Just as the Civil Rights Act of 1964 set out to eradicate intentional discrimination and ended up giving preferments, the Voting Rights Act of 1965 was intended to eliminate literacy tests and other barriers to black voting and has become an instrument to induce racially proportionate electoral *results*. Americans are finding that their right to elect their own leaders or to abide by majority rule may be challenged unless it produces racially proportionate results. This pursuit of racial results has created another new preferment. Blacks are permitted to vote racially, but whites are not. Whenever majority rule fails to result in minority electoral successes, courts can step in and impose remedies in the form of racially gerrymandered districts, cumulative voting schemes, and other circumventions of majority rule.

The purpose of the 1965 Voting Rights Act was to guarantee black access to the voting booth. With civil rights protests in the headlines, President Johnson told a joint session of Congress in March 1965 that the purpose of his bill was to eliminate "illegal barriers to the right to vote." The bill moved swiftly through Congress. After passing both houses with overwhelming majorities (in the House the margin of victory was 328–74, in the Senate, 79–18), Johnson held a nationally televised signing ceremony at the U.S. Capitol on August 6. He signed the bill in a room off the Senate chamber where, 104 years before, Lincoln had signed a bill freeing slaves pressed into service under the Confederacy.

Rather than banning literacy tests directly, the new law's core was a "triggering" provision authorizing the attorney general to suspend for five years "any test or device" used "as a prerequisite for voting or registration" in states in which less than 50 percent of the persons of voting age registered to vote or voted in the November 1964 presidential election. Moreover, the jurisdictions covered by this formula were required to obtain preclearance from the attorney general or the U.S. District Court for the District of Columbia for any new "voting qualification or prerequisite to voting, or standard, practice or procedure with respect to voting." Twenty-one states had literacy tests in 1965, but only seven Southern states were covered by the bill's registration and voting trigger.

Testifying before the House Judiciary Committee, Attorney General Nicholas Katzenbach declared that "the whole bill is really aimed at getting people registered." Responding to a question from California Democrat James C. Corman at the Judiciary Committee hearings about whether the bill would reach actions other than voter registration, such as changes in qualifications for office, Assistant Attorney General Burke Marshall replied, "The problem that the bill was aimed at was the problem of registration, Congressman. If there is a problem of another sort, I would like to see it corrected, but that is not what we were trying to deal with in the bill."

In a few short years, the Voting Rights Act's purpose was achieved as voter registration among Southern blacks soared. Over a million names were added to the voting rolls. The percentage of registered voting-age blacks in Mississippi jumped from 6.7 to 60 percent in only two years. Every other "covered" state made vast strides in black voter registration, all exceeding 51 percent by 1967.

In 1969, just as the statute attained its aim, the Supreme Court rewrote the law in the case of *Allen v. State Board of Elections*. In one of his last opinions, Chief Justice Earl Warren said for the Court's majority that the voting act "was aimed at the subtle, as well as the obvious, state regulations which have the effect of denying citizens their right to vote because of their race." Warren reasoned that "the right to vote can be affected by a dilution of voting power as well as by an absolute prohibition on casting a ballot." Changes in representation from legislative districts to at-large elections, the drawing of legislative districts, and even adjustments in the procedures for write-in voting, could all nullify the ability of racial minorities to "elect the candidate of their choice just as would prohibiting some of them from voting."

Justice John Marshall Harlan (grandson) dissented that the Court's opinion was "untrue to the statute's language" and "is unsupported by the legislative history." In his own dissent, Justice Hugo Black noted the preposterousness of both the Voting Rights Act and the majority opinion. He said the Constitutional Convention would have failed if the founding fathers had proposed giving the federal government the power to stop the passage of state laws until Washington had approved them.

By interpreting the Voting Rights Act as guaranteeing racially proportionate electoral outcomes, the Supreme Court made it an instrument for electoral preferments. Abigail Thernstrom wrote in the Spring 1979 issue of the *Public Interest* that "*Allen* set the tone for all future Voting Rights Act litigation. It permanently blurred the distinction between disenfranchisement and dilution, and between equality of political opportunity and equality of electoral result." With amendments in 1970, 1975, and 1982, the

Voting Rights Act now covers all states and includes Hispanics as well as blacks.[1] As with the 1964 Civil Rights Act after *Griggs*, statistics became everything in voting rights litigation.

Although the 1982 amendments stated that "nothing in this section establishes a right to have members of a protected class elected in numbers equal to their proportion in the population," electoral preferments were in the cards. In the 1986 case of *Thornburg v. Gingles*, the Supreme Court, in a ruling written by Justice Brennan, established what Justice O'Connor lamented as "an entitlement to roughly proportional representation." In 1994 in *Holder v. Hall*, Justice Clarence Thomas criticized the Court for making proportionality the driving principle of the Voting Rights Act. Critical Race Theorist Lani Guinier reached the same conclusion. She told her National Public Radio audience on the day of the decision that the Court had endorsed "proportionality as a baseline."

In a fifty-nine–page analysis, Justice Thomas, joined by Justice Antonin Scalia, decried the emergence and expansion of the proportionality requirement: "In construing the Act to cover claims of vote dilution, we have converted the Act into a device for regulating, rationing, and apportioning political power among racial and ethnic groups." This, Thomas said, requires the Supreme Court to become "a centralized politburo appointed for life to dictate to the provinces the 'correct' theories of democratic representation, the 'best' electoral systems for securing truly 'representative' government, the 'fairest' proportions of minority political influence." Thomas also attacked the "pernicious" premise that ideas and political interests are race-based. This premise, he says, logically leads to "segregating the races into political home-

---

[1] The 1970 amendment banned all literacy tests directly, thereby eliminating the original purpose of the "triggering" mechanism used to reform the original seven covered states. However, applying the Court's "vote dilution" standard, Justice Department "coverage" of these states continued.

lands that amounts, in truth, to nothing short of a system of political apartheid."

In a democracy, all votes are diluted. The votes of textile workers, for example, are diluted when Congress passes tariff reductions that sacrifice textile jobs for lower-priced imported apparel. The votes of high income earners are diluted when Congress passes tax bills raising income tax rates. The examples are endless.[2] Economists such as Anthony Downs, Gordon Tullock, and Nobel Prize winner George J. Stigler have noted that the probability that a person's vote will change the outcome of an election is so small that "the rational voter should stay at home." As all individual votes are diluted in the political marketplace, any effort to maximize the effectiveness of black and Hispanic votes gives these preferred minorities a privileged position relative to everyone else.

In the United States today, Democrats and Republicans routinely gerrymander electoral districts in efforts to produce electoral results favorable to their party. While it is permissible for Democrats to district out white Republicans and for Republicans to district out white Democrats, *Allen* and subsequent Supreme Court cases prevent reapportionments that would district out, or dilute, blacks and Hispanics. In practice, minimizing the dilution of preferred minority votes has meant maximizing preferred minority electoral results even when the consequence is to dilute the effective exercise of the electoral franchise by other ethnic groups.

In *United Jewish Organizations of Williamsburgh v. Carey*, for example, the Supreme Court rejected the reapportionment challenge of 30,000 Hasidic Jews living as a community in Williamsburgh, New York. The plaintiffs claimed that New York State's reapportionment plan diluted "the value of each plaintiff's

---

[2] Perhaps the ultimate form of vote dilution occurs when administrative agencies ignore clear statutory language, as when the EEOC turned a color-blind civil rights act into a mandate for racial quotas.

franchise by halving its effectiveness" by splitting the Hasidic community in half to maximize black voting strength. Justice Byron White's majority opinion essentially said that blacks are a favored group worthy of preferments, but Jews are not. Chief Justice Warren Burger dissented that "the result reached by the Court today in the name of the Voting Rights Act is ironic. The use of a mathematical formula tends to sustain the existence of ghettos by promoting the notion that political clout is to be gained or maintained by marshalling particular racial, ethnic, or religious groups in enclaves." The "mechanical" racial gerrymandering "moves us one step farther away from a truly homogeneous society" and marks a "retreat from the ideal of the American 'melting pot.'"

The reapportionments that pass muster are those that maximize the number of minority districts. During the Bush administration, lawyers from the Justice Department and the Republican party aligned with civil rights activists to push for minority districts after the 1990 census on the theory that by putting minorities in specified districts, the remaining districts would be more likely to vote Republican. This "unholy alliance," as described by NAACP lawyer Dennis Hayes, led to snakelike congressional districts connecting black-occupied houses.

There may be a limit, at least temporarily, to the extent to which racial gerrymandering can be pursued. In the 1993 case of *Shaw v. Reno*, the Supreme Court sent back to a lower court for reconsideration a North Carolina reapportionment scheme that had created a 160-mile-long black congressional district no wider in places than two lanes of Interstate 85. Similarly, on June 29, 1995, the Supreme Court in *Miller v. Johnson* condemned Georgia's racially gerrymandered 11th Congressional District, which connects black neighborhoods in metropolitan Atlanta with black precincts in Savannah, 260 miles to the east on the Atlantic coast. The Court found Georgia's 11th District unacceptable because "race was the predominant factor" in its creation under a

Justice Department "max-black" plan. The same day, however, in *DeWitt v. Wilson*, the Court upheld California's nine racially gerrymandered minority Congressional Districts. The Court has created a subjective area of permissible racial gerrymandering bordered by the requirement that minority votes not be diluted and a prohibition against odd and unusually shaped districts that reflect efforts to maximize minority representation at all costs.

In April 1994, U.S. District Judge Joseph H. Young found another way to impose racial proportionality. He decreed that a cumulative voting scheme had to be used in place of the at-large voting system for the Worcester County, Maryland, Board of Commissioners. Judge Young concluded from social science testimony that candidates favored by the county's blacks, who constituted 21 percent of the population, consistently lost commissioner elections because their votes were diluted by whites. Young found evidence of "racial polarization" in the fact that fewer whites than blacks voted for Jesse Jackson in Democratic presidential primaries. He discovered additional evidence of impermissible white racial voting in Maryland's failure to ratify the Fifteenth Amendment after the Civil War and in Worcester County's resistance to *Brown v. Board of Education* in the 1950s.

To remedy this Voting Rights Act violation, Young ordered that the at-large voting system, in which voters voted for five candidates, had to be changed to a cumulative voting system in which voters could cast all five votes for one candidate. Applying a "coefficient" called the "threshold of exclusion," which "identifies the percentage of the electorate that any group must exceed to elect a candidate of its choice regardless of how the rest of the electorate votes,"[3] Young decreed that a preferred minority in Worcester County was entitled to guaranteed racial representation if it

---

[3] Young said that, using cumulative voting, the "threshold of exclusion" was one divided by one plus the number of seats.

exceeded 16.7 percent of the votes. This requirement seems to pertain even if blacks prefer a white candidate. This privilege has not been extended to whites in black- or Hispanic-controlled cities.

Racial gerrymandering and cumulative voting schemes are just the first steps of a policy that demands racially proportionate results for preferred minorities. Once in office, preferred minority legislators experience vote dilution when they are outvoted by the white majority. Gaining their proportion of seats does not guarantee proportionate legislative results. To correct this "inequity," a supermajority requirement is imposed. The seven-member city council of Mobile, Alabama, cannot pass any ordinance with less than 71.4 percent of its vote. The supermajority requires that the majority of four whites gain the support of at least one of the three black members to achieve any result.

In Mobile, the 4–3 racial split resulted in a supermajority of five to ensure a share of outcomes for blacks. Had the split been 5–2, a supermajority of six would have been required. A split of 6–1 would have required unanimity. Nobel economics prize winner James M. Buchanan has noted that the unanimity rule would maximize the utility of legislative action by eliminating outcomes in which there are losers.

But not even the unanimity rule would satisfy the results-oriented requirements that judges have dug out of the Voting Rights Act. Under a unanimity rule, the preferred minority member could successfully block legislative action proposed by whites, but his own proposals would not be guaranteed legislative success. A federal judge could brand this failure as an example of "racial polarization" because whites did not vote for minority proposals. Ultimately, the implication of the results orientation of voting rights jurisprudence is that the preferred minority members get what they want. The tyranny of the minority, or rule by the preferred estate, is the logical outcome.

The U.S. Congress cannot forever hope to escape the results-oriented requirement imposed on Mobile's city council. Minority members of the U.S. Congress lack the votes to guarantee proportionate outcomes under majority rule. There is no reason why Congress should be immune from supermajority requirements or cumulative voting on bills. Before we continue on a path that leads either to legislative paralysis or to rule by a preferred estate, we should remember that just as everyone's votes are diluted in the election of government officials, elected legislators themselves find their votes diluted. The U.S. Congress is a ship with 535 oarsmen rowing in 535 different directions. The only way anything ever gets done is through a process called logrolling, in which legislators trade votes with one another. Logrolling is made possible because legislators have a free hand in choosing how to vote on any given issue. Even though a legislator from a farm district has no incentive to support an inner-city project, the legislator can trade support for the inner-city project in exchange for a city legislator's vote for farm price supports.

As each legislator represents a multitude of interests, the end results of logrolling are often unpredictable. Large industries such as tobacco producers that hire sophisticated lobbyists and make hefty campaign contributions still find themselves on the losing side of congressional votes. Labor unions and the textile industry could not stop the North American Free Trade Agreement (NAFTA). Scientists and the state of Texas lost the supercollider, the oil interests lost the depletion allowance, and the real estate industry lost its tax deductions. There are many losers in the legislative process, but the Voting Rights Act is being interpreted to mean that preferred minorities must not be among the losers.

We could regain sanity by realizing that most legislative issues are not black vs. white and that race and gender interests are no more deserving of preferments than class or economic interests. If we persist in creating a political system built upon racial preferments, democracy will be the casualty. The Voting

Rights Act is already being interpreted by judges to mean that preferred minorities are entitled by virtue of race to a proportionate share of leadership positions. As a result of court cases in Jackson, Tennessee, and Calhoun County, Alabama, the chairmanships of the city and county commissions respectively are required to rotate racially regardless of election outcomes to guarantee that preferred minorities share equally with other commissioners the position of chairperson of the commission. Will this preferment be extended to the Speaker of the House, the Senate majority leader, the Chief Justice? There is no reason to expect that the Voting Rights Act will not unfold to the limits of its logic.

CHAPTER NINE

The Proliferation of Privilege

Brown v. Board of Education, which set aside the democratic process to achieve a more integrated society, has instead led to separation and group privileges. In place of equality under the law and a color-blind society in which people are judged by their merit, we are confronted with the rise of new preferments based on race and gender. A new status-based legal system is evolving that allocates jobs, promotions, university admissions, board memberships, bonuses and awards, mortgage financing, voting outcomes, university tenure, access to training programs and gifted programs, and even reprimands and disciplinary action proportionately by race and gender.

This reappearance in the late twentieth century of status-based law, the antithesis of liberalism, was not the goal of the Myrdalian social engineers who took it upon themselves to hurry along racial integration. The quotas and various special dispensations were seen by those who helped to bring them about—such as Joseph Califano, who served in the Johnson and Carter administrations, and Laurence Silberman, who served in Nixon's administration—as temporary bootstrap measures to push blacks along faster. Once the process was begun, this winking at the law was supposed to stop. Califano, who was proud to have pushed for "the preference of blacks over whites for slots in colleges, jobs, and promotion" in the Johnson White House (and helped to solidify quotas as Jimmy Carter's HEW Secretary), wrote in 1989 that affirmative action was intended "only as a temporary expedient to speed blacks' entry into the social and economic mainstream." Its job was to pry "open some important doors for blacks, but it was never conceived as a permanent program and its time is running out."

Nixon officials who helped to institutionalize quotas later confessed to having engaged in self-deception. Silberman used an elaborate legal analysis to distinguish the Philadelphia Plan's "preferences" from illegal quotas. In 1977 he deplored his mistake: "I now realize that the distinction we saw between goals and timetables on the one hand, and unconstitutional quotas on the other, was not valid. Our use of numerical standards in pursuit of equal opportunity has led ineluctably to the very quotas, guaranteeing equal results, that we initially wished to avoid." Even those who were never fooled by euphemisms believed that the quotas were temporary. Nat Hentoff wrote in his book, *The New Equality*, that "compensatory special efforts for the Negro" are a "transitional tactic." As late as 1989, former EEOC Chairwoman Eleanor Holmes Norton still claimed that quotas "remain transitional and [will] fall into disuse once the job is done."

Today quotas are no longer seen as a temporary bootstrapping operation. They are justified as a new kind of entitlement necessary to indemnify minorities for past wrongdoing and to combat white racism. We are witnessing in the name of "diversity"—the new word for quotas—the development of a new constitutional right to proportional representation by race and gender in every aspect of life.

The belief that such an important entitlement as employment preferments could be revoked was based on careless and ahistorical thinking. History's compelling lesson is that privileges once granted are not easily rescinded. Marc Bloch's classic study, *Feudal Society*, shows how quickly temporary measures become rooted in permanence. Bloch reports that "every act, especially if it was repeated three or four times, was likely to be transformed into a precedent—even if in the first instance it had been exceptional or even frankly unlawful." A lord at Ardres once owned a bear that entertained the local inhabitants by fighting dogs. The inhabitants enjoyed the bear so much that they undertook to feed it bread. Long after the bear had died, the lord continued to exact the loaves of bread. In England, feudal tenants, whose ancestors were responsible for guarding the lord's castle, often had to pay dues in place of castle-guard service "for centuries after the castles themselves had crumbled into ruins."

Feudal privileges originated as temporary prerogatives of the king's bureaucracy. The chieftains who ascended to power after the fall of Rome divided the military and administrative responsibilities of governance among loyal followers. Because the absence of a money economy precluded paying salaries to these vassals, the medieval kings granted control of estates within their delegated territories to sustain them. These grants were sometimes called "fiefs," which then meant "to hand over temporarily, to lend," and initially they were revocable at the will of the king.

After Charlemagne's death in 814, his successors found themselves unable to revoke the temporary grants of privilege. The vassals developed greater independence from the king and increasingly held their positions for life. As time passed, these temporary privileges became the hereditary property rights of a new aristocratic class.

Disturbed by the erosion of his government's powers, one of Charlemagne's successors, Charles the Bald, tried in vain in 867 to take the county of Bourges from a rebellious vassal. Not long thereafter, to solidify his vassals' support for a military campaign, Charles issued the *placitum* of Quierzy in which he renounced his formal power to revoke fiefs, thus giving his imprimatur to what was already a customary privilege.

Initially, after kings realized that they lacked the ability to block their vassals' sons from inheriting the office, they retained for a period the right to confirm the heir in the office. A ceremony would be held in which the heir would accept his title as if it were still conveyed by the king. Eventually, even this legal pretense lapsed, swept away by the privileged entitlements that took a millennium to shatter.

As Oliver Wendell Holmes wrote in 1897, the deepest human instincts lay the "foundation of the acquisition of rights by lapse of time." Having been around for a generation, quotas are now protected by squatter's rights. The legal term for squatter's rights is "adverse possession." The doctrine says that the holders of property not legally their own can nevertheless keep it if sufficient time lapses. Holmes said that the "true explanation" for title by adverse possession is that "man, like a tree in the cleft of a rock, gradually shapes his roots to his surroundings, and when the roots have grown to a certain size, can't be displaced without cutting at his life."

Concerns about upsetting the applecart led Justice John Paul Stevens to extend quotas in the 1987 *Johnson* case even though he knew that Congress forbade them in the 1964 Civil Rights Act. Stevens admitted in his concurrence that even though "petitioner would unquestionably prevail" if Congress' original " 'color-blind' rhetoric" controlled, he decided to vote with a construction of the act "at odds with my understanding of the actual intent of the authors of the legislation" because "*Bakke* and *Weber* have been decided and are now an important part of the fabric of our law."

Stung by swift congressional rebuke of its *Wards Cove, Wilks,* and other 1989 civil rights decisions that put a brake on quotas, it is doubtful that the Supreme Court will again take the lead against quotas. When Justice Clarence Thomas headed the EEOC during the Reagan administration, he wrote that "quick-fix solutions, such as the appointment of another Justice with the right views, are not enough to ensure protection of our freedoms" and eliminate "hiring-by-the-numbers policies."

In 1990 Senator Sam Nunn withdrew his opposition to abortion on the grounds that women had exercised the right for seventeen years and it now was theirs under the doctrine of adverse possession. The Supreme Court took Nunn's view in 1992 when the Justices refused to overturn *Roe v. Wade*, despite serious reservations about the legal basis for the ruling, on the grounds that women had acquired squatter's rights to abortions: "An entire generation has come of age free to assume *Roe*'s concept of liberty in defining the capacity of women to act in society, and to make reproductive decisions," ruled the plurality opinion.

After being in effect for three decades, quotas are no longer rationalized as temporary expedients. The demand for legally mandated racial diversity means the expansion of quotas. Anyone who still believes that quotas are a temporary policy to push integration to a self-sustaining level is suffering from what the late philosopher Sidney Hook called a "pernicious illusion." "In human affairs," Hook wrote, "nothing is so likely to become permanent as the temporary."

Once implanted, quotas expand to the limits of their logic. Inevitably, subsequent expansions surprise and dismay those who thought that they had a limited application under control. Ever since *Brown*, the champion of each phase of the Supreme Court's postwar civil rights jurisprudence tried unsuccessfully to put brakes on the next step. Justice Felix Frankfurter balked at coercive measures like busing to integrate schools. Justice William O. Douglas pushed for busing, but he rejected quotas. Douglas said there was a "crucial difference" between busing to achieve racial balance and college admissions quotas. He reasoned that busing did not exclude anyone from a public school, but admissions quotas did. Justice William Brennan, the Court's quota architect, saw no difference between achieving racial balance by busing or by admissions quotas. But he was shocked by campus speech codes, which were instituted to appease disaffected minority students brought in to fill quotas. A year after his retirement Brennan expressed astonishment in an interview with Nat Hentoff—"I'll be damned!"—when informed that Stanford's speech code was supported by the Black Law Students Association, the Asian Law Association, the Native American Law Students Association, and the Jewish Law Students Association. Events had bypassed Brennan's liberal views to such an extent that he had become a reactionary. Brennan found himself in agreement with conservative Republican Representative Henry Hyde's bill to strike down the restrictive codes, and he expressed his opinion that the Court "ought to just abolish all of them."

Quotas have been opposed on the grounds that reverse discrimination violates the 1964 Civil Rights Act and the equal protection clause of the Constitution, but much more is at stake than simply reverse discrimination. Before our very eyes, a resurrection of feudalism is taking place in which individuals are no longer citizens of society, but members of estates with corresponding racial and gender privileges engrafted into law. The preferments have expanded far beyond collegiate admissions and employment hiring and have metastasized into generalized application.

One reason societies are surprised by their own developments is that there is always a vocal element denying the obvious. Long after quotas were institutionalized, some people were still denying that there were any quotas. Quota allegations were said to be scurrilous exaggerations designed to keep minorities in their places. A survey in the March 13, 1989, issue of *Fortune* magazine, however, revealed the pervasiveness of employment quotas. Only 14 percent of Fortune 500 companies hired on talent and merit alone; 18 percent admitted having racial quotas, while 54 percent used the euphemism "goals."

Five years later on January 31, 1994, *Business Week* featured a cover story, "White Male & Worried," which reported on the growing resentments of white males over reverse discrimination. The article quoted a white male, who had been passed over by preferred minorities and women, lamenting his "wrong pigment, wrong plumbing." Corporate consultant Harris Sussman told *Business Week* that "'White male' is what I call the newest swear word in America." The magazine reported that Sussman's own appearance at a corporate diversity seminar had been opposed by women and blacks because they saw no reason to "devote any time at all to white men."

Companies fill their quotas by recruiting at special minority job fairs set up by university placement offices. Many firms do not wait until graduation to pursue preferred minorities. Bell South targets minority freshmen to build a "pool of qualified minority candidates," which is then nurtured by special minority summer internship programs. According to the August 14, 1995, *Business Week*, Texaco and Dow Chemical "are building ties with minorities as early as high school." When forced to lay off workers, companies avoid discrimination lawsuits by using sophisticated statistical tests to ensure that the layoff list does not include too many people in legally protected groups.

Today, corporate managers' evaluations, bonuses, and promotions depend on their success at meeting "diversity goals" by hiring and promoting women and preferred minorities. Hughes Aircraft, for example, docked the bonuses of executives in two divisions by 10 percent because of bad grades on their "diversity report cards." Women and preferred minorities also receive special access to management through various grievance committees, which monitor workplace sensitivity and the advancements of women and preferred minorities.

The pressure on purchasing agents in industry and government to buy from minority suppliers has spawned special directories of minority-owned firms. The Thomas Publishing Company has a telephone keypad service in which purchasers can search through 3,500 product categories and get female and minority contractor information via fax within an hour. Corporations also choose outside law firms, not by their ability to cut deals or win lawsuits, but by their racial makeups. To boost their prospects, many big law firms, such as Jones, Day, Reavis & Pogue, have formed alliances with minority firms.

Some government set-aside programs cloak their racial nature under the guise of preferences for "socially and economically disadvantaged" individuals. However, these preferences apply "presumptively" to racial and ethnic minorities, while whites have to prove by "clear and convincing evidence" that they face "diminished capital and credit opportunities" to qualify. The presumption of disadvantage received by "protected minorities" is often farcical. Hispanic businessman Felix Granados is president of FAIC Securities, a prosperous financial firm that was set up by Florida's Fanjul family, owners of a $500 million sugarcane fortune, to take advantage of municipal bond set-asides for minorities. Mr. Granados defended the wealthy Fanjul family's claim to the set-aside by telling *Forbes* (March 13, 1995) that the relevant category "isn't 'economically disadvantaged.' It's 'minority.' And with a last name like Fanjul, that's just what they are."

Quotas are de rigueur for advertising that relies on models. The *New York Times* requires that real estate ads display a racially balanced mixture of models. Georgetown Law Professor Girardeau A. Spann, who is black, won an $850,000 verdict from an Arlington, Virginia, real estate developer whose condominium advertisements displayed only white models. As part of the settlement, the *Washington Post*, a co-defendant, agreed to a 25 percent black model requirement in its real estate ads. Imagine the ridicule that would have been heaped on the head of anyone who had predicted that civil rights legislation would lead to the specification of the permissible percentage of white models in real estate ads. Today such quotas are necessary not only to ward off lawsuits from minorities who could otherwise claim to be potential customers discouraged by racism, but also as evidence in employee discrimination suits that the business is diversity oriented.

Civil rights advocates in 1964 would have been astonished to hear that their handiwork would result in the requirement that mortgage lending criteria have no disparate impact on minorities and that this would be measured by the rejection rates of mortgage applications. As Nobel Prize winning economist Gary Becker has noted, statistical disparities in lending, like every other area, have many explanations other than racial discrimination. If mortgage lenders were discriminating, minority loans would have lower default rates than loans to whites. Lower default rates would be a sign that stricter, discriminatory, standards were being applied to minorities. In turn, that would mean that loans made to minorities would be more profitable than those made to whites. Yet no evidence exists that minority mortgage loans have lower default rates. Thus, there is no evidence of discrimination. Indeed, the evidence is to the contrary. In November 1994, Federal Reserve Board and other economists released an extensive study of 220,000 FHA mortgage loans from 1986 to 1989. The study found that black borrowers had higher default rates than whites. These results suggest that mortgage lenders feel pressured to give preferential treatment to protected minorities despite the higher risks.

But evidence has become irrelevant. The question is no longer one of discrimination but of preferment, and preferments require no evidence. They are a right. Just as discrimination ceased to require intent and could be established by statistical disparity, discrimination remedies themselves have been transmuted into preferments. In 1993 Shawmut National Corporation's acquisition plans were blocked by federal regulators until its subsidiary, Shawmut Mortgage Company, entered into a consent agreement with the Justice Department to racially norm its mortgage lending criteria in order to guarantee racial proportionality in mortgage lending.

Ten federal agencies quickly moved to incorporate the consent agreement in the growing body of regulations governing the allocation of mortgages and credit. In the jointly issued "Policy Statement on Discrimination in Lending" (March 8, 1994), loan criteria, regardless of intent, that "disproportionately and adversely" affect minority credit access are grounds for lawsuit. Just as employers have had to hire, promote, and discipline by racial proportion to avoid lawsuits, lenders must now allocate mortgages by race.

The Shawmut ruling was followed by an even more expansive interpretation of disparate impact. The Chevy Chase Federal Savings Bank in suburban Maryland was forced by the Justice Department to open four new branches in "majority African-American census tracts." As part of the settlement, Chevy Chase had to budget advertising for black publications, increase employment quotas, and provide below-market loans to blacks with interest rates "at either one percent less than the prevailing rate or one-half percent below the market rate combined with a grant to be applied to the downpayment requirement," to quote from the Justice Department's press release.

In April 1995 the Justice Department forced the American Family Mutual Insurance Company to sell property insurance to preferred minorities on uneconomic terms dictated by federal bureaucrats, thus setting aside the fundamental actuarial principle of risk-based premiums. Minorities have also acquired the right to force whites to enter into contracts with them. Like the 1964 Civil Rights Act, the Fair Housing Act of 1968 had a "Mrs. Murphy's" exemption for small owner-occupied boarding houses and another for the sale or lease by the owner of single-family owner-occupied housing. But in *Jones v. Alfred H. Mayer, Co.*, the Court trumped the Fair Housing Act with a new interpretation of an 1866 statute. The 1866 law had been enacted in order to give blacks the same rights as whites to enforce voluntary, mutually agreed contracts. The Court "discovered" in the 102-year-old law the right of blacks to force whites to enter into contracts involuntarily. In the 1976 case of *Runyon v. McCrary*, this right was extended from housing to private schools. For blacks, these rulings changed the right to make and enforce contracts with other willing parties into the privilege of requiring unwilling parties to enter into contracts with them. The 1991 Civil Rights Act wrote this privilege into the law.

Minority preferments also govern the allocation of government contracts, broadcast licenses, and scientific research grants. Having filled all economic channels, the preferments are flowing into nonpecuniary dimensions. Federal government managers now find that their task of holding subordinates accountable has been complicated by rules that require disciplinary actions to be racially proportioned. We can expect these new preferments to spread to the private sector as courts use the federal government's policies as a comparative baseline of proper institutional behavior in civil rights lawsuits.

The FBI has embraced a strict quota regime in which merit and bonus awards must be racially apportioned, along with promotions, access to training programs, appointments to SWAT and hostage rescue teams, and disciplinary actions. According to a consent decree settling a discrimination suit against the FBI brought by black agents, discipline cannot be "initiated against any group of employees at a statistically significant higher rate than any other group." Performance reviews must be race-normed, too, to prevent statistically significant disparities on the basis of race.

At the Department of Housing and Urban Development, for

managerial personnel to obtain an "outstanding rating," managers must be actively engaged in "promoting diversity." According to agency officials, this means that managers must be active members of minority, feminist, or homosexual organizations, act to ensure the career advancement of those with diversity status, and "volunteer as a mentor to instill the value of diversity."

The U.S. Merit Systems Protection Board, which oversees the civil service, now measures merit in terms of a civil servant's support for quotas. Duward Sumner, a spokesperson for the Merit Board, says that to qualify for the top performance evaluation, a bureaucrat must suggest ways to recruit more minorities. The same requirements now apply to top-level federal policymakers. Nominees must pass an FBI security clearance, which includes ascertaining whether the person has any ethnic or gender biases. Candidates who have shown insensitivity by expressing doubts about quotas or laughing at the wrong jokes don't qualify.

Alexis de Tocqueville described freedom of association as a "natural right of man" that "seems to me by nature almost as inalienable as individual liberty." Only federal employees who qualify as "protected minorities," however, are permitted by the U.S. government to exercise this right. The Coalition of Federal White Aviation Employees has been seeking recognition by the Federal Aviation Administration since 1992 without success. FAA employees are even forbidden from reading literature from the coalition. In contrast, the Council of African-American Employees, the National Asian Pacific American Association, the Gay, Lesbian or Bisexual Employees group, and the Native American/Alaska Native Coalition are officially recognized with access to bulletin boards, photocopying privileges, electronic mail, telephone voice mail, and permission to hold meetings in government facilities on government time.

In 1994 the federal Office of Personnel Management launched investigations into why minorities are disciplined and discharged at a higher rate than whites. It is reasonable that employees who are hired with lower, or "normed," qualifications to fill quotas would generally perform less well on the job and thus be more likely to receive correction. But James B. King, the director, worries that racially disproportionate disciplinary actions are a sign of institutionalized racism. A similar investigation at the Internal Revenue Service led to the development of a statistical model to determine the "evenly divided" level of disciplinary actions that supervisors are to uphold.

These developments should not surprise us. Once racism is designated as the cause of all differences, the use of quotas as corrective actions leads logically to group preferments. As the famed jurist Benjamin Cardozo said, in law there is a tendency for a principle to unfold to the limits of its logic. Preferments in university admissions soon spread to all other aspects of academic life. Just as the physically challenged or disabled have reserved parking places in parking lots, minorities have reserved positions on law reviews. In the 1920s and 1940s, blacks such as Charles Hamilton Houston and William T. Coleman, Jr., earned their way into Harvard Law School and onto its prestigious *Law Review* on the basis of merit. What they earned has since become a preferment.

Accreditation itself has become a tool for coercing preferments. Traditionally, accreditation depended on such factors as the percentage of faculty with Ph.D. degrees, the size of library collections, and financial resources. Now it depends on the promotion of multicultural curricula, the proportion of protected minorities on the faculty, and the proportion of minorities in graduating classes.

In 1991 the Middle States Association deferred the accreditation of Baruch College of the City University of New York and Westminster Theological Seminary in Philadelphia because of their "cultural diversity" shortcomings. Middle States charged that the "minority representation" of Baruch's faculty was inadequate and its "rate of retaining minority students was too low."

Westminster was assailed for having no women members on its governing board. This was because board membership was limited to ordained ministers, and Westminster Theological Seminary did not believe that women could be ordained. Secretary of Education Lamar Alexander pressured Middle States to back down in 1991, but the cat was out of the bag.

In February 1994 the Western Association of Schools and Colleges (WASC), which accredits colleges in California, Hawaii, and U.S. territories in the Pacific, adopted a diversity policy to promote the use of racial, ethnic, and sexual criteria in admissions, faculty hiring, and curriculums. The diversity statement's attack on academic freedom was too much for Stanford University, hitherto a leader in the diversity movement. Stanford's president declared that the university "will not... endorse WASC's continuing attempts to intrude upon institutional autonomy and integrity." But Stanford cannot resist what the FBI and General Motors cannot.

The world beyond the academy is no less awash in preferments. Symphony orchestras once had audition screens to prevent race from being a factor. Now that race must be a factor, the screens have come down.

This brief summary has far from exhausted the examples of quota privileges now accorded to preferred minorities. An attitude favoring ubiquitous proportionality has clearly emerged among civil rights activists. The U.S. Capitol art collection is under attack for having too many statues and paintings of white males. Of course, most of the statues and paintings represent former members of Congress who were white males, but that is considered proof of the race and gender hegemony that is in need of correction. The Metropolitan Museum of Art in New York City has also been attacked for having too few holdings by women and minority artists. At the 1993 annual conference of the College Art Association, a female professor from Boston University accused one speaker of "quotationage"—quoting too many male authorities.

Government quota requirements to counter "underrepresentation" in federal job categories are so strict that qualifications have become meaningless. On November 18, 1994, Catherine Crier reported on ABC-TV's "20/20" news program that U.S. Forest Service job postings for firefighting positions specified that "only unqualified applicants will be considered" and that "only applicants who do not meet standards will be considered." This meant that the jobs went to women, who filled 179 out of 184 openings during the hiring period. Calling the policy "quota lunacy," Representative Wally Herger (R-CA) said, "It is not a civil right to land a job for which one is unqualified. This is ridiculous."

In November 1994 William Jeffers, the Federal Aviation Administration's director for air traffic control, said that his agency was committed to filling "one out of every two vacancies with a diversity selection." To facilitate filling the quota, the FAA issued a "diversity handbook" for managers and supervisors in the summer of 1995. According to the handbook, "the merit promotion process is but one means of filling vacancies, which need not be utilized if it will not promote your diversity goals." One FAA job announcement quoted in the *Washington Times* (August 16, 1995) said: "Applicants who meet the qualification requirements... cannot be considered for this position.... Only those applicants who do not meet the Office of Personnel Management requirements... will be eligible to compete." To screen out qualified applicants "who meet the specialized experience requirements for the target position," the FAA has invented something it calls "qualification analysis." In other words, if you are qualified, you aren't.

Quotas have even taken precedence over military effectiveness and national defense. Morale and cohesion have been sacrificed to the sexual tensions and rivalries that result from mixing women with men aboard ships at sea, and gender quotas for fighter pilots have caused rigorous performance standards to be compromised. The physical standards for the service academies and military training have been reduced to accommodate the presence of women.

Gender quotas are even forcing universities to drop their football teams. As part of a discrimination settlement with the National Organization for Women, San Francisco State University terminated its football team in March 1995. The school was guilty of having a higher proportion of female students than female athletes. Dropping a male sport—football—and adding more women's sports achieved the required proportionality. Similarly, the same month U.S. District Judge Raymond Pettine found that Brown University discriminated against women because the ratio of female to male athletes was not "substantially proportionate" to the student body (women constituted 51 percent of the student body and 44 percent of the athletes). Brown's percentage of female athletes with ten female varsity teams was unusually high. "Remember Brown is ahead of the game," Brown attorney Beverly Ledbetter warned, "If they think we have a problem, other schools are in big trouble."

Originally, affirmative action meant that if the scores of a black candidate and a white candidate were equal, the black would be chosen. Then, with race-norming, blacks with lower scores would be chosen. Now whites are simply prevented from even taking the tests. In February 1994 the Los Angeles Fire Department turned away thousands of white applicants from taking its job test. Too many whites were expected to pass, a result that would conflict with a court order that 50 percent of those passing be minorities. One aspiring firefighter, Doug Maxwell, said, "I think it's discrimination. They have said to my face, you can't take the test because you are white."

Assaults are now being made on crime and punishment for having disparate impact on blacks. It is only logical that the demand for equal results rejects racial disproportion among criminal defendants and among the inmate population. Demands have already been made for the affirmative action records of prosecutors' offices in legal challenges to law enforcement that has a disparate impact. In 1991 the Minnesota Supreme Court struck down a crack cocaine law because of its disparate impact. The increased emphasis on prosecuting nebulous "white collar" crime, rather than following criminal evidence wherever it leads, reflects a growing pressure for racial balance in criminal prosecutions.

The Myrdalian assumption of white racism is now cited as a mitigating factor in the defense of blacks who have committed racial murders. Attorney William L. Kunstler said that "black rage" over systematic discrimination "was the catalyst for the insanity" that caused his client, Colin Ferguson, to go on a shooting spree on a Long Island commuter train in 1993 that killed six people and wounded nineteen others. Florida Supreme Court Justice Rosemary Barkett was appointed by President Clinton and confirmed by the Senate as a federal circuit court judge despite her view that punishments for murder must be race-normed. In Barkett's view, black defendant Charles Kenneth Foster drew a death sentence because of "aversive racism," not because he slit the throat and spine of a white victim on a Florida beach. In opposing the death sentence for Jacob John Dougan, who stabbed and shot a white "devil," Barkett argued that the murder was a

> social awareness case. Wrongly, but rightly in the eyes of Dougan, this killing was effectuated to focus attention on a chronic and pervasive illness of racial discrimination and of hurt, sorrow, and rejection. Throughout Dougan's life his resentment to bias and prejudice festered. His impatience for change, for understanding, for reconciliation matured to taking the illogical and drastic action of murder. His frustrations, his anger, and his obsession of injustice overcame reason.

The victim was a symbolic representative of the class causing
the perceived injustice.[1]

In the District of Columbia's federal court system, a "Task
Force on Gender, Race and Ethnicity" condemned race and gender
imbalances in employment, case win ratios, pretrial release rates,
and, of course, sentencing. Quotas are likely to prevail in the
administration of justice, just as they have in university admissions, hirings, promotions, the allocation of credit, and intra-
agency disciplinary actions.

Under a regime of preferments, careers are not "open to the
talents," but are limited by race and gender proportionality. The
distribution of careers by race is now a feature of legislative proposals. For example, the Clinton administration's health care plan
required racial balance in medical specialties.

By their nature quotas imply estates and unequal privileges.
We have been trained to see quotas as guaranteeing access for
minorities, but the other side of this coin is that quotas impose limits on white males. What is a preferment for one estate is a limit
on the other, and the contrast between privilege and limitation
brings out the disparate rankings of the racial estates.[2]

Once we accept the premise that all disparities result from
racism, the logical implication is that the distribution of income
will be adjusted each year to achieve racial proportionality. This is
the inevitable result of the path that we have taken. It will signify
the completion of the new feudal order that is being constructed
on the basis of racial and gender estates.

---

[1] Female defendants have successfully used the "abusive male" defense to escape
punishment for sexually mutilating their husbands.

[2] Gradations of privilege are forming within the class of "protected minorities."
Sharon Taxman, a Jewish schoolteacher in Piscataway, New Jersey, was laid off
to make room for a black woman. Though privileged on a gender basis, she was
bumped on a racial basis.

The New Marxists

T he pervasive reverse discrimination so characteristic of America today could, perhaps, be discounted if the result were a more integrated society. The pursuit of diversity, however, has resurrected separateness. We have already witnessed the appearance of voluntary segregation by blacks on college campuses and the separate management tracks established by corporate America in behalf of minorities and women. The ever-deepening wedge of separation is also driving the racial gerrymandering that is turning some congressional voting districts into thin lines drawn to connect black-occupied housing. University of Pennsylvania Law Professor Lani Guinier argues for black separateness and solidarity to counter "legislative vote dilution." She goes so far as to doubt that a black Republican representative could qualify as a black representative, because "only a representative sponsored by the black community and electorally accountable to it would count for purposes of a legislative bloc-voting analysis."

Guinier's view is standard fare among Critical Race Theorists, who argue that color blindness is "cultural genocide" for blacks. Critical Race Theorists are not so far out of the mainstream. Columbia Law School Dean Lance Liebman told the *New York Times* that "critical race theory is one of the most important intellectual movements in legal scholarship." A bibliography published in the *Virginia Law Review* lists 217 entries written by sixty-two authors from the most prestigious law schools. America's future legal elite—those who will become our lawyers, legislators, judges, and politicians—are being graded on how well they absorb this ideology. Some of Guinier's proposals have already been implemented by Reagan and Bush administration appointees. William Bradford Reynolds, Reagan's assistant attorney general for civil rights, approved the imposition of a supermajority on the Mobile, Alabama, city commission. His successor in the Bush administration, John Dunne, approved cumulative voting schemes for thirty-five jurisdictions and presided over the racial gerrymandering of congressional districts. If this movement continues to exert influence, our future as a unified people is in doubt.

Critical Race Theory is a legal ideology that justifies shriveling the democratic process and displacing equality before the law with race and gender privileges. Hegemony is a popular word among Critical Race Theorists, or Crits. The term was once used in foreign policy discussions to describe the Soviet Union's sway over its satellites and vulnerable neighboring states. Today hegemony refers to the superstructure of cultural, legal, political, and economic relationships that allegedly brainwash racial minorities into accepting their own oppression. Meritocracy, or the belief that people advance according to ability, is one villain of the piece. The concept of merit, the theory goes, not only implies "white male standards," but also serves the pretense that the elevated positions of white males are not based on their exclusion of minorities and women. The myth of the meritocratic society causes the oppressed to attribute their lack of success to their own unworthiness, while training white males to view their unjust domination as the natural result of applied ability.

Another villain is the myth of neutral legal principles. Critical legal and race theorists employ a technique that they call "trashing" to expose the hidden white male agenda behind every so-called neutral legal principle. For example, they "deconstruct" contract doctrine to show that it is really a tool for oppression. Freely negotiated contracts between a white male and a woman or a racial minority cannot be fair because the differing power positions of the parties don't permit them to bargain in equally unconstrained ways. For Crits, as for Marx, law is merely what serves the interest of a dominant group, defined today in terms of race or gender interests instead of the old Marxist economic or class interests.

Crits maintain that far from fostering a color-blind society, equality before the law perpetuates racism by opposing the remedial quotas and privileges necessary to shatter the hegemonic superstructure. Sidney Willhelm wrote in the *Michigan Law Review* that "the very idea of Equality, of treating Blacks and Whites alike, is racist because it fails to take account of over three hundred years of racist oppression. Equal opportunity is a myth because it ignores the tremendous advantages that Whites retain."

Like Myrdal, Crits deny that democracy produces moral outcomes. Goodwill cannot produce improvements in the positions of minorities because racism is simply the societal norm. It is so subconsciously ingrained that all whites are racists even if they have no racist intent. They are "aversive racists," unaware of the unconscious exercise of their prejudice.

Crits maintain that blacks cannot be integrated politically because whites will not vote for them. Any black who is elected by white votes, such as Virginia Governor Douglas Wilder, is dismissed as an "inauthentic black" who is marred by a "false consciousness."

Lani Guinier views such blacks as lacking the "voice of color." They fail to view the world through the "prism of race" and are "just physically black," lacking the requisite "cultural and psychological view of group solidarity." Uncle Toms doing the master's bidding, they cannot represent black interests.

In place of majority rule, Guinier proposes a result-oriented politics geared toward producing equal outcomes. She would achieve this by race-norming voting to give blacks an effective veto over the majority.[1] She would use such devices as cumulative voting, supermajorities, proportional representation, and gerrymandered districts to increase the weight of black votes. All of this is necessary to "re-orient our political imagination away from the chimera of achieving a physically integrated legislature in a color-blind society."

If it weren't for special pleading on the basis of race, Guinier's proposals could be seen as extensions of the protections against a runaway majority that are provided by the Constitution, federalism, a bicameral legislature, and the requirement for a 60 percent vote to cut off Senate debate. There are a variety of class, religious, ethnic, economic, and other interests that could claim protection against majority decisions: The incomes and estates of

---

[1] Race-norming began as the practice of curving employment and university admission tests to give minorities higher grades for lower raw scores. For example, when the Chicago police force took an exam for promotion of 500 officers to the rank of sergeant in 1987, the initial test scores yielded 416 successful whites, 66 blacks, and 18 Hispanics, but the scores were tinkered with to promote 332 whites, 138 blacks, and 30 Hispanics. The informal adjustment practices were later formalized by the U.S. Department of Labor. After receiving unfavorable publicity during the debate over the 1991 Civil Rights Act, the practice again became informal. Currently, it is known as "test-banding," in which preferences are given to blacks over whites within a range of raw scores. In the electoral context, racially normed voting weights black votes disproportionately to white votes so that individual black votes carry greater weight than individual white votes in congressional, state legislative, city council, school board, county commissioner, and state judicial elections.

successful people are discriminatorily taxed at progressive rates that do not apply to the majority; Mormons have been forced to abandon polygamy; homosexuals complain that the government does not recognize their same-sex marriages; Christians feel that their rights to express their faith publicly have been curtailed; people with welfare entitlements could claim a veto against dispossession; and whites in black-controlled political jurisdictions could claim supermajority and cumulative voting protections.

To avoid racial privileges, the protections against majority rule would have to be extended to every interest. There is something to be said for arrangements that would force government to do less but with greater support. But there is a fundamental problem with organizing a society around disparate interest groups. The concept of citizenship disappears as estates form around class, ethnic, and religious interests and then contest for favors from government.

Even liberalism's cherished First Amendment is under attack. Liberalism's opposition to regulating the content of speech has been attacked as a "neutrality trap" that fosters racism by shielding racist speakers and concepts. Within academia, politically correct speech codes routinely nullify the First Amendment. Critical Race Theorists are fighting to expand these new regulations to society as a whole.

For Crits, white male hegemony is most apparent in the economy, where the job market, mortgage market, executive offices, and the distribution of income and wealth are said to be heavily stacked against minorities. Crits find Adam Smith's belief that competitive markets match opportunity with merit a laughable concept. Like the legal system and the myth of meritocracy, Crits charge that the economy perpetuates white supremacy by maintaining the existing distribution of resources. In place of earned rewards, Crits advocate health care, day care, job training, and housing as basic entitlements. In general, Crits argue for government economic intervention to rectify the historical oppression of blacks.

One implication of Critical Race Theory is apartheid in the justice system. Black defendants require black judges, juries, prosecutors, lawyers, and police officers; otherwise "aversive racism" would miscarry justice. This is fine as far as it goes. But how could disputes, criminal or civil, be adjudicated between whites and blacks, or males and females, when we are operating on the Marxist premise that law serves only specific race and gender interests? Where does one go for a divorce? To a female court or a male court? Does a black/white dispute go to the black court or to the white court? One sometimes gets the impression that what the Critical Race Theorists are driving toward is a system in which minorities make all of the decisions, like Marx's proletariat. But it is a mean philosophy that says putting the shoe on the other foot is a move to a just system. The rejection of goodwill has taken us into a blind alley in which the goal is to reverse the hegemonic roles in an unjust system. We are so philosophically impoverished that revenge has become identified with moral progress.

It has been said many times that ideas have consequences. We are fifty years after Myrdal. Where will we be fifty years from now? The consequence of Myrdal is clear. *Brown* set in motion forces that have enfeebled the democratic process. The consequence of Critical Race Theory should be equally clear. What began as a demand for desegregation has developed into a powerful force leading to apartheid or violence.

For decades before the rise of the Nazi Party, German intellectuals demonized Jews and criticized "Judeo-Roman law" for suppressing the authentic German voice. Germany was the first country to achieve universal adult literacy. Between 1870 and 1933 it was the world's best-educated nation, with the best universities in almost every discipline. It was in this high-powered intellectual atmosphere that anti-Semitism became a popular pursuit. In 1879

Heinrich von Treitschke, a member of Germany's progressive National Liberal Party and a distinguished professor at the University of Berlin, wrote in his widely circulated intellectual journal, *Preussische Jahrbücher*, that "even in circles of the most highly educated, among men who would reject with disgust any ideas of ecclesiastical intolerance or national arrogance, there resounds as if from one mouth: *The Jews are our misfortune!*" Treitschke's phrase became the expression of the German anti-Semitic movement.

In 1881 an association of German students presented Bismarck with an "Anti-Semites' Petition" containing 225,000 signatures. The petition asked for "the emancipation of the German people from a form of alien domination which it cannot endure for any length of time." A counterpetition drive failed. Anti-Semitism spread in Germany after the Anti-Semites' Petition. It was fueled anew in the 1890s with the publication of politician Otto Böckel's book, *The Despairing Struggle of the Aryan Peoples with Jewry*, and it grew louder when Germany began losing World War I. The Jews were blamed for everything that went wrong. Succumbing to political pressure caused by rumors that Jews were putting Germans on the front lines while maintaining cushy jobs in the War Ministry bureaucracy, Germany undertook a religious census of the armed forces in 1916—despite its illegality under the equal protection guarantees of Germany's Reichstag Act of 1869.

After the war, anti-Semitism became more prevalent as Jews were blamed for "stabbing Germany in the back." College students and their teachers were vocal anti-Semites. Historian Paul Johnson says that "a key element in the Nazi triumph was the generation of schoolteachers who matured in the last decade of the nineteenth century, were infected with *Volkisch* anti-Semitism, and had become senior teachers by the 1920s." Two-thirds of the votes in Berlin student elections in 1921 were for anti-Semitic candidates.

The anti-Semitic forgery, *Protocols of the Elders of Zion*, was a German bestseller and the focus of many intellectual discussions within Germany. One journalist wrote: "In Berlin I attended several meetings which were entirely devoted to the *Protocols*. The speaker was usually a professor, a teacher, an editor, a lawyer or someone of that kind. The audience consisted of members of the educated class, civil servants, tradesmen, former officers, ladies, above all students, students of all faculties and years of seniority.... Passions were whipped up to the boiling point." With anti-Semitism deeply rooted within Germany's opinion-shaping elites, Adolf Hitler was able to step onto the scene.

Hitler believed in the "voice of color" and promised that his National Socialist Party would establish "Nordic, Teutonic, Germanic law" premised on "volk and race." Within months of attaining power in 1933, Hitler promulgated the "Law Against the Overcrowding of German Schools and Institutions of Higher Learning," which limited the percentage of Jewish students to "the proportion of non-Aryans within the Reich German population."

The next steps followed logically from the assumption that Jewish racial consciousness diverged from the interests of the German population. "Non-Aryan" civil servants were dismissed, and "non-Aryans" were prevented from entering the bar or serving as jurors, judges, university lecturers, entertainers, or journalists. In German courts, a Jew could only be a defendant. The Nazis' race-based legal system led to the near extermination of the Jews. The Final Solution was the logical consequence of the premise that Jewish racial consciousness could not be trusted to serve any but Jewish interests. Thus, there was no place for Jews in German society.

Like German anti-Semitism, the demonization of the white male is an *intellectual* movement. When University of Pennsylvania professor Houston Baker, president of the 30,000-member Modern Language Association, declares that "Whitemale Western initiatives have been the most globally insidious and unmercifully bloody manifestations of colonialism, imperialism, and racism" ever known, he provokes applause. Such extraordinary accusations, which would once have been dismissed as the ravings of a lunatic, are the cutting edge of scholarship and the basis of legal theories whose exponents are nominated to such posts as assistant attorney general for civil rights.

The demonization of the white male delegitimizes him. Charles Krauthammer has described the loss of moral authority of heterosexual white males, which undermines their rights and creates more space for quotas. One sixteen-year-old white male high school student from Dover, Massachusetts, wrote to *Time* magazine in response to the depiction on its cover of the white male as a pig in a business suit: "It seems as if today it is a crime to be a white male. We are obliged to apologize for everything and to everybody."

The delegitimization, in turn, creates space for insensitivity and hatred. Academic life today is replete with ad hominem attacks on white heterosexual males that parallel those used by Nazis against Jews and by Marx and Lenin against class enemies. Lenin routinely dehumanized class enemies as vermin, snakes, and leeches to make it easier to exterminate them. Hitler's descriptions of Jews as maggots, parasites, apes, swindlers, and eternal bloodsuckers had the same effect.

The negative characterizations of Jews listed in Gregory Martire and Ruth Clark's anti-Semitism index are increasingly applied to white males. Like Jews, white males are criticized for controlling the media, banking, and the government, for being indifferent to others not of their kind, for discriminating against others by hiring only white males, and for having too much power. The attack on white males is generic and does not differentiate between Ku Klux Klan members and doctrinaire white liberals who have led the assault on whites for their alleged racist ways.

The new enemy is "white culture," and the push to extirpate

books by DWMs—Dead White Males—from the curriculum of schools and colleges is reminiscent of the Nazi policy of purifying Germany by burning books. The traditional American educational curriculum is routinely condemned as the reflection of a white male European heterosexual mentality that, according to Stanford Professor Clayborne Carson, is "inescapably racist, indisputably sexist, and manifestly homophobic."

In a 1990 *New York Times* article, "Don't Celebrate 1492—Mourn It," Hans Konig damned Christopher Columbus for setting "into motion a sequence of greed, cruelty, slavery, and genocide that, even in the bloody history of mankind, has few parallels." Konig demands that we bring to an "end the phony baloney about the white man bringing Christianity, and about Columbus the noble son of the humble weaver." Syracuse University Professor Laurence Thomas is outraged that white males continue to enjoy public trust in American society even though "white males have committed more evil cumulatively than any other class of people in the world." Professor Thomas believes that "the Crusades, American slavery, and the two World Wars, including the Holocaust, should clinch this point." Smith College Professor Stanley Rothman has noted that any negative or offensive characterization of women and minorities is prohibited on campuses by rules against the "stereotyping" of any group except white males, who can be denounced with impunity as racist, sexist, villainous, and evil beyond belief. As George F. Will put it, "Only one group is ineligible for the privileged status of victim: there can be no limits on speech about white males."

New York City College Professor Leonard Jeffries, Jr., theorizes that white people are "ice people" and are "fundamentally materialistic, greedy, and intent on domination." In contrast, black people are "sun people" and are "essentially humanistic and communal." The moral judgments loaded into this characterization gain more power from the victim status of sun people. Jeffries thus provides a mechanism for portraying the overthrow of white culture as the achievement of justice.

No doubt Konig, Baker, Jeffries, and their numerous colleagues sound silly and ignoble, just as Marx and Hitler once sounded, but the consequences of their ideas are no less macabre. They affect the outlook of students and the behavior of juries, incite black extremist movements, and fuel persecutions of white students and professors that have left among the casualties free speech, open debate, and blacks who transcend racial-based thinking.

The reaction at Yale University to a speech to incoming undergraduates by Yale's dean, Donald Kagan, in 1990, shows how the new assumptions have penetrated the academy. Kagan said that in contrast to people in other countries, "Americans do not share a common ancestry and a common blood. They and their forebears come from every corner of the earth." Instead, they have in common "a system of laws and beliefs that shaped the establishment of the country, a system developed within the context of Western civilization." He urged students to study Western civilization as the source of representative democracy, laws that protect individual freedom, and the scientific revolution that has made life easier for everyone. "Do not fail to learn the great traditions that are the special gifts of Western civilization," he said, "which is the main foundation of our university and our country."

Kagan responded to claims that Western civilization's great works of literature and history are "relevant only to a limited group" by quoting W.E.B. Du Bois at the turn of the century:

I sit with Shakespeare and he winces not. Across the color line I walk arm in arm with Balzac and Dumas, where smiling men and welcoming women glide in gilded halls. From out of the caves of evening that swing between the strong-limbed earth and the tracery of the stars, I summon Aristotle

and Aurelius and what soul I will, and they come all gra-
ciously with no scorn or condescension. So, wed with Truth,
I dwell above the veil.

"For Du Bois," said Kagan, "the wisdom of the West's great writers was valuable for all, and he would not allow himself or others
to be deprived of it because of the accident of race."

Kagan's belief that Western ideals transcend race was too
much for members of the Yale community. The *Yale Daily News*
quoted students screaming "racist," "sexist," "narrow," and "out of
touch." Black student leaders said Kagan's remarks were "obnox-
ious" and called for a review of the school's " 'racist curriculum' to
root out any vestiges of white superiority and hegemony." The Yale
Women's Center, the Women's Art Collective, and Women's Action
Coalition joined the denunciatory chorus. Feminist activist
Katherine Pradt charged that Kagan has "legitimized a kind of
prejudice that masks itself in the demeanor and veneer of rational
discourse," which he uses "to wield power on campus." Professor
of history and women's studies, Cynthia Russett, said that the
speech reinforced faculty skepticism towards Kagan, most of whom
thought he should become "more sensitized toward his colleagues."

Sensitivity has become a one-way street. At a recent
University of Cincinnati race and gender sensitivity training program, the sensitivity trainer told a participating student that the
recent death of the student's father had removed a racist influence
from her life. This gratuitously insensitive remark produced no
academic petitions, hearings, or sensitivity training for the sensitivity trainer.

The general inference is that if only more white males would
die, the world would be a better place. We have not only heard this
kind of talk before, we have experienced its implementation on a
massive scale during the twentieth century. Are we destined to
repeat it in the twenty-first century?

In Germany the Jews were a small percentage of the population. In Russia and China class enemies were more numerous, but still fewer than the 41 percent of the United States population that American white males comprised in 1990 or the 24 percent some projections show for the year 2050. Although an outbreak of violence in the United States comparable to the extermination of class and race enemies seems farfetched, the systematic delegitimization of the white male targets this group for mistreatment. We already see the effects of a civil rights policy that limits white male access to universities, jobs, promotions, and government contracts. The 1991 Civil Rights Act codified this reverse discrimination and left white males without equal protection under the civil rights laws.

Out of *Brown* has come a system of racial preference and the destruction of the institutions of a liberal society. As time passes, this becomes more obvious. Observers are at work documenting the devastation in piecemeal ways by reporting on the parts of our civilization that are their specialties. Warren Farrell has written about the collapse of the criminal justice system under the assault of the feminists in his book, *The Myth of Male Power*. Dinesh D'Souza has documented the rising barriers to free speech in *Illiberal Education*. Allan Bloom chronicled the trivialization of the classics of Western civilization in *The Closing of the American Mind*. These are not unrelated developments. They all stem from the rejection of liberalism's premise that goodwill is the basis for relations among people. Without goodwill there can be only irreconcilable interests leading to apartheid or violence. What we have witnessed since *Brown* is not a happy journey toward racial integration, but the dismantling of the melting pot and the rise of the banners and battlements of group entitlements.

Racial entitlements are valuable, and to prevent fraud in the allocation of racial privileges U.S. citizens will have to be issued racial identity cards. The benefits of being a preferred minority are too great to rely on the current system of self-classification. As Berkeley Professor David Kirp has written: "Jobs are at stake. The temptation to lie outright about one's past has to be greater when careers are made to turn not on personal competence but instead on ethnic identity. If that's how the game is played, the cynics say, we'll bend the rules."

In 1978 twin brothers Paul and Philip Malone designated themselves "black" to benefit from a quota program in the Boston Fire Department. Their scores on the civil service exam had disqualified them as white applicants, but after learning that their maternal great-grandmother was black, they reapplied and were hired. A decade later, being one-eighth black—the same as Homer Plessy, namesake of the famous Supreme Court case—was deemed insufficient for the quota privileges, and the brothers were dismissed. In 1990 the San Francisco Fire Department was embroiled in a similar controversy over the level of Hispanic purity when firefighters were being promoted to become battalion chiefs. In 1994 Georgetown University Law School rescinded its acceptance of Raymond Tittman because, although his origins are African, he is not black.

More people than ever before are designating themselves as American Indians. Native-American births cannot explain the tripling of this self-designated category since the 1960 census. A March 5, 1991, *New York Times* article noted that "the growing realization that an Indian heritage can mean special benefits has motivated many Indians, and presumably some impostors, to openly assert an Indian background." One California contractor won a $19 million contract on the Los Angeles rapid transit system because he was one-sixty-fourth American Indian.

Like self-designation, ad hoc race determinations by employers and college admissions officers are open to abuse as institutions face strong economic incentives to exaggerate their minority employee populations to secure government largesse. Ultimately, the expanding system of racial privilege will require that a person's race be formally designated by the government.

Justice John Paul Stevens predicted as much. In a 1980 case upholding federal minority construction set-asides, Justice Stevens warned: "If the national government is to make a serious effort to define racial classes by criteria that can be administered objectively, it must study precedents such as the First Regulation to the Reich Citizenship Law of November 14, 1935." But even such thoroughgoing racist policies as Nazi Germany's and South African apartheid encountered insurmountable problems in unscrambling the human omelette. Ambiguities in family trees flummoxed even Nazi bureaucrats, and the South African parliament amended the 1950 Population Registration Act seven times because of unforeseen complications. It is difficult to see how the allocation of racial privileges in the United States can avoid a racial registry of the population.

In the face of these disturbing trends, there are hopeful countercurrents. In November 1993 University of Pennsylvania interim President Claire Fagin announced plans to scrap Penn's controversial speech code, which had given minorities a veto over free speech. She appointed a committee to devise a replacement that would encourage students to talk out their differences. If this outbreak of common sense catches on at Penn, long a center of political correctness and one of the first to fashion speech codes into a weapon against white males, goodwill might make a comeback against the dogma of implacable interests.

Fagin's decision to substitute discussion for regulation presumes goodwill. Otherwise, it is just more "endless talking," which Crit Richard Delgado says begins with racist premises, rehearses the dominant narrative, and ends up "inscribing its supremacist message even more deeply." Fagin's view that Penn must move away from a "very hyphenated world" and return to just being American assumes a common interest among the races and genders that is routinely denied by such faculty luminaries as Guinier and Baker. Fagin's call to replace the speech code with freedom of conscience is a marked change for the university where business law Professor Murray Dolfman was suspended and sentenced to sensitivity training for asking a black student which of the Constitution's amendments forbade slavery.

Even Blumrosen, who did so much to create the separate legal estates, is beginning to have second thoughts. In his book, *Modern Law: The Law Transmission System and Equal Employment Opportunity*, published in 1993, he is dismayed at the emergence of Critical Race Theory and feminist legal studies because they reject the "common theoretical foundation for civil rights activities." Blumrosen tries to corral the presumption of white racism that enabled him to elevate privilege above the law by asserting that blacks' access to higher jobs means that "we are not as racist as we were."

Ultimately, Critical Race Theory rejects the universalist principles of integration in favor of black separatism. As the logic of the thought unfolds, it is increasingly clear that the real hero is Malcolm X and not Martin Luther King, Jr., or Thurgood Marshall. Derrick Bell, who resigned from the Harvard Law School to protest the school's lack of a tenured nonwhite female, has interpreted *Brown* itself as a mere manifestation of white self-interest. It was nothing but crumbs, Bell says, that were given to achieve such opportunistic ends as boosting U.S. credibility in the Cold War struggle.

In a law review article, Bell wrote that if whites were to establish contact with an extraterrestrial civilization, they would sell all blacks into slavery and pay off the national debt. If extraterrestrials fail to appear, he predicts that a "Racial Preference Licensing Act" will be passed that will permit discrimination in exchange for a fee. The prevalence of racism, Bell says, guarantees that the statute will be a cash cow for the Treasury.

Despite this, Bell has been criticized for not being sufficiently pessimistic about racism in the United States. Professor Sidney Willhelm says that Bell "does not go far enough. His failure is in not recognizing that the Constitution itself is a racist document."

These indictments of liberalism's historic achievements as "perilously racist" institutions permit no common grounds upon which to build an integrated society. Moreover, any step toward integration that is successfully taken is automatically dismissed as an opportunistic fine-tuning of the hegemonic superstructure. With race interests perceived as so divergent, there is no longer a presumption of common interest. We are left with estates and their prerogatives. Separation is one possible outcome. Violence is another. This is the discouraging path that Myrdal and *Brown* set us upon.

CHAPTER ELEVEN

The Assault on Goodwill

T he December 7, 1993, edition of the *New York Times* reported that blacks and whites had joined together in a common cause. The black principal of an integrated Mississippi school had been fired for acquiescing to an overwhelming vote for prayer by the student body. Now black and white parents and students were united in demanding his reinstatement. Here were people acting democratically in a common cause, transcending their "race consciousness."

The *Times* thought it remarkable enough to merit a news story, but in real life such stories are not unusual. When we step back from the overheated rhetoric, when we shake loose from media coverage that portrays social pathology as the social norm, when we turn away from violent and cliché-ridden fantasies of Hollywood and look to our own lives and those of our neighbors, we know that there is still an enormous reservoir of goodwill— across racial boundaries as well as across the back fence— among Americans. It must be so, because without goodwill we find ourselves in Hobbes' war of all against all, and however bad things have gotten we are not there yet.

We must remind ourselves of this, lest the debunking of goodwill become a self-fulfilling prophesy. For if that happens, liberalism is lost. Liberalism is predicated on goodwill. Without goodwill, people of differing incomes, intelligence, ethnic origin, gender, and personality cannot live together in democracy and share in shaping the law that governs them all. In the absence of goodwill, there is nothing but the coercive power of government to mediate differences. Hostility reigns as each faction fights to control the state. Without goodwill, there can be no concept of government "of the people, by the people, and for the people." Jefferson's trust in the common man and Madison's trust in majority rule are illusions if goodwill is an illusion. This is why Marxian doctrines, which assert that goodwill is a veil that masks the economic interests of class, race, or gender, strike at the heart of liberalism.

Liberalism was scarcely one hundred years old when Karl Marx dismissed it as bourgeois cant. It was nothing, he said, but an ideological superstructure reflecting the economic class interests of capitalists. Marx and Engels poured unbridled scorn on the "bourgeois" notion that goodwill could unite all in a morality that transcended class interest. For Marx, there were as many moralities as there were classes and nothing to mediate between them but violence. Simone de Beauvoir summed up the Marxist view when she praised the Marquis de Sade for exposing "the bourgeois hoax which consists in erecting class-interests into universal principles."

When morality is reduced to class interest, there is no basis outside of class interest for preferring one class's morality to another's. Marx threw the selection of competing class interests to history. The proletariat was declared to be the ascending class, and this ascension gave legitimacy to its morality.

If one accepts a Marxian perspective, goodwill cannot be an effective force. The reason is simple. Moral consciousness cannot

transcend group interest. As Marx put it, "It is not the consciousness of men that determines their existence, but their social existence that determines their consciousness." Since each group
must thus act in its own interest, there is no humanistic basis upon
which to unite classes and cultivate effective reforms.

Marx thought he was being honest and realistic when he
declared that violence ("class struggle") mediates between class
moralities. Engels agreed. Moral theories, he wrote, are "as pow-
erless as Kant's 'Categorical Imperative.' As a matter of fact, every
class, as well as every profession, has its own system of morals and
breaks even this when it can do it without punishment. And love,
which is to unite all, appears today in wars, controversies, lawsuits, domestic broils, and mutual plunder."

Marx's doctrine of violence had a tremendous impact on the
twentieth century. Lenin took it a step further by making violence
the mediator between the Party and the proletariat. "The scientific concept of dictatorship," he wrote, "means neither more nor less
than unlimited power, resting directly on force, not limited by anything, not restricted by any laws, nor any absolute rules." Stalin
took it yet another step and made violence the mediator between
the Party and its members.

In the end, the inhumanity of its moral doctrine proved too
much for communist states, but even as they were disintegrating,
new Marxist assaults on goodwill were making headway in U.S.
legal philosophy. We seem destined to go through it all again as if
nothing had ever happened. Only this time it is race and gender
interests that disunite people and make goodwill impossible.

Critical Race Theory and radical feminism are Marxist to the
core. Crits see American democracy as an unjust combination by
whites to oppress blacks. The result, they believe, is a permanent
majority tyranny based on prejudice. Blacks are a minority that
always loses. Feminism applies the same denial of goodwill to the
genders. Catharine MacKinnon, for example, writes that "the liberal

state coercively and authoritatively constitutes the social order in the interest of men as a gender, through its legitimizing norms, relation to society, and substantive policies." MacKinnon is so insistent on the impossibility of goodwill between the genders that she refuses to take questions from men in the audiences of her collegiate speaking engagements.

If there is no presumption of goodwill, a critic's purpose cannot be to persuade, to correct an injustice, or to make a convincing case for freedom. For the new Marxists, as for the old, the essential element of criticism is indignation, and its essential task is denunciation. Marx wrote that criticism "is a weapon. Its object is an *enemy* it wants not to refute but to *destroy*." Lenin said that his language was "calculated not to convince but to break up the ranks of the opponent, not to correct the mistake of the opponent but to destroy him, to wipe his organization off the face of the earth." Against political enemies, Lenin conducted "a fight of extermination."

Once goodwill is thrown out, there is no possibility of reconciling differences or even discussing them. *Washington Post* columnist Richard Cohen, the epitome of a white liberal, has complained that as a white male writer, "I am being told to butt out, that since I am a member of the Oppressor Class, I may not comment." Polarization becomes so extreme that even something as natural as the sex act becomes impermissible. Andrea Dworkin describes sexual intercourse as "the pure, sterile, formal expression of men's contempt for women." She rejects even consensual marital heterosexual intercourse as female rape. Lesbianism and artificial insemination become the only legitimate uses of female sexuality.

To dismiss such views as extreme is to miss the point that they follow logically from any doctrine that reduces humankind to a disparate collection of class, race, or gender interests. Only the most dim prospects can flow from philosophies, legal doctrines, or

social policies predicated on such total determinism. If the materialistic basis of thought is so complete that ideas have no power to
reach beyond their specific class, race, or gender basis, the only
use of ideas is to stir up rebellion among the presumed oppressed
class, race, or gender. Talk is pointless, along with the First
Amendment. Democracy, law, everything becomes a sham. The
struggle for liberation is all—but once achieved nothing has happened but a reversal of roles. A feminist hegemony replaces a
male hegemony. A black hegemony replaces a white one. Unless
we assert that blacks or women are history's chosen vehicle,
putting the shoe on the other foot does not put society on the path
of moral progress. It is a poor cause that would overthrow white
male hegemony only to replace it with a black female hegemony.

It is certainly a peculiar cause for white male professors,
intellectuals, judges, and legislators to be engaged in. Either the
white males who are pursuing careers in Critical Race Theory and
policy have broken the mold and transcended their race interests,
or they do not truly believe the doctrines that they espouse and are
employing them as reformist weapons. The latter is a dangerous
tactic. Asserting the immorality of certain aspects of society has
often been the reformer's ploy. But when the total societal
arrangements are said to be immorally based on the hegemony of
a selfish interest group, there is nothing to reform.

Critical Race Theorists themselves are discovering this, as
their own work points increasingly toward separation, not integration. The Crits were elevated to fame by President Clinton's
nomination and subsequent withdrawal of Lani Guinier as assistant attorney general for civil rights. Clinton professed to discover,
belatedly, that her views were outside the political mainstream.
Guinier denied that her views were extreme. What got Guinier in
trouble was her extension of race-norming—which already had
been applied to employment tests and university admissions—to
voting. She wants to race-norm voting to provide minorities with a

veto to protect them from the tyranny of the majority. Guinier maintains that the United States doesn't really enjoy "one person, one vote" because the white majority votes racially, thus depriving blacks (and other minorities) of any influence on political outcomes. The disproportionate weighting of black votes implied by the veto is justified as an equal opportunity action that overcomes "the disproportionate power presently enjoyed by white voters."

Guinier was led to the minority veto because not even racially gerrymandered congressional districts and cumulative voting schemes can produce equal outcomes for minorities in a racially polarized political entity. If racism prevents democracy from delivering moral results, the minority veto can seem to be a logical response.

The tyranny of the majority has been addressed in many contexts. Recognizing that only a few people are out on the end of the bell curve, libertarians have expressed concerns about the exploitation of the economically successful by the masses and the assault on the gifted in the leveling-down approach in public education. Productive people are treated discriminatorily by progressive income taxation and estate taxation imposed in the name of "fairness" by majoritarian processes. Libertarians, however, have never asserted that this discriminatory exploitation was based on the lack of goodwill between poor and rich. Therefore, when this policy was taken to lengths that adversely affected the economy's performance and job opportunities, public policy could reassess its effects, reduce tax rates, and take a step back from "fairness" to achieve a wider goal.

Madison himself addressed the problem of majoritarian tyranny. He concluded that the alternative was far worse. Supermajority requirements, he argued, would transfer power from the majority to a handful and shatter the fundamental principle of free government. "It would be no longer the majority that would rule," he wrote "the power would be transferred to the minority." Since a smaller group would call the shots, minority rule would by its very nature be privileged. It would be a step back to aristocracy even if the few who comprised the supermajority were just and wise philosopher kings.

With Guinier, the tyranny of the minority becomes even more problematical. The assumption of racial ill will precludes any basis for arriving at policies that are in the common interest. Once society is split into warring factions, as in Yugoslavia, the outcome can only be apartheid or Lenin's "fight of extermination." Georgetown Law Professor Gary Peller has taken Critical Race Theory a step beyond Guinier. Supermajority requirements and other such devices operate within an "integrationist" ideology "that identifies progress with the transcendence of a racial consciousness about the world." The problem with integrationism, says Peller, is that it "links up with a broader set of liberal images—images that connect truth, universalism, and progress." Peller argues that there is no difference in the conservative and liberal approaches to racial justice. Both want to universalize institutional practices to erase the racial factor. Their goal is "to make social life neutral to racial identity." They only disagree on how far to extend preferences such as affirmative action.

Peller exposes integrationism as just another white construct. He argues that its pursuit has been at the expense of the vitality of the black community because, in short, integrationism conducts genocide against diversity. As there is no goodwill between the races, there cannot be diversity unless there is separation.

Peller faults integrationists for attempting to combat racism by transcending "the bias of particularity that they see as the root of racist consciousness." They have attempted to do this through the progressive rejection of local parochialism in favor of the impersonality of centralized authority. Peller sees such universalist aims as the ultimate racism because to combat particularity is to combat blackness. Peller notes that black nationalists such as Malcolm X had "anti-universalist assumptions" that defined the struggle against racism in terms of achieving local control "to liberate community institutions from outside, colonial rule." Black nationalists regard integration as a manifestation of white supremacist ideology and Thurgood Marshall as a "half-white son of a bitch."

However extreme these views sound, they flow logically from Myrdal's racist assumptions about American democracy. Integrationism destroys diversity by submerging blacks in white society. Peller praises "the reappearance of race consciousness in the scholarly work of critical race theorists" as an attempt to reopen a political discourse that was closed off by liberals in the 1960s. *Brown*'s denial of goodwill and rejection of the democratic process lead logically to apartheid.

Of course, we can suspend our logic and not get there, but why risk our future on the suspension (at what point?) of *Brown*'s logic? The logic is inherently dangerous and spreads paranoia. In 1991 Rutgers Law Professor Robert J. Cottrol and Tulane Law Professor Raymond T. Diamond defended the Second Amendment in the *Georgetown Law Journal* on the grounds that blacks require arms as protection against white racist institutions and as a necessary means for insurrection.

If scholarly minds are preparing for racial conflict, others may be, too. After all, there is a limit to racial preferences because at some point the majority becomes so disadvantaged that it will not tolerate their extension. Yet not only have preferences become an entitlement, many blacks regard their continual expansion as an entitlement. If minorities have been led to believe by years— even decades—of argument that preferences are necessary to overcome their oppression, quotas could not be terminated without conflict. The assault on goodwill logically leads to the displacement of citizenship by racial consciousness. Gunnar Myrdal is the father of the Crits. As long as he is our shepherd, the future is theirs.

The Struggle for a
Liberal Social Order

Doctrines that posit disparate, implacable interests lead to tyranny and violence. We cannot remain insouciant to the implications of the unpromising politics that the new Marxists are constructing. We must reclaim a liberal social order.

For a liberal social order to prevail, we need only to recognize the consequences of *Brown* and the Civil Rights Act. Pushed by impatience, we let the end justify the means. We set aside persuasion and the democratic process and gave up on goodwill and freedom of conscience. It has got us nowhere except to the unpromising Marxian conundrum of trying to construct a social order on the basis of irreconcilable interests. Equality before the law has given way to preferments. The founding fathers, white males all, are being stripped of moral authority, and the answer to the "tyranny of the majority" is said to be the tyranny of the minority.

There are signs, however, of a political reaction. People are getting as fed up with quotas as they were with segregation. On July 20, 1995, the regents of the University of California voted to end race-based admission at its campuses. On August 10, 1995, California Governor Pete Wilson sued his own state, challenging the constitutionality of the myriad race- and gender-quota privileges ensconced in the California Code. Momentum is building for a 1996 ballot initiative in California that would forbid quotas in state and local public education, employment, and contracting. Its key passage says, "Neither the State of California nor any of its political subdivisions or agents shall use race, sex, color, ethnicity or national origin as a criterion for either discriminating against, or granting preferential treatment to, any individual or group in the operation of the State's system of public employment, public education or public contracting."

Organizers expect little trouble gathering the 615,000 valid signatures necessary to get the "California Civil Rights Initiative" on the ballot, as pollsters estimate that 70 to 80 percent of Californians favor a rollback of the quota regime. Once on the ballot in 1996, the antiquota referendum is expected to win easily. Joel Kotkin of the Progressive Policy Institute reported in the August/September 1994 issue of *The New Democrat* that "even in the ultra-liberal Bay Area, more than 75 percent of whites oppose such practices, according to a recent analysis by the Survey Research Center at the University of California at Berkeley."

Many opponents of quotas hope that the initiative's momentum will take on national significance akin to that of California's Proposition 13 in the late 1970s, which began a national political wave culminating in Ronald Reagan's 1981 tax cuts. This would demonstrate a renewal of liberalism in which free people use the democratic process to reclaim democracy's twin partner, equality before the law.

The judiciary, however, might strike down the initiative as an expression of "aversive racism." In 1964 California citizens used the initiative process to amend the state's constitution to prevent the state from denying "the right of any person [to] decline to sell, lease or rent [real property] to such person or persons as he, in his absolute discretion, chooses." The U.S. Supreme Court used a Fourteenth Amendment argument to strike down the California initiative in the 1967 case of *Reitman v. Mulkey* on the grounds that, because the California initiative repealed state "fair housing" legislation barring racial discrimination in the sale or rental of private dwellings, the popular ballot initiative was racially motivated and, therefore, unconstitutional.

Even if the California initiative is sustained, its impact would be limited by its exception of federal quotas.

On the other hand, some recent court decisions have shown less support for quotas. For example, in 1994 the Fourth Circuit held the University of Maryland's scholarship program for blacks to be unconstitutional, and both the Sixth and Eleventh Circuits struck down hiring and promotion quotas for policemen and firemen created through consent decrees. On June 12, 1995, the Supreme Court applied the *Croson* ruling to federal set-asides and sent the *Adarand Constructors* case back to the lower court for a disparity study to justify the discrimination against the company. Notably, the Justices did not rule that reverse discrimination was inconsistent with the Equal Protection Clause of the Fourteenth Amendment. That same day the Justices placed some obstacles in the way of Judge Clark running the Kansas City school district to his liking. But the Court did not rescind or revisit its 1990 ruling permitting federal judges to order tax increases to finance their desegregation schemes.

Ultimately, the Supreme Court might resurrect the real meaning of the Fourteenth Amendment—equality before the law. However, of the nine members of the Supreme Court, only Justice Clarence Thomas has joined Justice Scalia's rejection of all manifestations of racial quotas. A protracted conflict may be in store between the people and the judiciary to resolve whether we are to be equal or privileged under the law.

As 1995 got under way, there were indications that the people may get some help from the politicians. Leading Republican presidential contender and Senate Majority Leader Robert J. Dole (R-Kan.) expressed doubts about quotas on NBC-TV's "Meet the Press" on February 5, 1995. Dole asked the Congressional Research Service to compile a list of all federal programs granting "a preference to individuals on the basis of race, sex, national origin, or ethnic background," including, but "not limited to, time-tables, goals, set-asides, and quotas." The Congressional Research Service responded with a thirty-two–page, single-spaced list describing more than 160 programs.

Some of the federal set-asides appear to have become entitlements. For example, Congress responded to widespread student loan defaults by cutting off loans to colleges whose students tended to default, but "historically black colleges and universities are exempted," according to the statute, thus creating a minority right to default. Minorities don't have to play by the same rules for regulatory approvals either. A statute gives automatic Federal Deposit Insurance Corporation (FDIC) approval to "minority-controlled bank acquisitions by minority-controlled holding companies without regard to asset size." Regulations encourage recipients of grants from the Departments of Agriculture, Commerce, Defense, Education, Health and Human Services, Housing and Urban Development, Interior, Justice, and Labor to use minority-owned banks. A Department of Agriculture regulation even states that "upon request, awarding agencies will furnish a listing of minority and women-owned banks."

Following Dole's remarks, Senator Phil Gramm (R-Tex.) upped the ante by declaring that if he were elected president, he would rescind Executive Order 11246, from which many federal quotas emanate. The Republican majority in the House of Representatives got into the fray by voting on February 21, 1995, to repeal a Federal Communications Commission tax deferment on capital gains for broadcast companies sold to minority-owned, or minority-fronted, companies. "We shouldn't be giving anyone special rights, special considerations over the rights of other Americans," Republican Conference Chairman John Boehner declared. Concerned by the disaffection of white male voters, President Clinton ordered a White House review of affirmative action, but his report called for mending rather than ending the system of racial preferences.

The political climate is changing. According to the *Washington Times*, Congressman Collin C. Peterson (D-Minn.) said, "I welcome hearings. We want to get into this. It's interesting that we can have people raise this issue and have hearings and not be ostracized. Two years ago if anyone would have said this, they would have strung them up." Defenders of quotas have expressed alarm. Theodore M. Shaw, associate director-counsel of the NAACP Legal Defense and Educational Fund, laments that "certainly the political landscape has changed. The prospect of Congress opening up affirmative-action programs for review is one that is a cause for concern."

To the contrary, it is a hopeful sign that Congress is beginning to realize that equal rights have been eroded by racial privileges, but there may be less here than meets the eye. Quotas are too extensive to be dislodged by a rescission of Executive Order 11246. Even the "Equal Opportunity Act of 1995," proposed on July 27, 1995, by Senator Dole and Rep. Charles T. Canady (R-Fla.), eliminates only "racial and gender preferences" in the federal government and by federal contractors, leaving intact the private sector quotas that *Griggs* and *Weber* created. Moreover, both Senators Dole and Gramm, like most congressional Republicans who are now questioning the legitimacy of racial quotas, voted for the 1991 Civil Rights Act, which codified in statutory law the disparate impact standard created by bureaucrats and judges. The Republicans, of course, may not have understood the implications of their vote. When White House Legal Counsel C. Boyden Gray assured Republicans that voting to codify the disparate impact standard would not legalize quotas, he repeated Chief Justice Burger's twenty-year-old mistake in *Griggs* of trying to go by statistics without having quotas. The impossibility of this position was made clear by the *Weber* decision in 1979. Yet here was the Bush White House arguing, and Republicans voting, as if *Weber* had never occurred.

Senator Dole tried to contain the quota implications of the 1991 act by inserting an interpretative memo into the *Congressional Record* that claimed the legislation affirmed the Supreme Court's *Wards Cove* decision. But his memo was contradicted by a counter-memo inserted by Senator John Danforth (R-Mo.). Danforth's memo, described as "the exclusive legislative history," states that the 1991 act affirms *Griggs* and "the other Supreme Court decisions prior to *Wards Cove*." This bodes ill for an anti-quota interpretation of the latest civil rights act. If bureaucrats and jurists could turn an airtight anti-quota piece of legislation like the 1964 Civil Rights Act into an instrument for quotas, they can have a field day with the 1991 act, which overturns intent and finds discrimination in statistical under-representation.

Quota opponents face vehement and entrenched opposition. One anonymous Republican lawyer quoted in the February 25, 1995, *New York Times* said that GOP lawmakers "really don't have the stomach to take this stuff on. It will be incredibly divisive, and they're worried about angering women." On February 21, 1995, the *Los Angeles Times* noted that, "in the past, confrontations over affirmative action have often proved to be false starts" and observed that despite opposing quotas, President Ronald Reagan left office with his administration having done "little to change the underlying policies." When the Supreme Court began reining in quotas in 1989, the Bush administration ran for the hills.

Considering the headway that equality of result has made in undermining equality before the law, the pervasiveness of quotas, and the lack of understanding of their origins and implications, the fight to reclaim law from privilege has barely begun. Ultimately, either quotas will go or democracy will, because legal privileges based on status are incompatible with democracy's requirement of equal standing before the law.

B I B L I O G R A P H Y

Articles and Books

Abernathy, Charles F. *Civil Rights: Cases and Materials*. St. Paul: West, 1980.

———. *Civil Rights and Constitutional Litigation. Cases and Materials*. 2d ed. St. Paul: West, 1992.

———. "Title VI and the Constitution: A Regulatory Model for Defining 'Discrimination.' " *Georgetown Law Journal* 70, no. 1 (October 1981): 1–49.

———. "When Civil Rights Go Wrong: Agenda and Process in Civil Rights Reform." *Temple Political and Civil Rights Law Review* 2, no. 2 (spring 1993): 177–208.

Abernathy, Ralph David. *And the Walls Came Tumbling Down*. New York: Harper & Row, 1989.

Abram, Morris B. "Affirmative Action: Fair Shakers and Social Engineers." *Harvard Law Review* 99, no. 6 (April 1986): 1312–1326.

———. "What Constitutes Civil Rights?" *New York Times Magazine*, 10 June 1984.

Abrams, Elliott. "The Quota Commission." *Commentary*, October 1972.

Abrams, Willie. "A Reply to Derrick Bell's *Racial Realism*." *Connecticut Law Review* 24, no. 2 (winter 1992): 517–532.

Ackermann, Bruce A. "Beyond *Carolene Products*." *Harvard Law Review* 98, no. 4 (February 1985): 713–746.

Adelson, Joseph. "Living With Quotas." *Commentary*, May 1978.

Adler, Jerry, Mark Starr, Farai Chideya, Lynda Wright, Pat Wingert, Linda Haac. "Taking Offense: Is this the new enlightenment on campus or the new McCarthyism?" *Newsweek*, 24 December 1990.

Aleinikoff, T. Alexander. "A Case for Race-Consciousness." *Columbia Law Review* 91, no. 5 (June 1991): 1060–1125.

———. "The Constitution in Context: The Continuing Significance of Racism." *University of Colorado Law Review* 63, no. 2 (1992): 325–373.

———. "Re-Reading Justice Harlan's Dissent in *Plessy v. Ferguson*: Freedom, Antiracism, and Citizenship." *University of Illinois Law Review* 1992, no. 4 (1992): 961–977.

Aleinikoff, T. Alexander, and Samuel Issacharoff. "Race and Redistricting: Drawing Constitutional Lines After *Shaw v. Reno*." *Michigan Law Review* 92, no. 3 (December 1993): 588–651.

Alexander, Larry. "What Makes Wrongful Discrimination Wrong? Biases, Preferences, Stereotypes, and Proxies." *University of Pennsylvania Law Review* 141, no. 1 (November 1992): 149–219.

Allen, W. B. "A New Birth of Freedom: Fulfillment or Derailment?" In Robert A. Goldwin and Art Kaufman, eds. *Slavery and Its Consequences: The Constitution, Equality, and Race*. Washington, D.C.: American Enterprise Institute, 1988.

Alter, Robert. "The Persistence of Reading." *Partisan Review* 15, no. 4 (1993): 510–516.

Altman, Andrew. *Critical Legal Studies: A Liberal Critique*. Princeton: Princeton Univ. Press, 1990.

Ambrose, Stephen E. *Eisenhower: Soldier and President*. New York: Simon and Schuster, 1990.

Amerine, Larry F. "Voting Rights Act of 1965 Suspends State Literacy Tests and Authorizes Federal Voting Registrars in Literacy-Test States Where Less Than Fifty Percent of the Population Registers or Votes." *Texas Law Review* 44, no. 7 (July 1966): 1411–1416.

Anderson, David E. "The Jurisprudence of Justice Rehnquist: Government by Constitution and Consensus." *The Intercollegiate Review* 17, no. 1 (fall/winter 1981): 17–30.

Anderson, Elijah. *Streetwise: Race, Class, & Change in an Urban Community*. Chicago: Univ. of Chicago Press, 1990.

Anderson, Lorrin. "The Siege of Yonkers: Federal Judges, Urban Blight." *National Review*, 13 May 1991.

Anderson, Martin. *Impostors in the Temple: American Intellectuals Are Destroying Our Universities and Cheating Our Students of Their Future*. New York: Simon & Schuster, 1992.

———. *Revolution*. San Diego: Harcourt Brace Jovanovich, 1988.

Ansley, Frances Lee. "Stirring the Ashes: Race, Class and the Future of Civil Rights Scholarship." *Cornell Law Review* 74, no. 6 (September 1989): 993–1077.

Arad, Yitzhak, Yisreal Gutman, and Abraham Margaliot, eds. *Documents on the Holocaust: Selected Sources on the Destruction of the Jews of Germany and Austria, Poland, and the Soviet Union*. Jerusalem: Yad Vashem, 1981.

Arblaster, Anthony. *Democracy*. Minneapolis: Univ. of Minnesota Press, 1987.

Armor, David J. *Forced Justice: School Desegregation and the Law*. New York: Oxford Univ. Press, 1995.

Assembly Judiciary Committee, California State Legislature. *Discrimination and Affirmative Action: Are There Any Facts Out There?: Report of the Hearing of May 4, 1995*. Sacramento, California: Assembly Publications Office, 1995.

Ayers, Edward L. *The Promise of the New South: Life After Reconstruction*. New York: Oxford Univ. Press, 1992.

Baker, C. Edwin. "Neutrality, Process, and Rationality: Flawed Interpretations of Equal Protection." *Texas Law Review* 58, no. 6 (August 1980): 1029–1096.

Baker, Houston A., Jr. *Black Studies Rap and the Academy*. Chicago. Univ. of Chicago Press, 1993.

———. "Letters: Professor Baker Replies." *Pennsylvania Gazette*, April 1990.

———. "Whose 'Crisis' Is It Anyway?: A word on dire prophecies and new sounds in the humanities." *Pennsylvania Gazette*, December 1989.

Baldwin, Frances Elizabeth. *Sumptuary Legislation and Personal Regulation in England*. Baltimore: Johns Hopkins Press, 1926.

Baldwin, James, Nathan Glazer, Sidney Hook, and Gunnar Myrdal. "Liberalism and the Negro: A Round-Table Discussion." *Commentary*, March 1964.

Baltzell, E. Digby. *The Protestant Establishment: Aristocracy & Caste in America*. New York: Random House, 1964.

Barnes, Fred, and Grover Norquist. "The Politics of Less: A Debate on Big-Government Conservatism." *Policy Review*, winter 1991.

Barnes, James A. "Minority Poker." *National Journal*, 4 May 1991.

Barnes, Robin D. "Politics and Passion: Theoretically a Dangerous Liaison." Review of *Reflections of An Affirmative Action Baby*, by Stephen L. Carter, and *The*

Alchemy of Race and Rights, by Patricia J. Williams. *Yale Law Journal* 101, no. 7 (May 1992): 1631–1659.

————. "Race Consciousness: The Thematic Content of Racial Distinctiveness in Critical Race Scholarship." *Harvard Law Review* 103, no. 8 (June 1990): 1864–1871.

————. "Realist Review." *Connecticut Law Review* 24, no. 2 (winter 1992): 553–565.

Bartlett, Katharine T., and Rosanne Kennedy, eds. *Feminist Legal Theory: Readings in Law and Gender*. Boulder: Westview, 1991.

Bass, Jack. *Unlikely Heroes: The Dramatic Story of the Southern Judges of the Fifth Circuit Who Translated the Supreme Court's Brown Decision into a Revolution for Equality*. New York: Simon and Schuster, 1981.

Bauer, Yehuda. *A History of the Holocaust*. New York: Franklin Watts, 1982.

Becker, Gary S. *The Economics of Discrimination*. Chicago: Univ. of Chicago Press, 1957. 2d ed. 1971.

————. "The Evidence Against Banks Doesn't Prove Bias." *Business Week*, 19 April 1993.

————. "How Bad Studies Get Turned Into Bad Policies." *Business Week*, 26 June 1995.

Beer, William R. "Accreditation by Quota: The Case of Baruch College." *Academic Questions* 3, no. 4 (fall 1990): 47–52.

Bell, Derrick. "Britain, Blacks, and Busing." Review of *Doing Good by Doing Little: Race and Schooling in Britain*, by David L. Kirp. *Michigan Law Review* 79, no. 4 (March 1981): 835–855.

————. *Faces at the Bottom of the Well: The Permanence of Racism*. New York: Basic Books, 1992.

————. "Foreword: The Final Civil Rights Act." *California Law Review* 79, no. 3 (May 1991): 597–611.

————. "Law, Litigation, and the Search for the Promised Land." Review of *The NAACP: Legal Strategy Against Segregated Education, 1925–1950*, by Mark V. Tushnet. *Georgetown Law Journal* 76, no. 1 (October 1987): 229–236.

————. "Racial Realism." *Connecticut Law Review* 24, no. 2 (winter 1992): 363–379.

Bell, Derrick A., Jr. "After We're Gone: Prudent Speculations on America in a Post-Racial Epoch." *St. Louis University Law Journal* 34, no. 3 (spring 1990): 393–405.

————. "*Brown v. Board of Education* and the Interest-Convergence Dilemma."

Harvard Law Review 93, no. 3 (January 1980): 518–533.

———. *Race, Racism and American Law*. 2d ed. Boston: Little, Brown, 1980.

———. "Racism: A Prophecy for the Year 2000." *Rutgers Law Review* 42, no. 1 (fall 1989): 93–108.

———. "Serving Two Masters: Integration Ideals and Client Interests in School Desegregation Litigation." *Yale Law Journal* 85, no. 4 (March 1976): 470–516.

Bell, Derrick, and Preeta Bansal. "The Republican Revival and Racial Politics." *Yale Law Journal* 97, no. 8 (July 1988): 1609–1621.

Belton, Robert. "The Dismantling of the Griggs Disparate Impact Theory and the Future of Title VII: The Need for a Third Reconstruction." *Yale Law & Policy Review* 8, no. 2 (1990): 223–256.

Belz, Herman. *Affirmative Action from Kennedy to Reagan: Redefining American Equality*. Washington, D.C.: Washington Legal Foundation, 1984.

———. *Equality Transformed: A Quarter-Century of Affirmative Action*. New Brunswick: Transaction, 1991.

Bennett, William J., and Terry Eastland. *Counting By Race: Equality from the Founding Fathers to Bakke and Weber*. New York: Basic Books, 1979.

———. "Why Bakke Won't End Reverse Discrimination." *Commentary*, September 1978.

Berg, Richard K. "Equal Employment Opportunity Under the Civil Rights Act of 1964." *Brooklyn Law Review* 31, no. 1 (December 1964): 62–97.

Berger, Brigitte. "Multiculturalism and the Modern University." *Partisan Review* 15, no. 4 (1993): 516–526.

Berger, Raoul. *Government by Judiciary: The Transformation of the Fourteenth Amendment*. Cambridge: Harvard Univ. Press, 1977.

Berkovec, James A., Glen B. Canner, Stuart A. Gabriel, and Timothy H. Hannan. "Discrimination, Default, and Loss in FHA Mortgage Lending." Washington, D.C.: Federal Reserve, November 1994.

Berman, Phyllis, and Alger, Alexandra. "The set-aside charade." *Forbes*, 13 March 1995.

Berns, Walter. *Taking the Constitution Seriously*. New York: Simon & Schuster, 1987.

Bernstein, David. "The Supreme Court and 'Civil Rights' 1886–1908." *Yale Law Journal* 100, no. 3 (December 1990): 725–744.

Bernstein, David E. "Roots of the 'Underclass': The Decline of Laissez-Faire

Jurisprudence and the Rise of Racist Labor Legislation." *American University Law Review* 43, no. 1 (fall 1993): 85–138.

Berry, Mary Frances. *Black Resistance White Law: A History of Constitutional Racism in America.* New York: Allen Lane, 1994.

Bickel, Alexander M. "The Civil Rights Act of 1964." *Commentary*, August 1964.

————. "The Decade of School Desegregation: Progress and Prospects." *Columbia Law Review* 64, no. 2 (February 1964): 193–229.

————. *The Least Dangerous Branch: The Supreme Court at the Bar of Politics.* 2d ed. New Haven: Yale Univ. Press, 1986.

————. *The Morality of Consent.* New Haven: Yale Univ. Press, 1975.

————. "The Original Understanding and the Segregation Decision." *Harvard Law Review* 69, no. 1 (November 1955): 1–65.

————. "Reapportionment & Liberal Myths." *Commentary*, June 1963.

————. *The Supreme Court and the Idea of Progress.* 1970. Reprint. New Haven: Yale Univ. Press, 1978.

Billacois, Francois. *The Duel: Its Rise and Fall in Early Modern France.* New Haven: Yale Univ. Press, 1990.

Black, Charles L., Jr. "The Lawfulness of the Segregation Decisions." *Yale Law Journal* 69, no. 3 (January 1960): 421–430.

Blacksher, James U., and Larry T. Menefee. "From *Reynolds v. Sims* to *City of Mobile v. Bolden*: Have the White Suburbs Commandeered the Fifteenth Amendment?" *Hastings Law Journal* 34, no. 1 (September 1982): 1–64.

Blackstone, William. *Commentaries on the Laws of England.* Reprint. Oxon, England: Professional Books Limited, 1982.

Blanton, James. "A Limit to Affirmative Action?" *Commentary*, June 1989.

Blits, Jan H. "The Silenced Partner: Linda Gottfredson and the University of Delaware." *Academic Questions* 4, no. 3 (summer 1991): 41–47.

Blits, Jan H., and Linda S. Gottfredson. "Employment Testing and Job Performance." *The Public Interest* no. 98 (winter 1990): 18–25.

————. "Equality or Lasting Inequality?" *Transaction/Society* 27, no. 3 (March/April 1990): 4–11.

Bliven, Bruce. "Black Skin & White Marble." *New Republic*, 20 December 1948.

————. "Judge Waring Moves North." *New Republic*, 5 May 1952.

Bloch, Farrell. *Antidiscrimination Law and Minority Employment: Recruitment Practices and Regulatory Constraints.* Chicago: Univ. of Chicago Press, 1994.

Bloch, Marc. *Feudal Society*. Chicago: Univ. of Chicago Press, 1961.

———. *French Rural History*. Berkeley: Univ. of California Press, 1966.

Bloom, Allan. *The Closing of the American Mind*. New York: Simon and Schuster, 1987.

———. "Western Civ—and Me: An Address at Harvard University." *Commentary*, August 1990.

Bloom, Allan, ed. *Confronting the Constitution: The Challenge to Locke, Montesquieu, Jefferson, and the Federalists from Utilitarianism, Historicism, Marxism, Freudianism, Pragmatism, Existentialism....* Washington, D.C.: AEI Press, 1990.

Bloomgarden, Lawrence. "Medical School Quotas and National Health." *Commentary*, January 1953.

Blow, Richard. "Mea Culpa." *New Republic*, 18 February 1991.

Blumrosen, Alfred W. "Anti-Discrimination in Action in New Jersey: A Law-Sociology Study." *Rutgers Law Review* 19, no. 2 (winter 1965): 187–287.

———. "The Binding Effect of Affirmative Action Guidelines." *Labor Lawyer* 1, no. 2 (spring 1985): 261–278.

———. *Black Employment and the Law*. New Brunswick: Rutgers Univ. Press, 1971.

———. "The Crossroads for Equal Employment Opportunity: Incisive Administration or Indecisive Bureaucracy?" *Notre Dame Lawyer* 49, no. 1 (October 1973): 46–62.

———. "How the Courts are Handling Reverse Discrimination Claims: Draft Report on Reverse Discrimination Commissioned by Labor Department." *Daily Labor Report* (BNA) No. 56, at E–1 (March 23, 1995).

———. "The Legacy of Griggs: Social Progress and Subjective Judgments." *Chicago-Kent Law Review* 63, no. 1 (1987): 1–41.

———. *Modern Law: The Law Transmission System and Equal Employment Opportunity*. Madison: Univ. of Wisconsin Press, 1993.

———. "Quotas, Common Sense, and Law in Labor Relations: Three Dimensions of Equal Opportunity." *Rutgers Law Review* 27 (1974): 675–703.

———. Review of *Legal Restraints of Racial Discrimination* by Michael Sovern. *U.C.L.A. Law Review* 14 (1967): 721–732.

———. "Society in Transition I: A Broader Congressional Agenda for Equal Employment—The Peace Dividend, Leapfrogging, and Other Matters." *Yale Law & Policy Review* 8, no. 2 (1990): 257–275.

———. "Society in Transition IV: Affirmation of Affirmative Action under the Civil Rights Act of 1991." *Rutgers Law Review* 45, no. 4 (summer 1993): 903–919.

———. "Strangers in Paradise: *Griggs v. Duke Power Co.* and the Concept of Employment Discrimination." *Michigan Law Review* 71 (November 1972): 59–110.

Bolick, Clint. *Changing Course: Civil Rights at the Crossroads*. New Brunswick, New Jersey: Transaction, 1988.

———. *Grassroots Tyranny: The Limits of Federalism*. Washington, D.C.: Cato Institute, 1993.

———. *Unfinished Business: A Civil Rights Strategy for America's Third Century*. San Francisco: Pacific Research Institute, 1990.

Bolick, Clint, and Mark B. Liedl. *Fulfilling America's Promise: A Civil Rights Strategy for the 1990s*. Washington, D.C.: Heritage Foundation, 1990.

Boorstin, Daniel J. *The Americans: The Colonial Experience*. New York: Random House, 1958.

Bork, Robert. "Civil Rights—A Challenge." *New Republic*, 31 August 1963.

Bork, Robert H. "Neutral Principles and Some First Amendment Problems." *Indiana Law Journal* 47, no. 1 (fall 1971): 1–35.

———. *The Tempting of America: The Political Seduction of the Law*. New York: Free Press, 1990.

Bovard, James. *Lost Rights*. New York: St. Martin's, 1994.

———. "Job-Breakers: The EEOC's assault on the workplace." *American Spectator*, March 1994.

Boyd, Thomas M. and Stephen J. Markman. "The 1982 Amendments to the Voting Rights Act: A Legislative History." *Washington & Lee Law Review* 40, no. 4 (fall 1983): 1347–1428.

Branch, Taylor. *Parting the Waters: America in the King Years, 1954–63*. New York: Simon and Schuster, 1989.

Brennan, William J., Jr. "Speech to the Text and Teaching Symposium, Georgetown University, October 12, 1985." In *The Great Debate: Interpreting Our Written Constitution*. Washington, D.C.: Federalist Society, 1986.

Brimelow, Peter. "Gender politics." *Forbes*, 14 March 1994.

Brimelow, Peter, and Joseph E. Fallon. "Controlling Our Demographic Destiny." *National Review*, 21 February 1994.

Brimelow, Peter, and Leslie Spencer. "The Hidden Clue: Media hoopla to the contrary, the evidence suggests that banks are color-blind when it comes to mortgage lending." *Forbes*, 4 January 1993.

————. "When Quotas Replace Merit, Everybody Suffers." *Forbes*, 15 February 1993.

"The Brixton Disorders, 10–12 April 1981: Report of an Inquiry by the Rt. Hon. the Lord Scarman, O.B.E." London: Her Majesty's Stationery Office, 1982.

Brooks, Roy L. *Rethinking the American Race Problem*. Berkeley: Univ. of California Press, 1990.

Brown, Kevin. "Has the Supreme Court Allowed the Cure for De Jure Segregation to Replicate the Disease?" *Cornell Law Review* 78, no. 1 (November 1992): 1–83.

Brown, Peter. *Minority Party: Why Democrats Face Defeat in 1992 and Beyond*. Washington, D.C.: Regnery Gateway, 1991.

Browne, Kingsley R. "The Civil Rights Act of 1991: A 'Quota Bill,' A Codification of *Griggs*, A Partial Return to *Wards Cove*, or All of the Above?" *Case Western Reserve Law Review* 43, no. 2 (winter 1993): 287–400.

Brownell, Herbert. *Advising Ike: The Memoirs of Attorney General Herbert Brownell*. Lawrence, Kansas: Univ. Press of Kansas, 1993.

Brustein, Robert. "Dumbocracy in America." *Partisan Review* 15, no. 4 (1993): 526 531.

Buchanan, James M., and Gordon Tullock. *The Calculus of Consent: Logical Foundations of Constitutional Democracy*. Ann Arbor: Univ. of Michigan Press, 1962.

Bunzel, John H. "Affirmative-action admissions: how it 'works' at U.C. Berkeley." *The Public Interest* no. 93 (fall 1988): 111–129.

————. "Exclusive Opportunities." *The American Enterprise*, March/April 1990.

Burleigh, John. "*The Supreme Court vs. the Constitution*." Review of *Government by Judiciary* by Raoul Berger. *Public Interest* no. 50 (winter 1978): 151–157.

Burnham, Philip. "Selling Poor Steven: The Struggles and torments of a forgotten class in antebellum America: black slaveowners." *American Heritage*, February/March, 1993.

Burnham, Walter Dean. *Democracy in the Making: American Government and Politics*. Englewood Cliffs, New Jersey: Prentice-Hall, 1983.

Burress, Richard T. *We the People: The Story of Our Constitutional Convention*. Stanford: Hoover Institution, n.d.

Burt, Robert A. "Alex Bickel's Law School and Ours." *Yale Law Journal* 104, no. 7 (May 1995): 1853–1873.

————. *The Constitution in Conflict*. Cambridge: Belknap, Harvard Univ. Press, 1992.

Bush, George. "Remarks on Signing the Civil Rights Act of 1991, November 21, 1991." *Public Papers of the Presidents of the United States: George Bush, 1991.* Vol. 2. Washington, D.C.: U.S. Government Printing Office, 1992.

Bush, Michael. *Noble Privilege.* New York: Holmes & Meier, 1983.

Byrne, Jeffrey S. "Affirmative Action for Lesbians and Gay Men: A Proposal for True Equality of Opportunity and Workforce Diversity." *Yale Law & Policy Review* 11, no. 1 (1993): 47–108.

Byrne, J. Peter. "Racial Insults and Free Speech Within the University." *Georgetown Law Journal* 79, no. 3 (February 1991): 399–443.

Cahn, Edmond. "Jurisprudence." *New York University Law Review* 30 (January 1955): 150–169.

Califano, Joseph A., Jr. "Tough Talk for Democrats." *New York Times Magazine*, 8 January 1989.

———. *The Triumph & Tragedy of Lyndon Johnson: The White House Years.* New York: Simon & Schuster, 1991.

Cantor, Norman F. *The Civilization of the Middle Ages.* New York: HarperCollins, 1993.

———. *Medieval Lives: Eight Charismatic Men and Women of the Middle Ages.* New York: HarperCollins, 1994.

Cantril, Hadley, ed. *Public Opinion 1935–1946.* Princeton: Princeton Univ. Press, 1951.

Capaldi, Nicholas. *Out of Order: Affirmative Action and the Crisis of Doctrinaire Liberalism.* Buffalo: Prometheus Books, 1985.

———. "Twisting the Law." *Policy Review*, spring 1980.

Capers, I. Bennett. "Sex(ual Orientation) and Title VII." *Columbia Law Review* 91, no. 5 (June 1991): 1158–1187.

Caplan, Lincoln. *The Tenth Justice: The Solicitor General and the Rule of Law.* New York: Alfred A. Knopf, 1987.

Cardozo, Benjamin, N. *The Nature of the Judicial Process.* New Haven: Yale Univ. Press, 1921.

Carey, George W. *The Federalist: Design for a Constitutional Republic.* Urbana, Illinois: Univ. of Illinois Press, 1989.

———. *In Defense of the Constitution.* Cumberland, Virginia: James River Press, 1989.

Carlson, Tucker. "D.C. Blues: The Rap Sheet on the Washington Police." *Policy Review*, winter 1993.

Carr, William. "Nazi Policy Against the Jews." In Richard Bessel, ed., *Life in the Third Reich*. New York: Oxford Univ. Press, 1987.

Carter, Stephen L. Foreword to *The Tyranny of the Majority: Fundamental Fairness in Representative Democracy*, by Lani Guinier. New York: Free Press, 1994.

———. "Living Without the Judge." *Yale Law Journal* 101, no. 1 (October 1991): 1–6.

———. *Reflections of an Affirmative Action Baby*. New York: Basic Books, 1991.

Cazel, Fred A., Jr., ed. *Feudalism and Liberty: Articles and Addresses of Sidney Painter*. Baltimore: Johns Hopkins Press, 1961.

Chambers, J. Le Vonne, and Barry Goldstein. "Title VII at Twenty: The Continuing Challenge." *Labor Lawyer* 1, no. 2 (spring 1985): 235–259.

Chambers, Mortimer, Raymond Grew, David Herlihy, Theodore K. Rabb, and Isser Woloch. *The Western Experience*. 2 vols. New York: Alfred A. Knopf, 1974.

Chavez, Linda. "Demystifying Multiculturalism." *National Review*, 21 February 1994.

———. "The Real Aim of the Promoters of Cultural Diversity Is To Exclude Certain People and to Foreclose Debate." *Chronicle of Higher Education*, 18 July 1990.

Chesler, Mark A. *Social Science in Court: Mobilizing Experts in the School Desegregation Cases*. Madison: Univ. of Wisconsin Press, 1988.

Clark, Kenneth B. "The Desegregation Cases: Criticism of the Social Scientist's Role." *Villanova Law Review* 5, no. 2 (winter 1959–60): 224–240.

———. "The Role of Race." *New York Times Magazine*, 5 October, 1980.

———. "The Social Scientists, The Brown Decision, and Contemporary Confusion." In Friedman, Leon. *Argument: The Oral Argument Before the Supreme Court in Brown v. Board of Education of Topeka, 1952–55*. New York: Chelsea House, 1969.

Clegg, Roger, ed. *Racial Preferences in Government Contracting*. Washington, D.C.: National Legal Center for the Public Interest, 1993.

Clurman, Morton. "How Discriminatory are College Admissions?" *Commentary*, June 1953.

Cohen, Carl. "Justice Debased: The Weber Decision." *Commentary*, September 1979.

———. *Naked Racial Preference*. Lanham, Maryland: Madison, 1995.

———. "Why Racial Preference Is Illegal and Immoral." *Commentary*, June 1979.

Cohen, Richard. "A Whiter Shade of Male." *Washington Post Magazine*, 12 August 1990.

Cohen, Robin. *Endgame in South Africa: The Changing Structures and Ideology of Apartheid*. London: James Currey, 1986.

Cohodas, Nadine. *Strom Thurmond & the Politics of Southern Change*. New York: Simon & Schuster, 1993.

Coleman, Trevor W. "Doubting Thomas: Some of Clarence Thomas' former supporters feel betrayed." *Emerge*, November 1993.

Coleman, William T., Jr. "Mr. Justice Marshall: A Substantial Architect of the United States Constitution for Our Times." *Yale Law Journal* 101, no. 1 (October 1991): 7–11.

Collier, Peter, and David Horowitz. *Destructive Generation: Second Thoughts About the '60s*. New York: Summit, 1989.

Congressional Quarterly, *Nixon: First Year of His Presidency*. Washington, D.C.: Congressional Quarterly Press, 1970.

Congressional Research Service. "Memo to Honorable Robert Dole: Compilation and Overview of Federal Laws and Regulations Establishing Affirmative Action Goals or Other Preference Based on Race, Gender, or Ethnicity." Washington, D.C.: Library of Congress, 17 February 1995.

Conot, Robert E. *Justice at Nuremberg*. New York: Harper & Row, 1983.

"Constitutional Scholars' Statement on Affirmative Action After *City of Richmond v. J.A. Croson Co.*" *Yale Law Journal* 98, no. 8 (June 1989): 1711–1715.

Conway, David. *A Farewell to Marx: An Outline and Appraisal of his Theories*. London: Penguin Books, 1987.

Cook, Anthony E. "The Temptation and Fall of Original Understanding." Review of *The Tempting of America: The Political Seduction of the Law*, by Robert Bork. *Duke Law Journal* 1990, no. 5 (November 1990): 1163–1206.

Cooper, Charles J. "*Wards Cove Packing Company v. Atonio*: A Step Toward Eliminating Quotas in the American Workplace." *Harvard Journal of Law & Public Policy* 14, no. 1 (winter 1991): 84–92.

Cose, Ellis. *A Man's World: How Real Is Male Privilege—And How High Is Its Price?* New York: HarperCollins, 1995.

———. *The Rage of a Privileged Class*. New York: HarperCollins, 1993.

Cottrol, Robert J., and Raymond T. Diamond. "The Second Amendment: Toward an Afro-Americanist Reconsideration." *Georgetown Law Journal* 80, no. 2 (December 1991): 309–361.

Cover, Robert M. "The Origins of Judicial Activism in the Protection of Minorities." *Yale Law Journal* 91, no. 7 (June 1982): 1287–1316.

Cox, Archibald. *The Court and the Constitution*. Boston: Houghton Mifflin, 1987.

Craig, Gordon A. *The Germans*. New York: Meridian, 1982.

Crenshaw, Kimberlé Williams. "Demarginalizing the Intersection of Race and Sex: A Black Feminist Critique of Antidiscrimination Doctrine, Feminist Theory, and Antiracist Politics." In Katharine T. Bartlett and Rosanne Kennedy, eds. *Feminist Legal Theory: Readings in Law and Gender*. Boulder: Westview, 1991.

————. "Race, Reform, and Retrenchment: Transformation and Legitimation in Antidiscrimination Law." *Harvard Law Review* 101, no. 7 (May 1988): 1331–1387.

Crenshaw, Kimberlé, Harold Cruse, Peter Gabel, Catharine A. MacKinnon, Gary Peller, and Cornel West. "Roundtable: Doubting Thomas." *Tikkun*, September/October 1991.

Culp, Jerome McCristal, Jr. "Posner on Duncan Kennedy and Racial Difference: White Authority in the Legal Academy." *Duke Law Journal* 41, no. 2 (April 1992): 1095–1114.

Cumming, Valerie. *Royal Dress: The Image and the Reality, 1580 to the Present Day*. New York: Holmes & Meier, 1989.

Cunningham, Roger A., William B. Stoebuck, and Dale A. Whitman. *The Law of Property*. St. Paul: West, 1984.

Current, Richard N., T. Harry Williams, and Frank Freidel. *American History: A Survey*. 4th ed. New York: Alfred A. Knopf, 1975.

Currie, David P. *The Constitution in the Supreme Court: The First Hundred Years 1789–1888*. Chicago: Univ. of Chicago Press, 1985.

————. *The Constitution in the Supreme Court: The Second Century 1888–1986*. Chicago: Univ. of Chicago Press, 1990.

D'Souza, Dinesh. *The End of Racism: Principles for a Multicultural Society*. New York: Free Press, 1995.

————. *Illiberal Education: The Politics of Race and Sex on Campus*. New York: Free Press, 1991.

————. " 'PC' So Far." *Commentary*, October 1991.

Dabney, Virginius. *Virginia: The New Dominion, A History from 1607 to the Present*. Charlottesville: Univ. Press of Virginia, 1971.

Dahl, Robert Alan. *A Preface to Democratic Theory*. Chicago: Univ. of Chicago Press, 1956.

Dahrendorf, Ralf. *Society and Democracy in Germany*. Munich: R. Piper, 1965. Reprint. New York: Norton, 1979.

Dalton, Clare. "Deconstructing Contract Doctrine." In Katharine T. Bartlett and Rosanne Kennedy, eds. *Feminist Legal Theory: Readings in Law and Gender*. Boulder: Westview, 1991.

Daly, John Charles, William B. Allen, Drew S. Days, III, Benjamin L. Hooks, and William Bradford Reynolds. *Affirmative Action and the Constitution*. Washington, D.C.: American Enterprise Institute, 1987.

Damask, Nicholas A., and Craig Cobane. "Inside the Sensitivity Laboratory: Mind Control, Multicultural-Style." *Campus*, winter 1994.

Damon, William. "Learning How to Deal with the New American Dilemma: We Must Teach Our Students About Morality and Racism." *Chronicle of Higher Education*, 3 May 1989.

Daniels, Edmund D., and Michael David Weiss. " 'Equality' over Quality." *Reason*, July 1991.

Davidson, Chandler, ed. *Minority Vote Dilution*. Washington, D.C.: Howard Univ. Press, 1984.

Davidson, Chandler, and Bernard Grofman, eds. *Quiet Revolution in the South: The Impact of the Voting Rights Act 1965–1990*. Princeton: Princeton Univ. Press, 1994.

Davis, Bernard D. *Storm over Biology: Essays on Science, Sentiment and Public Policy*. Buffalo: Prometheus Books, 1986.

Davis, Flora. *Moving the Mountain: The Women's Movement in America Since 1960*. New York: Simon & Schuster, 1991.

Davis, Michael D., and Hunter R. Clark. *Thurgood Marshall: Warrior at the Bar. Rebel on the Bench*. New York: Birch Lane Press, 1992.

Davis, Peggy C. "Law as Microaggression." *Yale Law Journal* 98, no. 8 (June 1989): 1559–1577.

Dawidowicz, Lucy S., "In Berlin Again." *Commentary*, August 1986.

———. *The War Against the Jews*. 2d ed., New York: Seth Press, 1986.

Dawidowicz, Lucy S., ed. *A Holocaust Reader*. New York: Behrman House, 1976.

Days, Drew S., III. "*Brown* Blues: Rethinking the Integrative Ideal." *William and Mary Law Review* 34, no. 1 (fall 1992): 53–74.

———. "Fullilove." *Yale Law Journal* 96, no. 3 (January 1987): 453–485.

De Beauvoir, Simone. *The Marquis de Sade*. London: Evergreen, 1954 and New York: Grove Press, 1953.

DeBenedictis, Don J. "Changing Faces: Coming to Terms With Growing Minority Populations." *ABA Journal*, April 1991.

de Tocqueville, Alexis. *Democracy in America*. Reprint. New York: Doubleday Anchor, 1969.

——. *The Old Regime and the French Revolution* Reprint. Garden City, New York: Doubleday Anchor, 1955.

Decter, Midge. "E Pluribus Nihil: Multiculturalism and Black Children." *Commentary*, September 1991.

——. "Ronald Reagan & the Culture War." *Commentary*, March 1991.

Delbanco, Andrew. "The Politics of Separatism." *Partisan Review* 15, no. 4 (1993): 534–542.

Delgado, Richard. "Affirmative Action as a Majoritarian Device: Or, Do You Really Want to Be a Role Model?" *Michigan Law Review* 89, no. 5 (March 1991): 1222–1231.

——. "Approach Avoidance: In Law School Hiring: Is the Law a WASP?" *St. Louis University Law Journal* 34, no. 3 (spring 1990): 631–642.

——. "Critical Legal Studies and the Realities of Race—Does the Fundamental Contradiction Have a Corollary?" *Harvard Civil Rights–Civil Liberties Law Review* 23, no. 2 (summer 1988): 407–413.

——. "Derrick Bell's *Racial Realism*: A Comment on White Optimism and Black Despair." *Connecticut Law Review* 24, no. 2 (winter 1992): 527–532.

——. "Enormous Anomaly? Left–Right Parallels in Recent Writing About Race." Review of *And We Are Not Saved: The Elusive Quest for Racial Justice*, by Derrick Bell, *Reflections of An Affirmative Action Baby*, by Stephen L. Carter, *The Content of Our Character: A New Vision of Race in America*, by Shelby Steele, and *The Alchemy of Race and Rights*, by Patricia Williams. *Columbia Law Review* 91, no. 6 (October 1991): 1547–1560.

——. "The Ethereal Scholar: Does Critical Legal Studies Have What Minorities Want?" *Harvard Civil Rights–Civil Liberties Law Review* 22, no. 2 (spring 1987): 301–322.

——. "The Imperial Scholar: Reflections on a Review of Civil Rights Literature." *University of Pennsylvania Law Review* 132, no. 3 (March 1984): 561–578.

——. "Recasting the American Race Problem." Review of *Rethinking the American Race Problem*, by Roy L. Brooks. *California Law Review* 79, no. 5 (October 1991): 1389–1400.

——. "Rodrigo's Chronicle." Review of *Illiberal Education: The Politics of Race and Sex on Campus*, by Dinesh D'Souza. *Yale Law Journal* 101, no. 6 (April 1992): 1357–1383.

——. "Rodrigo's Fourth Chronicle: Neutrality and Stasis in Antidiscrimination Law." Review of *Faces at the Bottom of the Well: The Permanence of Racism*, by

Derrick Bell, *The Hollow Hope: Can Courts Bring About Social Change?*, by Gerald N. Rosenberg, *Turning Right: The Making of the Rehnquist Supreme Court*, by David G. Savage, and *Race Against the Court: The Supreme Court and Minorities in Contemporary America*, by Girardeau A. Spann. *Stanford Law Review* 45, no. 4 (April 1993): 1133–1160.

————. "Rodrigo's Ninth Chronicle: Race, Legal Instrumentalilsm, and the Rule of Law." *University of Pennsylvania Law Review* 143, no. 2 (December 1994): 379–416.

————. "When a Story is Just a Story: Does Voice Really Matter?" *Virginia Law Review* 76, no. 1 (February 1990): 95–111.

————. "Zero-Based Racial Politics and an Infinity-Based Response: Will Endless Talking Cure America's Racial Ills?" *Georgetown Law Journal* 80, no. 5 (June 1992): 1879–1890.

Delgado, Richard, and Jean Stefancic. "Critical Race Theory: An Annotated Bibliography." *Virginia Law Review* 79 no. 2 (March 1993): 461–516.

Detlefsen, Robert R. *Civil Rights Under Reagan*. San Francisco: ICS Press, 1991.

"Developments in the Law—Employment Discrimination and Title VII of the Civil Rights Act of 1964." *Harvard Law Review* 84, no. 5 (March 1971): 1109–1316.

Dickstein, Morris. "Correcting PC." *Partisan Review* 15, no. 4 (1993): 542–549.

Dimond, Paul R. *Beyond Busing: Inside the Challenge to Urban Segregation*. Ann Arbor: Univ. of Michigan Press, 1985.

Dobrzynski, Judith H. "The 'Glass Ceiling': A Barrier to the Boardroom, Too." *Business Week*, 22 November 1993.

Donnelly, Elaine. *Special Report: Double Standards in Naval Aviation*. Livonia, Michigan: Center for Military Readiness, 25 April 1995.

Donohue, John J., III, and James Heckman. "Continuous Versus Episodic Change: The Impact of Civil Rights Policy on the Economic Status of Blacks." *Journal of Economic Literature* 24 (December 1991): 1603–1643.

Dorn, James A. "Economic Liberty and Democracy in East Asia." *Orbis* 37, no. 4 (fall 1993): 599–619.

Douglas, William O. *The Court Years*. New York: Random House, 1980.

Doyle, William. *The Oxford History of the French Revolution*. New York: Oxford Univ. Press, 1989.

Drinan, Robert F. "Another Look at Affirmative Action." *America*, 9 February 1985.

Dudziak, Mary L. "Desegregation as a Cold War Imperative." *Stanford Law Review* 41, no. 1 (November 1988): 61–120.

Duignan, Peter. *The United States: A Hopeful Future*. Stanford: Hoover Institution, 1993.

Dugard, John. *Human Rights and the South African Legal Order*. Princeton: Princeton Univ. Press, 1978.

Dugger, Ronnie. "These Are the Times: On Being a Southern Liberal." *Commentary*, April 1964.

Dworkin, Andrea. *Intercourse*. New York: Free Press, 1987.

Dworkin, Ronald. "How to Read the Civil Rights Act." *New York Review of Books*, 19 December 1979.

———. *A Matter of Principle*. Cambridge: Harvard Univ. Press, 1985.

———. *Taking Rights Seriously*. Cambridge: Harvard Univ. Press, 1977.

Eastland, Terry. "George Bush's Quota Bill: The Dismaying Impact of *Griggs*." *Policy Review*, summer 1991.

———. "Racial Preferences in Court (Again)." *Commentary*, January 1989.

Eastland, Terry, ed. *Benchmarks: Great Constitutional Controversies in the Supreme Court*. Washington, D.C.: Ethics and Public Policy Center, 1995.

Eaton, William. *Who Killed the Constitution: The Judges v. the Law*. Washington, D.C.: Regnery Gateway, 1988.

Edelman, Peter B. "The Next Century of Our Constitution: Rethinking Our Duty to the Poor. *Hastings Law Journal* 39, no. 1 (November 1987): 1–61.

Edsall, Thomas Byrne. "Tricky Dixie." Review of *Strom Thurmond and the Politics of Southern Change*. *New Republic*, 5 April 1993.

Edsall, Thomas Byrne, and Mary D. Edsall. *Chain Reaction: The Impact of Race, Rights, and Taxes on American Politics*. New York: Norton, 1991.

Eisler, Kim Isaac. *A Justice For All: William J. Brennan, Jr., and the Decisions that Transformed America*. New York: Simon & Schuster, 1993.

Ekirch, Arthur A., Jr. *The American Democratic Tradition: A History*. New York: Macmillan, 1963.

———. *The Decline of American Liberalism*. New York: Longman's, Green, 1955.

Elman, Philip. "Response." *Harvard Law Review* 100, no. 8 (June 1987): 1949–1957.

———. "The Solicitor General's Office, Justice Frankfurter, and Civil Rights Litigation, 1946–1960: An Oral History." Interviewed by Norman Silber. *Harvard Law Review* 100, no. 4 (February 1987): 817–852.

Elshtain, Jean Bethke. "Lessons from Amherst: Dragnet or Agenda for Action." *Commonweal*, 25 March 1988.

Ely, John Hart. "Another Such Victory: Constitutional Theory and Practice in a World Where Courts Are No Different From Legislatures." *Virginia Law Review* 77, no. 4 (May 1991): 833–854.

———. "The Constitutionality of Reverse Racial Discrimination." *University of Chicago Law Review* 41, no. 4 (summer 1974): 723–741.

———. *Democracy and Distrust: A Theory of Judicial Review*. Cambridge, Harvard Univ. Press, 1980.

Emerson, Ralph Waldo. *Self-Reliance*. 1841. Reprint. In Charles W. Eliot, ed. *Harvard Classics*, vol. 5. New York: P.F. Collier & Son, 1909.

Epstein, Richard A. *Forbidden Grounds: The Case Against Employment Discrimination Laws*. Cambridge: Harvard Univ. Press, 1992.

———. "The Paradox of Civil Rights." *Yale Law & Policy Review*. 8, no. 2 (1990): 299–319.

Epstein, Richard A., and Erwin Chemerinsky. "Forum: Should Title VII of the Civil Rights Act of 1964 Be Repealed?" *Law &: Southern California Interdisciplinary Law Journal* 2, no. 2 (summer 1993): 349–366.

Erler, Edward J. "Sowing the Wind: Judicial Oligarchy and the Legacy of *Brown v. Board of Education*." *Harvard Journal of Law and Public Policy* 8, no. 2 (spring 1985): 399–426.

Eskridge, William, N., Jr. "Reneging on History? Playing the Court/Congress/President Civil Rights Game." *California Law Review* 79, no. 3 (May 1991): 613–683.

Eskridge, William, N., Jr., and Philip P. Frickey. *Cases and Materials on Legislation: Statutes and the Creation of Public Policy*. St. Paul: West, 1988.

Faille, Christopher C. *The Decline and Fall of the Supreme Court*. Westport, Conn.: Praeger, 1995.

Fairman, Charles. "Foreword: The Attack on the Segregation Cases." *Harvard Law Review*. 70, no. 1 (November 1956): 83–94.

Farber, Daniel A., and Philip P. Frickey. "Is *Carolene Products* Dead? Reflections on Affirmative Action and the Dynamics of Civil Rights." *California Law Review* 79, no. 3 (May 1991): 685–727.

Farber, Daniel A., William N. Eskridge, Jr., and Philip P. Frickey. *Cases and Materials on Constitutional Law: Themes for the Constitution's Third Century*. St. Paul: West, 1993.

Farnham, Alan. "Holding Firm on Affirmative Action." *Fortune*, 13 March 1989.

Farrell, Warren. *The Myth of Male Power*. New York: Simon & Schuster, 1993.

Fein, Bruce, Rex Lee, Jesse Choper, A. E. Dick Howard, and Burt Neuborne. "The Brennan Legacy: A Roundtable Discussion." *ABA Journal*, February 1991.

Felton, Eric. "The 'Incorrect' Insurrection at Harvard Law." *Insight*, 24 July 1991.

Finn, Chester E., Jr. "Quotas and the Bush Administration." *Commentary*, November 1991.

Fiscus, Ronald J. *The Constitutional Logic of Affirmative Action*. Durham, N.C.: Duke Univ. Press, 1992.

Fish, Stanley. *There's No Such Thing as Free Speech And It's a Good Thing, Too*. New York: Oxford Univ. Press, 1994.

Fisher, William W., III., Morton J. Horwitz, and Thomas A. Reed, eds. *American Legal Realism*. New York: Oxford Univ. Press, 1993.

Fiss, Owen M. "The Fate of an Idea Whose Time Has Come: Antidiscrimination Law in the Second Decade after *Brown v. Board of Education*." *University of Chicago Law Review* 41, no. 4 (summer 1974): 742–773.

Flagg, Barbara J. "Fashioning a Title VII Remedy for Transparently White Subjective Decisionmaking." *Yale Law Journal*, 104, no. 8 (June 1995). 2009–2051.

———. "'Was Blind, But Now I See:' White Race Consciousness and the Requirement of Discriminatory Intent." *Michigan Law Review* 91, no. 5 (March 1993): 953–1017.

Flick, Rachel. "Does Affirmative Action Really Work?" *Reader's Digest*, August 1991.

Foner, Eric. *Reconstruction: America's Unfinished Revolution, 1863–1877*. New York: Harper & Row, 1988.

Ford, Christopher A. "Administering Identity: The Determination of 'Race' in Race-Conscious Law." *California Law Review* 82, no. 5 (October 1994): 1231–1285.

Foreman, Clark. "Georgia Kills the Poll Tax." *New Republic*, 26 February 1945.

Forman, James, Jr. "Saving Affirmative Action." *The Nation*, 6 December 1991.

———. "Victory by Surrender: The Voting Rights Amendments of 1982 and the Civil Rights Act of 1991." *Yale Law & Policy Review* 10, no. 1 (1992): 133–176.

Francis, Samuel. "The Cult of Dr. King." *Chronicles*, May 1988.

Frankfurter, Felix. "Letter to Franklin D. Roosevelt, February 18, 1937." In *Who Speaks for the Constitution?: The Debate Over Interpretive Authority*. Washington, D.C.: Federalist Society, 1992.

Franklin, John Hope. *The Color-Line: Legacy for the Twenty-First Century.* Columbia, Mo.: Univ. of Missouri, 1993.

Freeman, Alan. "Antidiscrimination Law: The View from 1989." In David Kairys, ed. *The Politics of Law: A Progressive Critique.* New York: Pantheon Books, 1990.

Freyer, Tony. *Hugo L. Black: and the Dilemma of American Liberalism.* Glenview, Ill.: Scott, Foresman, 1990.

Fried, Charles. "Affirmative Action After *City of Richmond v. J.A. Croson, Co.*: A Response to the Scholars' Statement." *Yale Law Journal* 99, no. 1 (October 1989): 155–161.

———. *Order & Law: Arguing the Reagan Revolution—A Firsthand Account.* New York: Simon & Schuster, 1991.

Friedman, Leon, ed. *Argument: The Oral Argument Before the Supreme Court in Brown v. Board of Education of Topeka, 1952–55.* New York: Chelsea House, 1969.

Friedman, Milton. *Capitalism and Freedom.* Chicago: Univ. of Chicago Press, 1962.

Gabel, Peter. "Affirmative Action and Racial Harmony." *Tikkun*, May/June 1995.

Galbraith, John Kenneth, Edwin Kuh, and Lester G. Thurow. "A Galbraith–Kuh–Thurow Reply." *New York Times Magazine*, 10 October 1971.

———. "The Galbraith Plan to Promote the Minorities." *New York Times Magazine*, 22 August 1971.

Galen, Michele. "White, Male, and Worried." *Business Week.* 31 January 1994.

Galen, Michele, with Ann Therese. "Diversity: Beyond the Numbers Game: Companies are stepping up programs to retain minorities." *Business Week,* 14 August 1995.

Gann, L. H., and Alvin Rabushka. "Racial Classification: Politics of the Future?" *Policy Review*, summer 1981.

Garrow, David J. *Bearing the Cross: Martin Luther King, Jr., and the Southern Christian Leadership Conference.* New York: William Morrow, 1986.

———. "Hopelessly Hollow History: Revisionist Devaluing of *Brown v. Board of Education.*" *Virginia Law Review* 80, no. 1 (February 1994): 151–160.

———. *Protest at Selma: Martin Luther King, Jr. and the Voting Rights Act of 1965.* New Haven: Yale Univ. Press, 1978.

Gates, Henry Louis, Jr. "Let Them Talk: Why civil liberties pose no threats to civil rights." Review of *Words That Wound: Critical Race Theory, Assaultive Speech and the First Amendment*, by Mari J. Matsuda, Charles R. Lawrence III, Richard Delgado, and Kimberlé Williams Crenshaw. *New Republic*, 20 & 27 September 1993.

Gellhorn, Walter, Clark Byse, Peter L. Strauss, Todd Rakoff, Roy A. Schotland. *Administrative Law: Cases and Comments.* 8th ed. Mineola, N.Y.: Foundation Press, 1987.

Geslewitz, Irving M. "Understanding the 1991 Civil Rights Act." *The Practical Lawyer* 38, no. 2 (March 1992): 57–69.

Gewirtz, Paul. "Discrimination Endgame." *New Republic*, 12 August 1991.

———. "Fine Print." *New Republic*, 18 November 1991.

———. "Thurgood Marshall." *Yale Law Journal* 101, no. 1 (October 1991): 13–18.

Gibbs, Nancy. "Bigots in the Ivory Tower: An alarming rise in hatred roils U.S. campuses." *Time*, 7 May 1990.

Giliomee, Hermann, and Lawrence Schlemmer. *From Apartheid to Nation-Building.* Cape Town: Oxford Univ. Press, 1989.

Girson, Rochelle. "Mutations in the Body Politic." *Saturday Review*, 29 August 1964.

Glasser, Ira. "Affirmative Action and the Legacy of Racial Injustice." In Phyllis A. Katz and Dalmas A. Taylor, eds. *Eliminating Racism: Profiles in Controversy.* New York: Plenum Press, 1988.

Glazer, Nathan. *Affirmative Discrimination: Ethnic Inequality and Public Policy.* New York: Basic Books, 1975.

———. "An Interview with Nathan Glazer." *New Perspectives*, fall 1985.

———. "Toward an Imperial Judiciary?" *Public Interest*, no. 41 (fall 1975): 104–123.

Gleckman, Howard, Tim Smart, Paula Dwyer, Troy Segal, and Joseph Weber. "Race in the Workplace: Is Affirmative Action Working?" *Business Week*, 8 July 1991.

Gold, Michael Evan. "*Griggs*' Folly: An Essay on the Theory, Problems, and Origin of the Adverse Impact Definition of Employment Discrimination and a Recommendation for Reform." *Industrial Relations Law Journal* 7, no. 4 (1985): 429–598.

Goldstein, Joseph. *The Intelligible Constitution: The Supreme Court's Obligation to Maintain the Constitution as Something We The People Can Understand.* New York: Oxford Univ. Press, 1992.

Goldwater, Barry M., with Jack Casserly. *Goldwater.* New York: Doubleday, 1988.

Goldwin, Robert A. *Why Blacks, Women, and Jews Are Not Mentioned in the Constitution, and other unorthodox views.* Washington, D.C.: AEI Press, 1990.

Goldwin, Robert A., and Art Kaufman, eds. *Slavery and Its Consequences: The*

Constitution, Equality, and Race. Washington, D.C.: American Enterprise Institute, 1988.

Goldwin, Robert A., and Robert A. Licht, eds. *The Spirit of the Constitution: Five Conversations*. Washington, D.C.: AEI Press, 1990.

Goode, Stephen. "On the Outs over Who Gets In." *Insight*, 9 October 1989.

Goodheart, Eugene. "PC or Not PC." *Partisan Review* 15, no. 4 (1993): 550–556.

Goodman, Walter. "The Capital Keeps Calm: When Washington Ended Segregation, There Was Less Protest Than Most People Expected." *New Republic*, 25 October 1954.

Gordon, Robert A. "Thunder From the Left." Review of *Storm over Biology: Essays on Science, Sentiment and Public Policy* by Bernard A. Davis. *Academic Questions* 1, no. 3 (summer 1988): 74–92.

Gordon, Robert W. "New Developments in Legal Theory." In David Kairys, ed. *The Politics of Law: A Progressive Critique*, rev. ed. New York: Pantheon Books, 1990.

Gosnell, Cullen B., Lane W. Lancaster, and Robert S. Rankin. *Fundamentals of American National Government*. New York: McGraw-Hill, 1955.

Gotanda, Neil. "A Critique of 'Our Constitution Is Color-Blind.'" *Stanford Law Review* 44, no. 1 (November 1991): 1–68.

Gottesman, Michael H. "Twelve Topics to Consider Before Opting for Racial Quotas." *Georgetown Law Journal* 79, no. 6 (August 1991): 1737–1767.

Graham, Hugh Davis. *The Civil Rights Era: Origins and Development of National Policy 1960–1972*. New York: Oxford Univ. Press, 1990.

———. *Civil Rights in the U.S.* University Park, Pennsylvania: Pennsylvania State University Press, 1994.

Graglia, Lino A. "Affirmative Discrimination." *National Review*, 5 July 1993.

———. *Disaster by Decree: The Supreme Court Decisions on Race and the Schools*. Ithaca: Cornell Univ. Press, 1976.

———. "Does Constitutional Law Exist?" *National Review*, 26 June 1995.

———. "Judicial Activism: Even on the Right, It's Wrong." *Public Interest*, no. 95 (spring 1989): 57–74.

———. "The 'Remedy' Rationale for Requiring or Permitting Otherwise Prohibited Discrimination: How the Court Overcame the Constitution and the 1964 Civil Rights Act." *Suffolk University Law Review* 22, no. 3 (fall 1988): 569–621.

———. "Title VII of the Civil Rights Act of 1964: From Prohibiting to Requiring Racial Discrimination in Employment." *Harvard Journal of Law & Public Policy* 14, no. 1 (winter 1991): 68–83.

Grano, Joseph D. "Free Speech v. the University of Michigan." *Academic Questions* 3, no. 2 (spring 1990): 7–22.

Gray, C. Boyden. "Disparate Impact: History and Consequence." *Louisiana Law Review* 54, no. 6 (July 1994): 1487–1505.

Gray, John. *Hayek on Liberty*. New York: Basil Blackwell, 1984.

———. *Liberalism*. Minneapolis: Univ. of Minnesota Press, 1986.

———. *Liberalisms: Essays in Political Philosophy*. London: Routledge, 1989.

The Great Debate: Interpreting Our Written Constitution. Washington, D.C.: Federalist Society, 1986.

Greenberg, Jack. *Crusaders in the Courts: How a Dedicated Band of Lawyers Fought for the Civil Rights Revolution*. New York: Basic Books, 1994.

———. *Race Relations and American Law*. New York: Columbia Univ. Press, 1959.

Greene, Linda S. "Civil Rights at the Millennium—A Response to Bell's Call for Racial Realism." *Connecticut Law Review* 24, no. 2 (winter 1992): 499–515.

Greenfeld, Helaine. "Some Constitutional Problems with the Resegregation of Public Schools." *Georgetown Law Journal* 80, no. 2 (December 1991): 363–386.

Greenfield, Kent Roberts. *Sumptuary Law in Nurnberg: A Study in Paternal Government*. Baltimore: Johns Hopkins Press, 1918.

Griffin, John Howard. *Black Like Me*. 1960. Reprint. New York: Penguin Books, 1976.

Grofman, Bernard, Lisa Handley, and Richard G. Niemi. *Minority Representation and the Quest for Voting Equality*. New York: Cambridge University Press, 1992.

Grofman, Bernard, and Chandler Davidson, eds. *Controversies in Minority Voting: The Voting Rights Act in Perspective*. Washington, D.C.: Brookings Institution, 1992.

Gross, Barry R. *Discrimination in Reverse: Is Turnabout Fair Play?* New York: New York Univ. Press, 1978.

Guinier, Lani. "[E]racing Democracy: The Voting Rights Cases." *Harvard Law Review* 108, no. 1 (November 1994): 109–137.

———. "Keeping the Faith: Black Voters in the Post-Reagan Era." *Harvard Civil Rights–Civil Liberties Law Review* 24, no. 2 (spring 1989): 393–435.

———. "No Two Seats: The Elusive Quest for Political Equality." *Virginia Law Review* 77, no. 8 (November 1991): 1413–1514.

———. "Of Gentlemen and Role Models." *Berkeley Women's Law Journal* 6, part 1 (1990–91): 93–106.

———. "Second Proms and Second Primaries: The Limits of Majority Rule." *Pennsylvania Gazette*, October 1993.

———. "The Triumph of Tokenism: The Voting Rights Act and the Theory of Black Electoral Success." *Michigan Law Review* 89, no. 5 (March 1991): 1077–1154.

———. *The Tyranny of the Majority: Fundamental Fairness in Representative Democracy*. New York: Free Press, 1994.

———. "Voting Rights and Democratic Theory: Where Do We Go From Here?" In *Controversies in Minority Voting*. Edited by Bernard Grofman and Chandler Davidson. Washington, D.C.: Brookings Institution, 1992.

———. "Who's Afraid of Lani Guinier?" *New York Times Magazine*, 27 February 1994.

Guinier, Lani, Michelle Fine, and Jane Balin, with Ann Bartow and Deborah Lee Stachel. "Becoming Gentlemen: Women's Experiences at One Ivy League Law School." *University of Pennsylvania Law Review* 143, no. 1 (November 1994): 1–110.

Gunther, Gerald. *Constitutional Law*. Westbury, N.Y.: Foundation Press, 1991.

Haack, Susan. "Knowledge and Propaganda: Reflections of an Old Feminist." *Partisan Review* 15, no. 4 (1993): 556–564.

Haar, Charles M., and Lance Liebman. *Property and Law*. 2d ed. Boston: Little Brown, 1985.

Hacker, Andrew. "The Myths of Racial Division: Blacks, Whites—and Statistics." *New Republic*, 23 March 1992.

———. *Two Nations: Black and White, Separate, Hostile, Unequal*. New York: Scribner, 1992.

Halberstam, David. *The Fifties*. New York: Villard Books, 1993.

Hall, Kermit L., ed. *The Oxford Companion to the Supreme Court of the United States*. New York: Oxford Univ. Press, 1992.

Halpern, Stephen C. *On the Limits of the Law: The Ironic Legacy of Title VI of the 1964 Civil Rights Act*. Baltimore: Johns Hopkins Univ. Press, 1995.

Hammerman, Herbert. "'Affirmative-Action Stalemate': A Second Perspective." *Public Interest,* no. 93 (fall 1988): 130–134.

Hannaford, Ivan. "The Idiocy of Race." *Wilson Quarterly* 28, no. 2 (spring 1994): 8–35.

Harbaugh, William. *Lawyer's Lawyer: The Life of John W. Davis*. New York: Oxford Univ. Press, 1973.

Harris, Angela P. "Race and Essentialism in Feminist Legal Theory." *Stanford Law Review* 42, no. 3 (February 1990): 581–616.

Harris, Cheryl I. "Whiteness as Property." *Harvard Law Review* 106, no. 8 (June 1993): 1707–1791.

Harris, Fred R., and Roger W. Wilkins, eds. *Quiet Riots: Race and Poverty in the United States*. New York: Pantheon, 1988.

Hart, H. L. A. *The Concept of Law*. Oxford: Oxford Univ. Press, 1961.

Hatch, Orrin. "Loading the Economy." *Policy Review*, spring 1980.

Haydu, Andy. Letter to the Editor. *Time*, 7 March 1994.

Hayek, Friedrich A. *The Constitution of Liberty*. Chicago: Univ. of Chicago Press, 1960.

———. *Law, Legislation and Liberty*. 3 vols. Chicago: Univ. of Chicago Press, 1979.

———. *The Road to Serfdom*. Chicago: Univ. of Chicago Press, 1944.

Hayman, Robert L., Jr. "The Color of Tradition: Critical Race Theory and Postmodern Constitutional Traditionalism." *Harvard Civil Rights–Civil Liberties Law Review* 30, no. 1 (winter 1995): 57–108.

Heilbroner, Robert L. *The Making of Economic Society*. 6th ed. Englewood Cliffs, New Jersey: Prentice-Hall, 1980.

Heller, Mikhail, and Aleksandr Nekrich. *Utopia in Power: The History of the Soviet Union from 1917 to the Present*. New York: Summit Books, 1986.

Helmholz, R. H. "Adverse Possession and Subjective Intent." *Washington University Law Quarterly* 61, no. 2 (summer 1983): 331–358.

Henry, William A., III. "Beyond the Melting Pot." *Time*, 9 April 1990.

———. "Upside Down in the Groves of Academe." *Time*, 1 April 1991.

Hentoff, Nat. "The Justice Breaks His Silence: For the First Time Since His Retirement, Supreme Court Justice William Brennan Delivers the Closing Argument on his Colleagues, the Constitution and What This Country Faces." *Playboy*, July 1991.

———. *The New Equality*. New York: Viking Press, 1964.

———. "The New Jacobins: Will the terror of political correctness spread from the campus to the 'real world?'" *Reason*, November 1991.

Herrnstein, R. J. "Still an American Dilemma." *Public Interest*, no. 98 (winter 1990): 3–17.

Hertzberg, Hendrik. "TRB From Washington: Wounds of Race." *New Republic*, 10 July 1989.

Hickock, Eugene W., and Gary L. McDowell. *Justice vs. Law: Courts and Politics in American Society*. New York: Free Press, 1993.

Hilberg, Raul. *The Destruction of the European Jews*. New York: Holmes & Meier, 1985.

Hill, Herbert. "The Role of Law in Securing Equal Employment Opportunity: Legal Powers and Social Change." *Boston College Industrial and Commercial Law Review* 7, no. 3 (spring 1966): 625–652.

Himmelfarb, Gertrude. *On Liberty & Liberalism: The Case of John Stuart Mill*. San Francisco: ICS Press, 1990.

Hitler, Adolf. *Mein Kampf*. New York: Reynal & Hitchcock, 1941.

Hobbes, Thomas. *Leviathan*. 1651. Reprint. C. B. Macpherson, ed. New York: Viking Penguin, 1982.

Hockett, Jeffrey D. "Justice Robert H. Jackson and Segregation: A Study of the Limitations and Proper Basis for Judicial Action." *Yearbook 1989: Supreme Court Historical Society*. Washington, D.C.: Supreme Court Historical Society, 1989.

Hogue, Arthur R. *Origins of the Common Law*. 1966. Reprint. Indianapolis: LibertyPress, 1985.

Holland, Kenneth M. "Equality and the Constitution: A Study in the Transformation of a Concept." In Robert A. Goldwin and Art Kaufman, eds. *Slavery and Its Consequences: The Constitution, Equality, and Race*. Washington, D.C.: American Enterprise Institute, 1988.

Hollander, Paul. "From Iconoclasm to Conventional Wisdom: The Sixties in the Eighties." *Academic Questions* 2, no. 4 (fall 1989): 31–38.

Holmes, Oliver Wendell. "The Path of the Law." *Harvard Law Review* 10, no. 8 (March 1897): 457–478.

Holzer, Henry Mark. *Sweet Land of Liberty? The Supreme Court and Individual Rights*. Costa Mesa, Calif.: Common Sense Press, 1983.

Hook, Sidney. Foreword to *Discrimination in Reverse: Is Turnabout Fair Play?* by Barry R. Gross. New York: New York Univ. Press, 1978.

———. "Meese's Major Failure." Letter to the Editor. *Policy Review*, summer 1989.

———. *Philosophy and Public Policy*. Carbondale, Illinois: Southern Illinois Univ. Press, 1980.

———. "Rationalizations for Reverse Discrimination." *New Perspective*, winter 1985.

Horne, Gerald. *Reversing Discrimination: The Case for Affirmative Action*. New York: International Publishers, 1992.

Horwitz, Morton, J. "The Jurisprudence of *Brown* and the Dilemmas of Liberalism." *Harvard Civil Rights–Civil Liberties Law Review* 14, no. 3 (fall 1979): 599–613.

———. *The Transformation of American Law 1870–1960: The Crisis of Legal Orthodoxy*. New York: Oxford Univ. Press, 1992.

Hughes, Samuel M. "The 'Misquoted Queen' Speaks Up." *Pennsylvania Gazette*, October 1993.

Hutchinson, Dennis J. "Unanimity and Desegregation: Decisionmaking in the Supreme Court, 1948–1958." *Georgetown Law Journal* 68, no. 1 (October 1979): 1–87.

Hyneman, Charles S. *The Supreme Court on Trial*. New York: Atherton Press, 1963.

Iannone, Carol, "Literature by Quota." *Commentary*, March 1991.

Issacharoff, Samuel. "Polarized Voting and the Political Process: The Transformation of Voting Rights Jurisprudence." *Michigan Law Review* 90, no. 7 (June 1992): 1833–1891.

Jackson, Robert H. *The Struggle for Judicial Supremacy: A Study of a Crisis in American Power Politics*. New York: Alfred A. Knopf, 1949.

Jackson, Samuel C. "EEOC vs. Discrimination, Inc." *The Crisis*, January 1968.

Jackson, Walter A. *Gunnar Myrdal and America's Conscience: Social Engineering and Racial Liberalism, 1938–1987*. Chapel Hill: Univ. of North Carolina Press, 1990.

Jaffa, Harry V. *Original Intent and the Framers of the Constitution: A Disputed Question*. Washington, D.C.: Regnery Gateway, 1994.

Jaroff, Leon. "Teaching Reverse Racism: A strange doctrine of black superiority is finding its way into school and college." *Time*, 4 April 1994.

Jarvis, Sonia R. "*Brown* and the Afrocentric Curriculum." *Yale Law Journal* 101, no. 6 (April 1992): 1285–1304.

Jencks, Christopher. *Rethinking Social Policy: Race, Poverty, & the Underclass*. Cambridge: Harvard Univ. Press, 1991.

Jeudwine, John W. *The Foundations of Society and the Land*. New York: Arno Press, 1975.

Johnson, Alex M., Jr. "Defending the Use of Quotas in Affirmative Action: Attacking Racism in the Nineties." *University of Illinois Law Review* 1992, no. 4 (1992): 1043–1073.

———. "The New Voice of Color." *Yale Law Journal* 100, no. 7 (May 1991): 2007–2064.

Johnson, Lyndon Baines. "Address Before a Joint Session of the Congress, November 27, 1963." In *Public Papers of the Presidents of the United States: Lyndon Baines Johnson, 1963–64*. Vol. 1. Washington, D.C.: U.S. Government Printing Office, 1965.

————. "Annual Message to the Congress on the State of the Union, January 7, 1964." In *Public Papers of the Presidents of the United States: Lyndon Baines Johnson, 1963–64*. Vol. 1. Washington, D.C.: U.S. Government Printing Office, 1965.

————. "Commencement Address at Howard University: 'To Fulfill These Rights,' June 4, 1965." In *Public Papers of the Presidents of the United States: Lyndon Baines Johnson, 1965*. Vol. 2. Washington, D.C.: U.S. Government Printing Office, 1966.

————. "Radio and Television Remarks Upon Signing the Civil Rights Bill, July 2, 1964." In *Public Papers of the Presidents of the United States: Lyndon Baines Johnson, 1963–64*. Vol. 2. Washington, D.C.: U.S. Government Printing Office, 1965.

————. "Remarks in the Capitol Rotunda at the Signing of the Voting Rights Act, August 6, 1965." In *Public Papers of the Presidents of the United States: Lyndon Baines Johnson, 1965*. Vol. 2. Washington, D.C.: U.S. Government Printing Office, 1966.

————. "Special Message to the Congress on the Right to Vote, March 15, 1965." In *Public Papers of the Presidents of the United States: Lyndon Baines Johnson, 1965*. Vol. 1. Washington, D.C.: U.S. Government Printing Office, 1966.

Johnson, Paul. *The Birth of the Modern: World Society 1815–1830*. New York: HarperCollins, 1991.

————. *A History of the Jews*. New York: Harper & Row, 1987.

————. *Modern Times: From the Twenties to the Nineties*, rev. ed. New York: HarperCollins, 1991.

Johnson, Sheri Lynn. "Unconscious Racism and the Criminal Law." *Cornell Law Review* 73, no. 5 (July 1988): 1016–1037.

Johnson, Stephen D. "Reverse Discrimination and Aggressive Behavior." *Journal of Psychology* 104, no. 1 (January 1980): 11–19.

Johnson, Theresa. "The Legal Use of Racial Quotas and Gender Preferences by Public and Private Employers." *Labor Law Journal* 40, no. 7 (July 1989): 419–425.

Kairys, David, ed. *The Politics of Law: A Progressive Critique*, rev. ed. New York: Pantheon, 1990.

Kagan, Donald. "An Address to the Class of 1994." *Commentary*, January 1991.

Kamisar, Yale. "The School Desegregation Cases in Retrospect." In Leon Friedman. *Argument: The Oral Argument Before the Supreme Court in Brown v. Board of Education of Topeka, 1952–55*. New York: Chelsea House, 1969.

Kaplan, John. "Equal Justice in an Unequal World: Equality for the Negro—the Problem of Special Treatment." *Northwestern University Law Review* 61, no. 3 (July–August 1966): 363–410.

Karlan, Pamela S. "Maps and Misreadings: The Role of Geographic Compactness in Racial Vote Dilution Litigation." *Harvard Civil Rights–Civil Liberties Law Review* 24, no. 1 (winter 1989): 173–248.

Karst, Kenneth L. *Belonging to America: Equal Citizenship and the Constitution.* New Haven: Yale Univ. Press, 1989.

———. *Law's Promise, Law's Expression: Visions of Power in the Politics of Race, Gender, and Religion.* New Haven: Yale Univ. Press, 1994.

Katz, Phyllis A., and Dalmas A. Taylor, eds. *Eliminating Racism: Profiles in Controversy.* New York: Plenum Press, 1988.

Keen, Maurice. *The Penguin History of Medieval Europe.* 1968. Reprint. New York: Penguin Books, 1991.

Kellogg, Peter John. "Northern Liberals and Black America: A History of White Attitudes, 1936–1952." Ph.D. diss., Northwestern University, 1971. Ann Arbor, Mich.: University Microfilms, 1971.

Kelly, Alfred H. "Clio and the Court: An Illicit Love Affair." *Supreme Court Review* (1965): 119–158.

Kelman, Mark. *A Guide to Critical Legal Studies.* Cambridge: Harvard Univ. Press, 1987.

Kendall, Willmoore. *John Locke and the Doctrine of Majority-Rule.* Urbana: Univ. of Illinois, 1965.

Kendall, Willmoore, and George W. Carey. *The Basic Symbols of the American Political Tradition.* Baton Rouge: Louisiana State Univ. Press, 1970.

Kennedy, Duncan. "A Cultural Pluralist Case for Affirmative Action in Legal Academia." *Duke Law Journal* 1990, no. 4 (September 1990): 705–757.

———. "Legal Education as Training for Hierarchy." In David Kairys, ed. *The Politics of Law: A Progressive Critique*, rev. ed. New York: Pantheon Books, 1990.

Kennedy, John F. "Radio and Television Report to the American People on Civil Rights, June 11, 1963." In *Public Papers of the Presidents of the United States: John F. Kennedy, 1963.* Washington, D.C.: Government Printing Office, 1964.

———. "Special Message to the Congress on Civil Rights and Job Opportunities, June 19, 1963." In *Public Papers of the Presidents of the United States: John F. Kennedy, 1963.* Washington, D.C.: Government Printing Office, 1964.

Kennedy, Randall. "A Reply to Philip Elman." *Harvard Law Review* 100, no. 8 (June 1987): 1938–1948.

———. "Persuasion and Distrust: A Comment on the Affirmative Action Debate." *Harvard Law Review* 99, no. 6 (April 1986): 1327–1346.

Kennedy, Randall L. "Racial Critiques of Legal Academia." *Harvard Law Review* 102, no. 8 (June 1989): 1745–1819.

Keppel, Ben. *The Work of Democracy: Ralph Bunche, Kenneth B. Clark, Lorraine Hansberry, and the Cultural Politics of Race.* Cambridge: Harvard Univ. Press, 1995.

Kerlow, Eleanor. *Poisoned Ivy: How Egos, Ideology, and Power Politics Almost Ruined Harvard Law School.* New York: St. Martin's, 1994.

Ketcham, Ralph, ed. *The Anti-Federalist Papers and the Constitutional Convention Debates.* New York: Mentor, 1986.

Kiernan, V.G. *The Duel in European History: Honour and the Reign of Aristocracy.* New York: Oxford Univ. Press, 1989.

Kimball, Roger. "From Farce to Tragedy." *Partisan Review* 15, no. 4 (1993): 564–569.

King, Martin Luther, Jr. "I Have a Dream." In *A Testament of Hope: The Essential Writings and Speeches of Martin Luther King, Jr.* Edited by James M. Washington. San Francisco: HarperCollins, 1986.

———. *"Playboy* Interview: Martin Luther King, Jr." In *A Testament of Hope: The Essential Writings and Speeches of Martin Luther King, Jr.* Edited by James M. Washington. San Francisco: HarperCollins, 1986.

Kinsley, Michael. "TRB from Washington: Quota Bill?" *New Republic,* 15 April 1991.

Kirkpatrick, Jeane J. "My Experience with Academic Intolerance." *Academic Questions* 2, no. 4 (fall 1989): 21–29.

Klarman, Michael. "An Interpretive History of Modern Equal Protection." *Michigan Law Review* 90, no. 2 (November 1991): 213–318.

Klarman, Michael J. *"Brown,* Racial Change, and the Civil Rights Movement." *Virginia Law Review* 80, no. 1 (February 1994): 7–150.

———. "How *Brown* Changed Race Relations: The Backlash Thesis." *Journal of American History* 81, no. 1 (June 1994): 81–118.

———. "The Puzzling Resistance to Political Process Theory." *Virginia Law Review* 77, no. 4 (May 1991): 747–832.

———. "Reply: *Brown v. Board of Education*: Facts and Political Correctness." *Virginia Law Review* 80, no. 1 (February 1994): 185–199.

Klein, Joe. "The Legacy of Summerton: *Brown v. Board of Education*: 40 years later, a visit to the town where it all began." *Newsweek,* 16 May 1994.

Kluger, Richard. *Simple Justice: The History of Brown v. Board of Education and Black America's Struggle for Equality.* New York: Alfred A. Knopf, 1976.

Kors, Alan Charles. "The Politicization of Extracurricular Life." *Academic Questions* 3, no. 2 (spring 1990): 36–40.

Korwar, Arati R. *War of Words: Speech Codes at Public Colleges and Universities.* Nashville, Tenn.: Freedom Forum First Amendment Center, 1994.

Kovarsky, Irving. "The Harlequinesque Motorola Decision and its Implications." *Boston College Industrial and Commercial Law Review* 7, no. 3 (spring 1966): 535–547.

Kramer, Hilton. "Confronting the Monolith." *Partisan Review* 15, no. 4 (1993): 569–573.

Krauthammer, Charles. "Defining Deviancy Up: The new assault on bourgeois life." *New Republic*, 22 November 1993.

Kristol, Irving. "How Hiring Quotas Came to the Campuses." *Fortune*, September 1974.

Kronman, Anthony T. *The Lost Lawyer: Failing Ideals of the Legal Profession.* Cambridge: Belknap Harvard, 1993.

LaNoue, George R. "The Demographic Premises of Affirmative Action." *Population and Environment* 14, no. 5 (May 1993): 121–140.

———. "Social Science and Minority 'Set-Asides.' " *Public Interest,* no. 110 (winter 1993): 49–76.

Lawrence, Charles R. III. "The Id, the Ego, and Equal Protection: Reckoning with Unconscious Racism." *Stanford Law Review* 39, no. 2 (January 1987): 317–388.

———. "If He Hollers Let Him Go: Regulating Racist Speech on Campus." *Duke Law Journal* 1990, no. 3 (June 1990): 431–483.

Lawson, Steven F. *In Pursuit of Power.* New York: Columbia Univ. Press, 1985.

Leflar, Robert A., and Wylie H. Davis. "Segregation in the Public Schools—1953." *Harvard Law Review* 67, no. 3 (January 1954) 377–435.

"Legal Realism and the Race Question: Some Realism About Realism on Race Relations." *Harvard Law Review* 108, no. 7 (May 1995): 1607–1624.

Lehman, David. "The Reign of Intolerance." *Partisan Review* 15, no. 4 (1993): 598–603.

Leibold, Peter M., Stephen A. Sola, and Reginald E. Jones. "Civil Rights Act of 1991: Race to the Finish—Civil Rights, Quotas, and Disparate Impact in 1991." *Rutgers Law Review* 45, no. 4 (summer 1993): 1043–1087.

Lemann, Nicholas. "Taking Affirmative Action Apart." *New York Times Magazine,* 11 June 1995.

Lempert, Richard O., and Stephen A. Saltzburg. *A Modern Approach to Evidence: Text, Problems, Transcripts, and Cases.* 2d ed. St. Paul: West, 1982.

Lenkowsky, Leslie. "College Today: The Students' Perspective." *Academic Questions* 2, no. 4 (fall 1989): 39–44.

Leo, John. "Counting by Race at Georgetown." *U.S. News & World Report,* 6 May 1991.

Lerner, Barbara. "Employment Discrimination: Adverse Impact, Validity, and Equality." *Supreme Court Review* (1979): 17–49.

Leslie, Connie. "Lessons from Bigotry 101: With plays, seminars and rules, schools attack bias. Some solutions can cause problems, too." *Newsweek,* 25 September 1989.

Levin, Michael. "Is Racial Discrimination Special?" *Policy Review* no. 22 (fall 1982): 85–95.

Lewis, Anthony. *Portrait of a Decade: The Second American Revolution.* New York: Random House, 1964.

Linde, Hans A. "Judges, Critics, and the Realist Tradition." *Yale Law Journal* 82, no. 2 (December 1972): 227–256.

Loevy, Robert D. *To End All Segregation: The Politics of the Passage of the Civil Rights Act of 1964.* Lanham, Md.: Univ. Press of America, 1990.

Lofgren, Charles A. *The Plessy Case: A Legal-Historical Interpretation.* New York: Oxford Univ. Press, 1987.

Lokos, Lionel. *The New Racism: Reverse Discrimination in America.* New Rochelle: Arlington House, 1971.

Loury, Glenn C. "Beyond Civil Rights." In Russell Nieli, ed. *Racial Preference and Racial Justice.* Washington, D.C.: Ethics and Public Policy Center, 1991.

———. " 'Matters of Color'—Blacks and the Constitutional Order." In Robert A. Goldwin and Art Kaufman, eds. *Slavery and Its Consequences: The Constitution, Equality, and Race.* Washington, D.C.: American Enterprise Institute, 1988.

———. "Self-censorship." *Partisan Review* 15, no. 4 (1993): 608–620.

Loury, Glenn C., J. Kenneth Blackwell, Robert L. Woodson, Buster Soaries, and Paul L. Pryde. *Black History Month 1990 at the Heritage Foundation.* Washington, D.C.: Heritage Foundation, 1990.

Lowi, Theodore J. *The End of Liberalism: Ideology, Policy, and the Crisis of Public Authority.* New York: Norton, 1969.

Lusky, Louis. *By What Right? A Commentary on the Supreme Court's Power to Revise the Constitution.* Charlottesville: Michie, 1975.

————. "Footnote Redux: A *Carolene Products* Reminiscence." *Columbia Law Review* 82, no. 6 (October 1982): 1093–1109.

————. "Minority Rights and the Public Interest." *Yale Law Journal* 52, no. 1 (December 1942): 1–41.

Lynch, Frederick R. *Invisible Victims: White Males and the Crisis of Affirmative Action.* New York: Greenwood Press, 1989.

————. "Workforce Diversity: PC's Final Frontier?" *National Review*, 21 February 1994.

Lynch, Frederick R., and William R. Beer. " 'You Ain't the Right Color, Pal': White Resentment of Affirmative Action." *Policy Review*, winter 1990.

Lynch, Timothy. "Our Legal System is a Minefield." *USA Today Magazine*, March 1994.

Lyons, Phil. "An Agency with a Mind of its Own: The EEOC's Guidelines on Employment Testing." *New Perspectives*, fall 1985.

Mabry, Marcus. "A View From the Front: My life as a member of the PC patrol." *Newsweek*, 24 December 1990.

————. *The New Right v. the Constitution.* Washington, D.C.: Cato Institute, 1986.

MacDonald, Heather. "The Diversity Industry: Cashing in on affirmative action." *New Republic*, 5 July 1993.

————. "The Diversity Principle." *Partisan Review* 15, no. 4 (1993): 620–630.

Macedo, Stephen. *Liberal Virtues: Citizenship, Virtue, and Community in Liberal Constitutionalism.* Oxford: Clarendon Press, 1990.

MacKinnon, Catharine A. "Feminism, Marxism, Method, and the State: Toward Feminist Jurisprudence." In Katharine T. Bartlett and Rosanne Kennedy, eds. *Feminist Legal Theory: Readings in Law and Gender.* Boulder: Westview, 1991.

Maine, Henry Sumner. *Ancient Law: Its Connection with the Early History of Society and its Relation to Modern Ideas.* 1861. Reprint. New York: Dorsett Press, 1986.

————. *Popular Government.* 1885. Reprint. Indianapolis: LibertyClassics, 1976.

Magee, Rhonda V. "The Master's Tools, From the Bottom Up: Responses to African-American Reparations Theory in Mainstream and Outsider Remedies Discourse." *Virginia Law Review* 79, no. 4 (May 1993): 863–916.

Maguire, J. M. Review of *An American Dilemma,* by Gunnar Myrdal. *Harvard Law Review* 58 (1944): 285–296.

Maguire, Timothy. "My Bout With Affirmative Action." *Commentary*, April 1992.

Manning, Robert D., and Stephen R. Domesick. "Title VII: Relationship and Effect on Executive Order No. 11246." *Boston College Industrial and Commercial Law Review* 7, no. 3 (spring 1966): 561–571.

Mansfield, Harvey C., Jr. *America's Constitutional Soul*. Baltimore: Johns Hopkins Univ. Press, 1991.

Marcus, Steven. "Soft Totalitarianism." *Partisan Review* 15, no. 4 (1993): 630–638.

Markman, Stephen. "Classifying the Races." *National Review*, 5 April 1985.

———. "Minority Rules." Review of *The Tyranny of the Majority*, by Lani Guinier. *National Review*, 21 March 1994.

Martire, Gregory, and Ruth Clark. *Anti-Semitism in the United States*. New York: Praeger, 1982.

Marx, Karl. "The Eighteenth Brumaire of Louis Bonaparte." In Karl Marx and Frederick Engels, *Selected Works*. Vol. 1. Moscow: Foreign Languages Publishing House, 1955.

———. "Toward the Critique of Hegel's Philosophy of Law." In *Writings of the Young Marx on Philosophy and Society*. Translated and edited by Lloyed D. Easton and Kurt H. Guddat. Garden City, N.Y.: Doubleday Anchor, 1967.

Mason, Alpheus Thomas. *Harlan Fiske Stone: Pillar of the Law*. New York: Viking Press, 1956.

Matsuda, Mari J. "Looking to the Bottom: Critical Legal Studies and Reparations." *Harvard Civil Rights–Civil Liberties Law Review* 22, no. 2 (spring 1987): 323–397.

———. "Pragmatism Modified and the False Consciousness Problem." *Southern California Law Review* 63, no. 6 (September 1990): 1763–1782.

———. "Public Response to Racist Speech: Considering the Victim's Story." *Michigan Law Review* 87, no. 8 (August 1989): 2320–2381.

Matsuda, Mari J., Charles R. Lawrence, Richard Delgado, and Kimberlé Williams Crenshaw. *Words That Wound: Critical Race Theory, Assaultive Speech and the First Amendment*. Boulder, Colo.: Westview Press, 1992.

Matthews, Anne. "Deciphering Victorian Underwear and Other Seminars." *New York Times Magazine*, 10 February 1991.

Mayhew, Leon H. *Law and Equal Opportunity: A Study of the Massachusetts Commission Against Discrimination*. Cambridge: Harvard Univ. Press, 1968.

McCarthy, Sarah J. "Cultural fascism: As a feminist I am outraged by attempts to turn flirting into a federal crime." *Forbes*, 9 December 1991.

McCaughey, Elizabeth. "No Exit: What the Clinton plan will do for you." *New Republic*, 7 February 1994.

————. "She's Baack! Clinton's plan on the ropes." *New Republic*, 28 February 1994.

McClaughry, John. "A Spirit of Liberty." *American Rifleman*, October 1986.

McClellan, James. *Liberty, Order and Justice: An Introduction to the Constitutional Principles of American Government*. Washington, D.C.: Center for Judicial Studies, 1989.

McConnell, Michael W. "The Fourteenth Amendment: A Second American Revolution or the Logical Culmination of the Tradition?" *Loyola of Los Angeles Law Review* 25, no. 4 (June 1992): 1159–1176.

————. "Originalism and the Desegregation Decisions." *Virginia Law Review* 81, no. 4 (May 1995): 947–1140.

McCormick, John. " 'Separate But Equal' Again? Kansas City: Black parents look for alternatives to desegregation." *Newsweek*, 16 May 1994.

McDonald, Forrest. *Novus Ordo Seclorum: The Intellectual Origins of the Constitution*. Lawrence, Kan.: Univ. Press of Kansas, 1985.

McDowell, Gary L. "Affirmative Inaction: The Brock–Meese Standoff on Federal Racial Quotas." *Policy Review*, spring 1989.

McGowan, William. "Race and Reporting." *City Journal*, summer 1993.

McGuigan, Patrick B., and Dawn M. Weyrich. *Ninth Justice: The Fight for Bork*. Washington, D.C.: Free Congress Foundation, 1990.

McLean, Edward B., ed. *Derailing the Constitution: The Undermining of American Federalism*. Bryn Mawr, Pa.: Intercollegiate Studies Institute, 1995.

McPherson, James M. "Reconstruction: The Second American Revolution." *Constitution*, fall 1990.

McWilliams, Carey. "The Climax of an Era." *The Nation*, 29 May 1954.

Mead, Lawrence M. *The New Politics of Poverty: The Non-Working Poor in America*. New York: Basic, 1992.

Meek, R. L., D. D. Raphael, and P. G. Stein, eds. *Adam Smith: Lectures on Jurisprudence*. 1978. Reprint. Indianapolis: LibertyPress, 1982.

Meese, Edwin. *With Reagan*. Washington, D.C.: Regnery Gateway, 1992.

Meigs, James B. "College Papers Do the Right-Wing Thing." *Rolling Stone*, 5 October 1989.

Meltzer, Bernard D. "The Weber Case: The Judicial Abrogation of the Antidiscrimination Standard in Employment." *University of Chicago Law Review* 47, no. 3 (spring 1980): 423–465.

Mensch, Elizabeth. "The History of Mainstream Legal Thought." In David Kairys, ed. *The Politics of Law: A Progressive Critique*, rev. ed. New York: Pantheon Books, 1990.

Mill, John Stuart. *Utilitarianism, Liberty, and Representative Government.* Reprint. London: J.M. Dent, 1947.

Miller, Arthur S., and Ronald F. Howell. "The Myth of Neutrality in Constitutional Adjudication." *University of Chicago Law Review* 27, no. 4 (summer 1960): 661–695.

Miller, Binney. "Who Shall Rule and Govern? Local Legislative Delegations, Racial Politics, and the Voting Rights Act." *Yale Law Journal* 102, no. 1 (October 1992): 105–203.

Miller, John J., ed. *Alternatives to Afrocentrism.* Washington, D.C.: Manhattan Institute, 1994.

Miller, John J., and Abigail Thernstrom. "Losing Race: California vs. affirmative action." *New Republic,* 26 June 1995.

Millon, David. "Objectivity and Democracy." *New York University Law Review* 67, no. 1 (April 1992): 1–66.

Miniter, Richard. "Campus Speech Wars: Waving the Tacky Shirt." *Insight,* 24 January 1994.

———. "Women's Successes Smash Business Myths." *Insight,* 21 February 1994.

Monroe, Sylvester. "Does Affirmative Action Help or Hurt?" *Time,* 27 May 1991.

Moore, W. John. "On the March Again?" *National Journal,* 12 December 1992.

Morgan, Edmund S. *The Birth of the Republic: 1763–1789.* Chicago: Univ. of Chicago, 1956.

Morison, Samuel Eliot. *The Oxford History of the American People.* Reprint. 3 vols. New York: Mentor, 1972.

Morris, Richard B. *Witnesses at the Creation: Hamilton, Madison, Jay and the Constitution.* 1985 Reprint. New York: Mentor, 1989.

Morrow, Lance. "Are Men Really That Bad?" *Time,* 14 February 1994.

Motley, Constance Baker. "My Personal Debt to Thurgood Marshall." *Yale Law Journal* 101, no. 1 (October 1991): 19–24.

Munk, Nina. "Fighting over the spoils." *Forbes,* 15 August 1994.

Munro, Don. "The Continuing Evolution of Affirmative Action Under Title VII: New Directions After the Civil Rights Act of 1991." *Virginia Law Review* 81, no. 2 (March 1995): 565–610.

Murray, Charles. *Losing Ground: American Social Policy 1950–1980*. New York: Basic Books, 1984.

Myrdal, Gunnar. *An American Dilemma: The Negro Problem and Modern Democracy*. 2 vols. New York: Harper & Row, 1944.

Neas, Ralph G. "The YLPR Interview: Ralph G. Neas." *Yale Law & Policy Review* 8, no. 2 (1990): 366–379.

"The Negro: His Future in America, A Special Section." *New Republic*, 18 October 1943.

Newman, Roger K. *Hugo Black: A Biography*. New York: Pantheon Books, 1994.

Nieli, Russell. *Racial Preference and Racial Justice: The New Affirmative Action Controversy*. Washington, D.C.: Ethics and Public Policy Center, 1991.

Nisenbaum, Steven. "Race Quotas." *Harvard Civil Rights Civil–Liberties Law Review* 8, no. 1 (January, 1973): 128–180.

Nixon, Richard. *Beyond Peace*. New York: Random House, 1994.

————. *RN: The Memoirs of Richard Nixon*. 2 vols. New York: Warner Books, 1979.

Norton, Eleanor Holmes. "At Liberty." *Constitution*, fall 1989.

————. *A Conversation with Eleanor Holmes Norton*. Washington, D.C.: American Enterprise Institute, 1979.

————. "The End of the Griggs Economy: Doctrinal Adjustment for the New American Workplace." *Yale Law & Policy Review*, 8, no. 2 (1990): 197–204.

————. "Equal Employment Law: Crisis in Interpretation—Survival Against the Odds." *Tulane Law Review* 62, no. 4 (March 1988): 681–715.

O'Brien, David M. *Storm Center: The Supreme Court in American Politics*. 3d ed. New York: Norton, 1993.

Oetken, J. Paul. "Form and Substance in Critical Legal Studies." *Yale Law Journal* 100, no. 7 (May 1991): 2209–2228.

Omond, Roger. *The Apartheid Handbook: A Guide to South Africa's Everyday Racial Policies*. Middlesex, England: Penguin Books, 1985.

O'Neil, Robert M. *Discriminating Against Discrimination: Preferential Admissions and the DeFunis Case*. Bloomington, Ind.: Indiana Univ. Press, 1975.

Patterson, Orlando. "The moral crisis of the black American." *Public Interest* no. 32 (summer 1973): 43–69.

Pearlstein, Mitchell B. "Affirmative Action: The Muddied Middle Ground." *Academic Questions* 4, no. 3 (summer 1991): 78–83.

Peck, Cornelius J. "The Equal Employment Opportunity Commission: Developments in the Administrative Process 1965–1975." *Washington Law Review* 51, no. 4 (October 1976): 831–65.

Pekelis, Alexander H. "The Supreme Court Today." *New Republic*, 17 April 1994.

Peller, Gary. "The Discourse of Constitutional Degradation." *Georgetown Law Journal* 81, no. 2 (December 1992): 313–341.

————. "Race Consciousness." *Duke Law Journal* 1990, no. 4 (September 1990): 758–847.

Peltason, J.W. *Fifty-Eight Lonely Men: Southern Federal Judges and School Desegregation*. Urbana: Univ. of Illinois Press, 1971.

Pennock, J. Roland. *Liberal Democracy: Its Merits and Prospects*. New York: Rinehart and Co., 1950.

Pertschuk, Michael, and Wendy Schaetzel. *The People Rising: The Campaign against the Bork Nomination*. New York: Thunder's Mouth Press, 1989.

Pildes, Richard H., and Richard G. Niemi. "Expressive Harms, 'Bizarre Districts,' and Voting Rights: Evaluating Election-District Appearances after *Shaw v. Reno*." *Michigan Law Review* 92, no. 3 (December 1993): 483–587.

Pilon, Roger. "Freedom, Responsibility, and the Constitution: On Recovering Our Founding Principles." *Notre Dame Law Review* 68, no. 3 (1993): 507–547.

————. "Uncivil Rights." *Regulation*, summer 1991.

Podhoretz, Norman. "Rape in Feminist Eyes." *Commentary*, October 1991.

Polanyi, Michael. "Beyond Nihilism." In *Knowing and Being: Essays by Michael Polanyi*. Edited by Marjorie Grene. Chicago: Univ. of Chicago Press, 1969.

————. "The Message of the Hungarian Revolution." In *Knowing and Being: Essays by Michael Polanyi*. Edited by Marjorie Grene. Chicago: Univ. of Chicago Press, 1969.

————. "On the Modern Mind." *Encounter*, May 1965.

Pole, J. R. *The Pursuit of Equality in American History*. 2d rev. ed. Berkeley: Univ. of California Press, 1993.

Pollack, Jack Harrison. *Earl Warren: The Judge Who Changed America*. Englewood Cliffs: Prentice-Hall, 1979.

Pollak, Louis H. "Racial Discrimination and Judicial Integrity: A Reply to Professor Wechsler." *University of Pennsylvania Law Review* 108, no. 1 (November 1959): 1–34.

Polsby, Daniel D., and Robert D. Popper. "Ugly: An Inquiry into the Problem of Racial Gerrymandering under the Voting Rights Act." *Michigan Law Review* 92, no. 3 (December 1993): 652–682.

Poole, Austin Lane. *Obligations of Society in XII and XIII Centuries: The Ford Lectures, Michaelmas Term 1944*. Oxford: Clarendon Press, 1946.

Posner, Richard A. *Cardozo: A Study in Reputation*. Chicago: Univ. of Chicago Press, 1990.

———. "The Decline of the Law as an Autonomous Discipline, 1962–1987." *Harvard Law Review* 100, no. 4 (February 1987): 761–80.

———. "Duncan Kennedy on Affirmative Action." *Duke Law Journal* 1990, no. 5 (November 1990): 1157–1162.

——— *Economic Analysis of Law*, 3d ed. Boston: Little Brown, 1986.

———. *The Economics of Justice*. Cambridge: Harvard Univ. Press, 1981.

———. *Law and Literature: A Misunderstood Relation*. Cambridge: Harvard Univ. Press, 1988.

———. "Law as Politics: Horwitz on American Law 1870–1960." Review of *The Transformation of American Law, 1870–1960: The Crisis of Legal Orthodoxy*. *Critical Review* 6, no. 4 (fall 1992): 559–574.

———. "Pragmatism versus the Rule of Law." Excerpts from Bradley Lecture. *AEI Newsletter*, March 1991.

———. *The Problems of Jurisprudence*. Cambridge: Harvard Univ. Press, 1990.

Posner, Richard A., ed. *The Essential Holmes: Selections from the Letters, Speeches, Judicial Opinions, and Other Writings of Oliver Wendell Holmes, Jr.* Chicago: Univ. of Chicago Press, 1992.

Post, Langdon. "Warren: The Myth and His Record." *New Republic*, 23 June 1952.

Powell, John A. "Racial Realism or Racial Despair?" *Connecticut Law Review* 24, no. 2 (winter 1992): 533–551.

Powell, Monica. "Law Review Adopts Affirmative Action." *Insight*, 29 May 1989.

Presser, Arlynn Leiber. "Broken Dreams." *ABA Journal*, May 1991.

Presser, Stephen B. *Recapturing the Constitution: Race, Religion, and Abortion Reconsidered*. Washington, D.C.: Regnery, 1994.

Puddington, Arch. "Seniority: Not For Whites Only." *New Perspectives*, fall 1984.

———. "What To Do About Affirmative Action." *Commentary*, June 1995.

Quirk, William J., and R. Randall Bridwell. *Judicial Dictatorship*. New Brunswick, N.J.: Transaction, 1995.

Raab, Earl. "Quotas by Any Other Name." *Commentary*, January 1972.

Rabkin, Jeremy A. "The Color of California." *The American Spectator*, May 1995.

Rachlin, Carl. "Title VII: Limitations and Qualifications." *Boston College Industrial and Commercial Law Review* 7, no. 3 (spring 1966): 473–494.

Ralston, Charles Stephen. "Court vs. Congress: Judicial Interpretation of the Civil Rights Act and Congressional Response." *Yale Law & Policy Review* 8, no. 2 (1990): 205–222.

Rauch, Jonathan. *Demosclerosis: The Silent Killer of American Government.* New York: Random House, 1994.

———. *Kindly Inquisitors: The New Attacks on Free Thought.* Chicago: Univ. of Chicago Press, 1993.

Ravitch, Diane. "The Ambiguous Legacy of Brown v. Board of Education." *New Perspectives*, summer 1984.

"Recent Statute: The Civil Rights Act of 1964." *Harvard Law Review* 78, no. 3 (January 1965): 684–696.

Reed, John Shelton, and Merle Black. "How Southerners Gave Up Jim Crow." *New Perspectives*, fall 1985.

Reed, Leonard. "What's Wrong with Affirmative Action?" *Washington Monthly*, January 1981.

Rehnquist, William H. *The Supreme Court: How it Was, How it Is.* New York: William Morrow, 1987.

Reisman, David. *The Political Economy of James Buchanan.* College Station: Texas A&M Univ. Press, 1990.

Report of the National Advisory Commission on Civil Disorders. New York: E.P. Dutton & Co., 1968.

Rhode, Deborah L. "Feminist Critical Theories." *Stanford Law Review* 42, no. 3 (February 1990): 617–638.

Ricketts, Glenn M. "Multiculturalism Mobilizes." *Academic Questions* 3, no. 3 (summer 1990): 56–62.

Riker, William H. *The Development of American Federalism.* Boston: Kluwer Academic Publishers, 1987.

Roback, Jennifer. "Racism and Rent Seeking." *Economic Inquiry* 27, no. 4 (October 1989): 661–681.

Roberts, Paul Craig, and Matthew A. Stephenson. *Marx's Theory of Exchange, Alienation, and Crisis.* 2d ed. New York: Praeger, 1983.

Roberts, Steven V. "The Bakke Case Moves to the Factory." *New York Times Magazine*, 25 February 1979.

Robison, Joseph B. "Outflanking Segregation." *New Republic*, 30 June 1952.

Roche, George. *The Balancing Act: Quota Hiring in Higher Education*. LaSalle, Ill.: Open Court, 1994.

Rodell, Fred. *Nine Men: A Political History of the Supreme Court of the United States from 1790 to 1955*. New York: Random House, 1955.

Roosevelt, Franklin D., Jr. "Business Opinion: Roosevelt tells how Government Will Press for Equal Employment." Letter to the Editor. *Nation's Business*, December 1965.

Rose, David L. "Twenty-Five Years Later: Where Do We Stand on Equal Employment Opportunity Law Enforcement?" *Vanderbilt Law Review* 42, no. 4 (1989): 1121–1182.

Rosen, Jeffrey. "Affirmative Action: A Solution." *New Republic*, 8 May 1995.

———. "The Book of Ruth: Judge Ginsburg's Feminist Challenge." *New Republic*, 2 August 1993.

———. "Reasonable Women." *New Republic*, 1 November 1993.

———. "Sentimental Journey: The emotional jurisprudence of Harry Blackmun." *New Republic*, 2 May 1994.

Rosenberg, Gerald N. "*Brown* is Dead! Long Live *Brown*! The Endless Attempt to Canonize a Case." *Virginia Law Review* 80, no. 1 (February 1994): 161–171.

———. *The Hollow Hope: Can Courts Bring About Social Change?* Chicago: Univ. of Chicago Press, 1991.

Rosenfeld, Michel. *Affirmative Action and Justice: A Philosophical and Constitutional Inquiry*. New Haven: Yale Univ. Press, 1991.

Ross, Alf. *Why Democracy?* Cambridge: Harvard Univ. Press, 1952.

Ross, Thomas. "Innocence and Affirmative Action." *Vanderbilt Law Review* 43, no. 2 (March 1990): 297–316.

Rossiter, Clinton, ed. *The Federalist Papers*. Reprint. New York: Penguin Books, 1961.

Roth, Byron M. *Prescription for Failure: Race Relations in the Age of Social Science*. New Brunswick, N.J.: Transaction, 1994.

———. "Social Psychology's 'Racism.' " *Public Interest*, no. 98 (winter 1990): 26–36.

———. "Symbolic Racism: The Making of a Scholarly Myth." *Academic Questions* 2, no. 3 (summer 1989): 53–65.

Rothman, Stanley. "Professors in the Ascendant." *Academic Questions* 2, no. 4 (fall 1989): 45–51.

———. "Who's a Bigot?" Review of *The Scar of Race*, by Paul M. Sniderman and Thomas Piazza. *National Review*, 2 May 1994.

Rothstein, Edward. "Roll Over Beethoven: The new musical correctness and its mistakes." *New Republic*, 4 February 1991.

Rowan, Carl T. "A Dialogue with Carl T. Rowan." *Emerge*, May 1991.

———. *Dream Makers, Dream Breakers: The World of Thurgood Marshall*. New York: Little, Brown, 1993.

Rubin, Theodore Isaac. *Anti-Semitism: A Disease of the Mind*. New York: Continuum, 1990.

Sackett, Victoria. "Ignoring the People." *Policy Review*, spring 1980.

Savage, David G. *Turning Right: The Making of the Rehnquist Supreme Court*. New York: John Wiley & Sons, 1992.

Scales-Trent, Judy. "Black Women and the Constitution: Finding Our Place, Asserting Our Rights." *Harvard Civil Rights–Civil Liberties Law Review* 24, no. 1 (winter 1989): 9–44.

Scalia, Antonin. "The Disease As a Cure." In Russell Nieli, ed. *Racial Preference and Racial Justice: The New Affirmative Action Controversy*. Washington, D.C.: Ethics and Public Policy Center, 1991.

Scanlan, James P. "Illusions of Job Segregation." *Public Interest*, no. 93 (fall 1988): 54–69.

Scheibla, Shirley. "Fairness by Fiat—Some Employees These Days Are More Equal Than Others." *Barron's*, 20 January 1970.

———. "Gentlemen's Agreement?—Government is Making Business Its Unwilling Partner in Bias." *Barron's*, 23 December 1969.

Schlei, Barbara Lindemann, and Paul Grossman. *Employment Discrimination Law*. Washington, D.C.: Bureau of National Affairs, 1976. 2d ed. 1983. Supplement 1991.

Schlesinger, Arthur M., Jr. *The Disuniting of America: Reflections on a Multicultural Society*. New York: W.W. Norton, 1992.

Schnapper, Eric. "Affirmative Action and the Legislative History of the Fourteenth Amendment." *Virginia Law Review* 71, no. 5 (June 1985): 753–798.

Schneider, Pauline A. "Gender, Race, and Ethnicity in the D.C. Circuit." *Washington Lawyer*, March/April 1995.

Schoenbrod, David. *Power Without Responsibility: How Congress Abuses the People Through Delegation*. New Haven: Yale Univ. Press, 1993.

"Scholars' Reply to Professor Fried." *Yale Law Journal* 99, no. 1 (October 1989): 163–168.

Schuck, Peter H. "What Went Wrong With the Voting Rights Act: The right to vote now means safe seats for minority candidates." *Washington Monthly*, November 1987.

Schuwerk, Robert P. "The Philadelphia Plan: A Study in the Dynamics of Executive Power." *University of Chicago Law Review* 39, no. 4 (summer 1972): 723–760.

Schwartz, Benjamin. "The Diversity Myth: America's Leading Export." *The Atlantic Monthly*, May 1995.

Schwartz, Bernard. *A History of the Supreme Court*. New York: Oxford Univ. Press, 1993.

———. *Super Chief: Earl Warren and his Supreme Court—A Judicial Biography*. New York: New York Univ. Press, 1983.

Schwartz, Bernard, ed. *Statutory History of the United States: Civil Rights*. 2 vols. New York: Chelsea House, 1970.

Schwartz, Herman. "The 1986 and 1987 Affirmative Action Cases: It's All Over But the Shouting." *Michigan Law Review* 86, no. 3 (December 1987): 524–576.

Schwemm, Robert G. *Housing Discrimination: Law and Litigation*. New York: Clark, Boardman Callaghan, 1990.

Seabury, Paul. "HEW & the Universities." *Commentary*, February 1972.

Sedler, Robert A. "The Constitution, Racial Preference, and the Equal Participation Objective." In Robert A. Goldwin and Art Kaufman, eds. *Slavery and Its Consequences: The Constitution, Equality, and Race*. Washington, D.C.: American Enterprise Institute, 1988.

Seidman, Louis Michael. "*Brown* and *Miranda*." *California Law Review* 80, no. 3 (May 1992): 673–753.

Senese, Donald J. "The IRS and the Private Schools: 'The Power to Tax Involves the Power to Destroy.' " *Policy Review*, spring 1979.

Shalit, Ruth. "Hate Story: Racial strife at law school." *New Republic*, 7 June 1993.

Sharpe, Ernest, Jr. "The Man Who Changed His Skin." *American Heritage*, February 1989.

Shepard, Scott. "Penn: The Most Poisoned Ivy?" *Campus*, fall 1993.

Sherry, Suzanna. "Civic Virtue and the Feminine Voice in Constitutional Adjudication." *Virginia Law Review* 72, no. 3 (April 1986): 543–616.

Shipp, E.R. "Filling the Gap: Some Parents Feel Church-Run and Independent Schools Pick Up Where Public Education Falls Short." *Emerge*, May 1994.

Shirer, William L. *The Rise and Fall of the Third Reich: A History of Nazi Germany*. New York: Simon and Schuster, 1960.

THE NEW COLOR LINE

Short, Thomas. "Big Brother at Delaware." *National Review*, 18 March 1991.——. "A 'New Racism' on Campus?" *Commentary*, August 1988.

Shulman, Stephen N., and Charles F. Abernathy. *The Law of Equal Employment Opportunity*. Boston: Warren, Gorham & Lamont, 1990.

Siegan, Bernard H. *The Supreme Court's Constitution: An Inquiry into Judicial Review and Its Impact on Society*. New Brunswick, N.J.: Transaction, 1987.

Silber, Norman, and Geoffrey Miller. "Toward 'Neutral Principles' in the Law: Selections from the Oral History of Herbert Wechsler." *Columbia Law Review* 93, no. 4 (May 1993): 854–931.

Silberman, R. Gaull. "The EEOC is Meeting the Challenge: Response to David Rose." *Vanderbilt Law Review* 42, no. 6 (November 1989): 1641–1646.

Simon, James F. *The Center Holds: The Power Struggle Inside the Rehnquist Court*. New York: Simon & Schuster, 1995.

Sindler, Allan P. *Bakke, DeFunis, and Minority Admissions: The Quest for Equal Opportunity*. New York: Longman, 1978.

Singer, James W. "Equal Employment Agencies Are Beginning to Shape Up." *National Journal*, 7 January 1978.

Skerry, Peter. "Borders and quotas: immigration and the affirmative-action state." *Public Interest* 96 (summer 1989): 86–102.

Sleeper, Jim. *The Closest of Strangers*. New York: Norton, 1990.

Smith, James P., and Finis R. Welch. *Closing the Gap: Forty Years of Economic Progress for Blacks*. Santa Monica: Rand Corporation, 1986.

Smith, Lillian. "Addressed to White Liberals." *New Republic*, 18 September 1944.

——. *Strange Fruit*. New York: Reynal & Hitchcock, 1944.

Smith, William French. *Law & Justice in the Reagan Administration: Memoirs of an Attorney General*. Stanford: Hoover Institution Press, 1991.

Sniderman, Paul M., and Thomas Piazza. *The Scar of Race*. Cambridge: Belknap Harvard, 1993.

Snyder, Jeffrey R. "A Nation of Cowards." *Public Interest,* no. 113 (fall 1993): 40–55.

Soifer, Aviam. "Protecting Civil Rights: A Critique of Raoul Berger's History." *New York University Law Review* 54, no. 3 (June 1979): 651–706.

Southern, David W. *Gunnar Myrdal and Black–White Relations: The Use and Abuse of An American Dilemma, 1944–1969*. Baton Rouge: Louisiana State Univ. Press, 1987.

Southern, R. W. *The Making of the Middle Ages*. New Haven: Yale Univ. Press, 1953.

Sovern, Michael I. *Legal Restraints on Racial Discrimination in Employment*. New York: Twentieth Century Fund, 1966.

Sowell, Thomas. " 'Affirmative Action' Reconsidered." *Public Interest*, no. 42 (winter 1976): 47–65.

———. "Are Quotas Good for Blacks?" *Commentary*, June 1978.

———. *Civil Rights: Rhetoric or Reality?* New York: William Morrow, 1984.

———. *A Conflict of Visions: Ideological Origins of Political Struggles*. New York: William Morrow, 1987.

———. *The Economics and Politics of Race*. New York: William Morrow, 1983.

———. *Inside American Education*. New York: Free Press, 1993.

———. *Judicial Activism Reconsidered*. Stanford: Hoover Institution, 1989.

———. *Knowledge & Decisions*. New York: Basic Books, 1980.

———. *Marxism: Philosophy and Economics*. New York: William Morrow, 1985.

——— "The New Racism on Campus." *Fortune*, 13 February 1989.

———. *Preferential Policies: An International Perspective*. New York: William Morrow, 1990.

———. "The Road to Hell is Paved with Good Intentions." *Forbes*, 17 January 1994.

———. "Scapegoating." *Forbes*, 11 April 1994.

———. "The skinny black Marine and the fat white Marine." *Forbes*, 8 November 1993.

———. *The Vision of the Anointed: Self-Congratulation as a Basis for Social Policy*. New York: Basic Books, 1995.

Spann, Girardeau A. "Pure Politics." *Michigan Law Review* 88, no. 7 (June 1990): 1971–2033.

———. *Race Against the Court: The Supreme Court and Minorities in Contemporary America*. New York: New York Univ. Press, 1993.

———. "Simple Justice." *Georgetown Law Journal* 73, no. 4 (April 1985): 1041–1081.

Stanfield, Rochelle L. "The Split Society." *National Journal*, 2 April 1994.

———. "The Wedge Issue." *National Journal*, 1 April 1995.

Steele, Shelby. *The Content of Our Character: A New Vision of Race in America*. New York: St. Martin's Press, 1990.

———. "The Recoloring of Campus Life: Student racism, academic pluralism, and the end of a dream." *Harper's*, February 1989.

Steinberg, Stephen. "How Jewish Quotas Began." *Commentary*, September 1971.

Stephanopoulos, George, and Christopher Edley, Jr. "Affirmative Action Review: Report to the President." Washington, D.C.: White House, 19 July 1995.

Steskal, Christopher. "Creating Space for Racial Difference: The Case for African-American Schools." *Harvard Civil Rights–Civil Liberties Law Review* 27, no. 1 (winter 1992): 187–218.

Stigler, George J. "Economic Competition and Political Competition." In Kurt R. Leube and Thomas Gale Moore, eds. *The Essence of Stigler*. Stanford: Hoover Institution Press, 1986.

Still, Edward. "Voluntary Constituencies: Modified At-Large Voting as a Remedy for Minority Vote Dilution in Judicial Elections." *Yale Law & Policy Review* 9, no. 2 (1991): 354–369.

Stone, Geoffrey R., Louis M. Seidman, Cass R. Sunstein, and Mark V. Tushnet. *Constitutional Law*. Boston: Little, Brown, 1986.

Stone, John, and Stephen Mennell, eds. *Alexis de Tocqueville: On Democracy, Revolution, and Society*. Chicago: Univ. of Chicago, 1980.

Stratton, Lawrence M., Jr. "Special Trial Judges, the Tax Court and the Appointments Clause: *Freytag v. Commissioner*." *The Tax Lawyer* 45, no. 2 (winter 1992): 497–511.

Strauss, David A. "The Illusory Distinction Between Equality of Opportunity and Equality of Result." *William and Mary Law Review* 34, no. 1 (fall 1992): 171–188.

———. "The Law and Economics of Racial Discrimination in Employment: The Case for Numerical Standards." *Georgetown Law Journal* 79, no. 6 (August 1991): 1619–1657.

Strayer, Joseph R. *Feudalism*. 1965 Reprint. Huntington, New York: Robert E. Krieger, 1965.

Strebeigh, Fred. "Defining Law on the Feminist Frontier." *New York Times Magazine*, 6 October 1991.

Strossen, Nadine. "Politically Correct Speech and the First Amendment." *Cato Policy Report*, March/April 1991.

———. "Regulating Racist Speech on Campus: A Modest Proposal." *Duke Law Journal* 1990, no. 3 (June 1990): 484–573.

Sullivan, Kathleen M. "Sins of Discrimination: Last Term's Affirmative Action Cases." *Harvard Law Review* 100, no. 1 (November 1986): 78–98.

Sunstein, Cass R. *Democracy and the Problem of Free Speech*. New York: Free Press, 1993.

———. *The Partial Constitution*. Cambridge: Harvard Univ. Press, 1993.

———. "The Spirit of the Laws." Review of *On Reading the Constitution*, by Laurence H. Tribe and Michael C. Dorf. *New Republic*, 11 March 1991.

———. "Three Civil Rights Fallacies." *California Law Review* 79, no. 3 (May 1991): 751–774.

———. "Voting Rites." Review of *The Tyranny of the Majority: Fundamental Fairness in Representative Democracy*, by Lani Guinier. *New Republic*, 25 April 1994.

Sykes, Charles J. *The Hollow Men: Politics and Corruption in Higher Education*. Washington, D.C.: Regnery Gateway, 1990.

———. *A Nation of Victims: The Decay of the American Character*. New York: St. Martin's Press, 1992.

———. *Profscam: Professors and the Demise of Higher Education*. Washington, D.C.: Regnery Gateway, 1988.

Taylor, Jared. *Paved with Good Intentions: The Failure of Race Relations in Contemporary America*. New York: Carroll & Graf, 1992.

Terkel, Studs. *Race: How Blacks and Whites Think and Feel about the American Obsession*. New York: New Press, 1992.

Thernstrom, Abigail. "Guinier Mess: Clinton's civil rights blooper." *New Republic*, 14 June 1993.

———. "Permaffirm Action: Reverse discrimination isn't dead." *New Republic*, 31 July 1989.

———. "*Shaw v. Reno:* Notes from a Political Thicket." In Roger Clegg and Leonard Leo, eds. *Public Interest Law Review 1994*. Washington, D.C.: National Legal Center for the Public Interest, 1994.

Thernstrom, Abigail M. "The odd evolution of the Voting Rights Act." *Public Interest*, no. 55 (spring 1979): 49–76.

———. "On the Scarcity of Black Professors." *Commentary*, July 1990.

———. " 'Voting Rights' Trap: The Danger of Resegregation." *New Republic*, 2 September 1985.

———. *Whose Votes Count? Affirmative Action and Minority Voting Rights*. Cambridge: Harvard Univ. Press, 1987.

Thomas, Clarence. "Civil Rights as a Principle Versus Civil Rights as an Interest."

In David Boaz, ed. *Assessing the Reagan Years*. Washington, D.C.: Cato Institute, 1988.

Thompson, Charles. "The Supreme Court Looks at Jim Crow." *New Republic*, 17 April 1950.

Thompson, James Westfall. *Economic and Social History of the Middle Ages*. 2 vols. 1928. Reprint. New York: Frederick Ungar, 1966.

Thoreau, Henry David. "Walden." In Owens, Lily, ed. *Works of Henry David Thoreau*. Reprint. 1906. New York: Avenel, 1981.

Thorpe, Lewis, trans. *Einhard and Notker the Stammerer: Two Lives of Charlemagne*. Reprint. New York: Penguin Books, 1969.

Tillyard, E. M. W. *The Elizabethan World Picture*. New York: Vintage, n.d.

Tobin, Gary A. *Jewish Perceptions of Antisemitism*. New York: Plenum Press, 1988.

Totenberg, Nina. "Discriminating to End Discrimination." *New York Times Magazine*, 14 April 1974.

Traub, James. "Can Separate Be Equal? New answers to an old question about race and schools." *Harper's*, June 1994.

———. "Ghetto Blasters: The case for all-black schools." *New Republic*, 15 April 1991.

Tribe, Laurence H. *American Constitutional Law*. 2d ed. Mineola, N.Y.: Foundation Press, 1988.

———. *Constitutional Choices*. Cambridge: Harvard Univ. Press, 1985.

———. "The Puzzling Persistence of Process-Based Constitutional Theories." *Yale Law Journal* 89, no. 6 (May 1980): 1063–1080.

Tucker, Jeffrey. "Uprooting Liberty." Review of *Grassroots Tyranny*, by Clint Bolick. *Chronicles*, March 1994.

Tushnet, Mark V. "Anti-Formalism in Recent Constitutional Theory." *Michigan Law Review* 83, no. 6 (May 1985): 1502–1544.

———. "Critical Legal Studies: A Political History." *Yale Law Journal* 100, no. 5 (March 1991): 1515–1544.

———. "The Degradation of Constitutional Discourse." *Georgetown Law Journal* 81, no. 2 (December 1992): 251–311.

———. *Making Civil Rights Law*. New York: Oxford Univ. Press, 1994.

———. *The NAACP's Legal Strategy against Segregated Education, 1925–1950*. Chapel Hill: Univ. of North Carolina Press, 1987.

———. "Reply." *Georgetown Law Journal* 81, no. 2 (December 1992): 343–350.

———. "The Significance of *Brown v. Board of Education.*" *Virginia Law Review* 80, no. 1 (February 1994): 173–184.

———. "Thurgood Marshall and the Brethren." *Georgetown Law Journal* 80, no. 6 (August 1992): 2109–2130.

———. "What Really Happened in *Brown v. Board of Education.*" *Columbia Law Review* 91, no. 8 (December 1991): 1867–1930.

Tushnet, Mark, ed. *The Warren Court in Historical and Political Perspective.* Charlottesville: Univ. Press of Virginia, 1993.

Unger, Roberto Mangabeira. *The Critical Legal Studies Movement.* Cambridge: Harvard Univ. Press, 1983.

U.S. Commission on Civil Rights. *Toward an Understanding of Johnson.* Washington, D.C., 1987.

U.S. Department of Justice. *Office of Legal Policy Report to the Attorney General. Redefining Discrimination: Disparate Impact and the Institutionalization of Affirmative Action.* Washington, D.C., 1987.

U.S. Department of Labor. *Opportunity 2000: Creative Affirmative Action Strategies for a Changing Workforce.* Washington, D.C.: U.S. Government Printing Office, 1988.

U.S. Equal Employment Opportunity Commission, *Legislative History of Titles VII and XI of the Civil Rights Act of 1964.* Washington, D.C.: U.S. Government Printing Office, 1968.

———. *White House Conference on Equal Employment Opportunity.* Washington, D.C.: U.S. Government Printing Office, 1965.

U.S. Equal Employment Opportunity Commission Archives, Washington D.C. "The Equal Employment Opportunity Commission During the Administration of President Lyndon B. Johnson: November 1963–January 1969." 1 November 1968.

Urofsky, Melvin I. *A Conflict of Rights: The Supreme Court and Affirmative Action.* New York: Scribners, 1991.

Vaas, Francis J. "Title VII: Legislative History." *Boston College Industrial and Commercial Law Review* 7, no. 3 (spring 1966): 431–472.

Van Alstyne, William. "Rites of Passage: Race, the Supreme Court, and the Constitution." *University of Chicago Law Review* 46, no. 4 (summer 1979): 775–810.

van den Haag, Ernest. "Affirmative Action and Campus Racism." *Academic Questions* 2, no. 3 (summer 1989): 66–68.

———. "Social Science Testimony in the Desegregation Cases: A Reply to Professor Kenneth Clark." *Villanova Law Review* 6, no. 1 (fall 1960): 69–79.

Vann Woodward, C. *The Strange Career of Jim Crow*. 3d rev. ed. New York: Oxford Univ. Press, 1974.

Vincent, John Martin. *Costume and Conduct in the Laws of Basel, Bern, and Zurich 1370–1800*. New York: Greenwood Press, 1935.

Vose, Clement E. *Constitutional Change: Amendment Politics and Supreme Court Litigation Since 1900*. Lexington, Mass.: Lexington Books, 1972.

Walsh, Michael. "Battle Fatigue." *Time*, 21 February 1994.

Walsh, William F. "Title by Adverse Possession." *New York University Law Quarterly* 16 (1939): 532–558.

Washington, James M., ed. *A Testament of Hope: The Essential Writings and Speeches of Martin Luther King, Jr.* San Francisco: HarperCollins, 1986.

Wasserstrom, Richard A. "Racism, Sexism, and Preferential Treatment: An Approach to the Topics." *UCLA Law Review* 24, no. 3 (February 1977): 581–622.

Wechsler, Herbert. "Toward Neutral Principles of Constitutional Law." *Harvard Law Review* 73, no. 1 (November 1959): 1–35.

Weiss, Michael. "Feminist Legal Theory Is Creating a Government Not of Laws but of Women." *Reason*, January 1992.

West, Cornel. "The Role of Law in Progressive Politics." In David Kairys, ed. *The Politics of Law: A Progressive Critique*. New York: Pantheon Books, 1990.

Whalen, Charles, and Barbara Whalen. *The Longest Debate: A legislative history of the 1964 Civil Rights Act*. Washington, D.C.: Seven Locks Press, 1985.

White, David M., and Richard L. Francis. "Title VII and the Masters of Reality: Eliminating Credentialism in the American Labor Market." *Georgetown Law Journal* 64, no. 6 (July 1976): 1213–1244.

White, G. Edward. "Earl Warren's Influence on the Warren Court." In *The Warren Court in Historical and Political Perspective*. Edited by Mark Tushnet. Charlottesville: Univ. Press of Virginia, 1993.

Whitman, Mark, ed. *Removing a Badge of Slavery: The Record of Brown v. Board of Education*. Princeton: Markus Wiener, 1993.

Who Speaks for the Constitution? The Debate Over Interpretive Authority. Washington, D.C.: Federalist Society, 1992.

Wiener, Jon. "Law Profs Fight the Power; Minority Legal Scholars." *The Nation*, 4 September 1989.

Wilbanks, William. *The Myth of a Racist Criminal Justice System*. Monterey: Brooks/Cole, 1987.

Wildavsky, Aaron. "The 'reverse sequence' in civil liberties." *Public Interest* no. 78

(winter 1985): 32–42.

———. "Robert Bork and the Crime of Inequality." *Public Interest* no. 98 (winter 1990): 98–117.

Wiley, Ed, III. "Black America's Quest for Education: The Euphoria of the 'Brown' Decision Has Faded to Reveal Recurring Problems of Access and Inequality." *Emerge*, May 1994.

Wilkinson, J. Harvie, III. *From Brown to Bakke: The Supreme Court and School Integration: 1954–1978*. New York: Oxford Univ. Press, 1979.

Will, George F. "From Topeka to Kansas City: They've gone about as far as they can go. Farther, actually." *Newsweek*, June 26, 1995.

———. *Restoration: Congress, Term Limits and the Recovery of Deliberative Democracy*. New York: Free Press, 1992.

Willhelm, Sidney. "The Supreme Court: A Citadel for White Supremacy." Review of *Race, Racism and American Law*, by Derrick A. Bell, Jr. *Michigan Law Review* 79, no. 4 (March 1981): 847–855.

Williams, Armstrong. *Beyond Blame: How We Can Succeed by Breaking the Dependency Barrier*. New York: Free Press, 1995.

Williams, Dennis A. "The Big Payback: Can We Be Compensated for Slavery with Cash?" *Emerge*, May 1991.

Williams, Joan C. "Deconstructing Gender." In Katharine T. Bartlett and Rosanne Kennedy eds. *Feminist Legal Theory: Readings in Law and Gender*. Boulder: Westview, 1991.

Williams, Juan. "The Triumph of Thurgood Marshall: The First Black Supreme Court Justice Looks Back on his Historic Career." *Washington Post Magazine*, 7 January 1990.

Williams, Kenny J. "Caste and Class in a University Town: Professor Kenny J. Williams Interviewed by Carol Iannone." *Academic Questions* 4, no. 2 (spring 1991): 41–61.

Williams, Patricia. *The Alchemy of Race and Rights*. Cambridge: Harvard Univ. Press, 1991.

———. "*Metro Broadcasting, Inc. v. FCC*: Regrouping in Singular Times." *Harvard Law Review* 104, no. 2 (December 1990): 525–546.

Williams, Patricia J. "Alchemical Notes: Reconstructing Ideals From Deconstructed Rights." *Harvard Civil Rights–Civil Liberties Law Review* 22, no. 2 (spring 1987): 401–433.

Williams, Walter. "The False Civil Rights Vision." *Georgia Law Review* 21, no. 5 (summer 1987): 1119–1139.

————. "False Civil Rights Vision and Contempt for Rule of Law." *Georgetown Law Journal* 79, no. 6 (August 1991): 1777–1782.

Williams, Walter E. *All It Takes Is Guts: A Minority View*. Washington, D.C.: Regnery Gateway, 1987.

Williams, Wendy W. "The Equality Crisis: Some Reflections on Culture, Courts, and Feminism." In Katharine T. Bartlett and Rosanne Kennedy, eds. *Feminist Legal Theory: Readings in Law and Gender*. Boulder: Westview, 1991.

Wilson, Douglas L. "Thomas Jefferson and the Character Issue." *Atlantic Monthly*, November 1992.

Wilson, James Q. *Essays on Character*. Washington, D.C.: AEI Press, 1991.

Wilson, William J. *The Declining Significance of Race: Blacks & Changing American Institutions*. 2d ed. Chicago: Univ. of Chicago, 1980.

————. *Power, Racism & Privilege: Race Relations in Theoretical & Sociohistorical Perspectives*. New York: Free Press, 1976.

Winter, Ralph. "TM's Legacy." *Yale Law Journal* 101, no. 1 (October 1991): 25–29.

Wittes, Benjamin, and Janet Wittes. "Group Therapy: Research by Quota." *New Republic*, 5 April 1993.

Wolfe, Alan. "The New American Dilemma: Understanding, and Misunderstanding, Race." Review of *Two Nations: Black and White, Separate, Hostile, Unequal*, by Andrew Hacker, *Rethinking Social Policy: Race, Poverty, and the Underclass*, by Christopher Jencks, *Streetwise: Race, Class, and Change in an Urban Community*, by Elijah Anderson, *The New Politics of Poverty: The Nonworking Poor in America*, by Lawrence Mead, *On Character: Essays*, by James Q. Wilson, and *Race: How Blacks and Whites Think and Feel about the American Obsession*, by Studs Terkel. *New Republic*, 13 April 1992.

Wolfe, Bertram D. *An Ideology in Power: Reflections on the Russian Revolution*. New York: Stein and Day, 1969.

————. *Three Who Made a Revolution*. 4th rev. ed. New York: Dial Press, 1964.

Wolfe, Christopher. *The Rise of Modern Judicial Review*, rev. ed. Lanham, Md.: Littlefield Adams, 1994.

Wolters, Raymond. *The Burden of Brown: Thirty Years of School Desegregation*. Knoxville: Univ. of Tennessee Press, 1984.

Wood, Gordon S. "The Democratization of the Mind in the American Revolution." In *The Moral Foundations of the American Republic*. 3d ed. Edited by Robert H. Horwitz. Charlottesville: Univ. Press of Virginia, 1986.

————. *The Radicalism of the American Revolution*. New York: Alfred A. Knopf, 1992.

Woodward, Bob, and Scott Armstrong. *The Brethren: Inside the Supreme Court.* New York: Simon & Schuster, 1979.

Workman, James. "Gender Norming: Quotas in the State Department." *New Republic*, 1 July 1991.

Wright, Bruce. *Black Robes, White Justice: Why Our Legal System Doesn't Work for Blacks.* New York: Lyle Stuart, 1987.

Wright, J. Skelly. "Color-Blind Theories and Color-Conscious Remedies." *University of Chicago Law Review* 47, no. 2 (winter 1980): 213–245.

Wynter, Leon E. "Managing Diversity Rises from Ashes of Affirmative Action." *Emerge*, November 1993.

Wyzanski, Charles E., Jr. Review of *An American Dilemma, the Negro Problem and Modern Democracy*, by Gunnar Myrdal. *Harvard Law Review* 58 (1944): 285–291.

Yarbrough, Tinsley E. *Judicial Enigma: The First Justice Harlan.* New York: Oxford Univ. Press, 1995.

Yates, Steven. *Civil Wrongs: What Went Wrong with Affirmative Action.* San Francisco: ICS Press, 1994.

Yudof, Mark G. "School Desegregation: Legal Realism, Reasoned Elaboration, and Social Science Research in the Supreme Court." *Law and Contemporary Problems* 42, no. 4 (Autumn 1978): 57–110.

Congressional Record

Case, Sen. Clifford. *Congressional Record* 110, pt. 6 (8 April 1964): 7212–13, 7247.

Celler, Rep. Emanuel. *Congressional Record* 110, pt. 2 (31 January 1964): 1517–1518.

———. *Congressional Record* 110, pt. 2 (8 February 1964): 2575, 2577–2578.

———. *Congressional Record* 110, pt. 12 (2 July 1964): 15896.

Clark, Sen. Joseph S. *Congressional Record* 110, pt. 6 (8 April 1964): 7212–13.

Danforth, Sen. John. *Congressional Record* 137, no. 155 (daily ed. October 25, 1991): S15276–S15277.

Dole, Sen. Robert. *Congressional Record* 137, no. 158 (daily ed. October 30, 1991): S15472–S15478.

Goldwater, Sen. Barry. *Congressional Record* 110, pt. 11 (18 June 1964): 14319.

Humphrey, Sen. Hubert H. *Congressional Record* 110, pt. 4 (17 March 1964): 5423.

———. *Congressional Record* 110, pt. 5 (30 March 1964): 6549, 6552–6553.

———. *Congressional Record* 110, pt. 6 (9 April 1964): 7420.

———. *Congressional Record* 110, pt. 10 (4 June 1964): 12707, 12722–12724.

———. *Congressional Record* 110, pt. 10 (13 June 1964): 13724.

Kennedy, Sen. Edward. *Congressional Record* 110, pt. 6 (9 April 1964): 7380.

Kuchel, Sen. Thomas N. *Congressional Record* 110, pt. 5 (30 March 1964): 6563.

Leadership Conference on Civil Rights. "Some Questions and Answers on the Civil Rights Bill." *Congressional Record* 110, pt. 6 (11 April 1964): 7711.

Lindsay, Rep. John. *Congressional Record* 110, pt. 2 (31 January 1964): 1540.

Muskie, Sen. Edmund. *Congressional Record* 110, pt. 11 (18 June 1964): 14328.

Selden, Rep. Armistead. *Congressional Record* 110, pt. 2 (1 February 1964): 1604.

Smith, Rep. Howard W. *Congressional Record* 110, pt. 2 (1 February 1964): 1623.

———. *Congressional Record* 110, pt. 2 (8 February 1964): 2564, 2577–2578.

———. *Congressional Record* 110, pt. 12 (2 July 1964): 15870.

Williams, Sen. Harrison. *Congressional Record* 110, pt. 7 (23 April 1964): 8921.

Williams, Sen. John. *Congressional Record* 110, pt. 11 (18 June 1964): 14331.

Court Cases

Adarand Constructors, Inc. v. Peña, 63 U.S.L.W. 4523 (U.S. June 12, 1995).

Aiken v. Memphis, 37 F. 3d 1155 (6th Cir. 1994).

Albemarle Paper Co. v. Moody, 422 U.S. 405 (1975).

Alexander v. Holmes County Board of Education, 396 U.S. 19 (1969).

Allen v. State Board of Elections, 393 U.S. 544 (1969).

Baker v. Carr, 369 U.S. 186 (1962).

Batson v. Kentucky, 476 U.S. 79 (1986).

Beer v. United States, 425 U.S. 130 (1976).

Belton v. Gebhart, 87 A.2d 862 (Del. Ch. 1952).

Berea College v. Kentucky, 211 U.S. 45 (1908).

Berkman v. City of New York, 812 F.2d 52 (2d Cir. 1987).

Board of Education of Oklahoma City Public Schools v. Dowell, 498 U.S. 237 (1991).

Bob Jones University v. United States, 461 U.S. 574 (1983).

Bolling v. Sharpe, 347 U.S. 497 (1954).

Briggs v. Elliott, 98 F. Supp. 529 (E.D.S.C. 1951).

Briggs v. Elliott, 103 F. Supp. 920 (E.D.S.C. 1952).

Briggs v. Elliott, 132 F. Supp. 776 (E.D.S.C. 1955).

Brown v. Board of Education of Topeka, 98 F. Supp. 797 (D. Kan. 1951).

Brown v. Board of Education of Topeka, 347 U.S. 483 (1954).

Brown v. Board of Education of Topeka, 349 U.S. 294 (1955).

Buchanan v. City of Jackson, 683 F. Supp. 1515 (W.D. Tenn. 1988).

Buchanan v. Warley, 245 U.S. 60 (1917).

Burton v. Wilmington Parking Authority, 365 U.S. 715 (1961).

Cane v. Worcester County, 840 F. Supp. 1081 (D. Md. 1994).

Cane v. Worcester County, 847 F. Supp. 369 (D. Md. 1994).

Cane v. Worcester County, 35 F. 3d 921 (4th Cir. 1994), *cert. denied*, 63 U.S.L.W. 2625 (U.S. Feb. 21, 1995).

Civil Rights Cases, 109 U.S. 3 (1883).

Columbus Board of Education v. Penick, 443 U.S. 449 (1979).

Connecticut v. Teal, 457 U.S. 440 (1982).

Contractors Association of Eastern Pennsylvania v. Secretary of Labor, 442 F.2d 159 (3d Cir. 1971), *cert. denied*, 404 U.S. 854 (1971).

Cooper v. Aaron, 358 U.S. 1 (1958).

Corry v. Stanford University, No. 740309 (Cal. App. Dep't Super. Ct. February 27, 1995).

Cumming v. Board of Education, 175 U.S. 528 (1899).

Davis v. Bandemar, 478 U.S. 109 (1986).

Davis v. County School Board of Prince Edward County, 103 F. Supp. 337 (E.D. Va. 1952).

Davis v. School Commissioners of Mobile County, 402 U.S. 33 (1971).

Dayton Board of Education v. Brinkman, 433 U.S. 406 (1977).

Dayton Board of Education v. Brinkman, 443 U.S. 526 (1979).

DeFunis v. Odegaard, 416 U.S. 312 (1974).

DeShaney v. Winnebago County Dept. of Social Services, 489 U.S. 189 (1989).

DeWitt v. Wilson, 63 U.S.L.W. 3917 (U.S. June 27, 1995).

Dillard v. Baldwin County Board of Education, 686 F. Supp. 1459 (M.D. Ala. 1988).

Dillard v. Crenshaw County, 831 F.2d 246 (11th Cir. 1987).

Dillard v. Crenshaw County, 679 F. Supp. 1546 (M.D. Ala. 1988).

Dothard v. Rawlinson, 433 U.S. 321 (1977).

Dougan v. State, 595 So.2d 1 (Fla. 1992).

Elmore v. Rice, 72 F. Supp. 516 (1947).

Firefighters v. Cleveland, 478 U.S. 501 (1986).

Firefighters v. Stotts, 467 U.S. 561 (1984).

Foster v. State, 614 So.2d 455 (Fla. 1992).

Franks v. Bowman Transportation Co., 424 U.S. 747 (1976).

Freeman v. Pitts, 503 U.S. 467 (1992).

Frontiero v. Richardson, 411 U.S. 677 (1973).

Fullilove v. Klutznick, 448 U.S. 448 (1980).

Furnco Construction Corp. v. Waters, 438 U.S. 567 (1978).

Gayle v. Browder, 352 U.S. 903 (1956).

Gebhart v. Belton, 91 A.2d 137 (Del. 1952).

Georgia v. United States, 411 U.S. 526 (1973).

Goldberg v. Kelly, 397 U.S. 254 (1970).

Gong Lum v. Rice, 275 U.S. 78 (1927).

Goss v. Board of Education of Knoxville, 373 U.S. 683 (1963).

Green v. New Kent County School Board, 391 U.S. 430 (1968).

Griffin v. Prince Edward County School Board, 377 U.S. 218 (1964).

Griggs v. Duke Power Co., 420 F.2d 1225 (4th Cir. 1970).

Griggs v. Duke Power Co., 401 U.S. 424 (1971).

Grove City College v. Bell, 465 U.S. 555 (1984).

Harper v. Virginia State Board of Elections, 383 U.S. 663 (1966).

Heart of Atlanta Motel v. United States, 379 U.S. 241 (1964).

Hills v. Gautreaux, 425 U.S. 284 (1976).

Holder v. Hall, 114 S. Ct. 2581 (1994).

Holmes v. City of Atlanta, 350 U.S. 879 (1955).

In Re Birmingham Reverse Discrimination Litigation, 20 F.3d 1525 (11th Cir. 1994), *cert. denied*, 63 U.S.L.W. 3753 (U.S. April 18, 1995).

International Brotherhood of Teamsters v. United States, 431 U.S. 324 (1977).

J.E.B. v. Alabama, 114 S. Ct. 1419 (1994).

Jenkins v. Missouri, 593 F. Supp. 1485 (W.D. Mo. 1984).

Jenkins v. Missouri, 807 F.2d 657 (8th Cir. 1986).

Johnson v. Committee on Examinations, 407 U.S. 915 (1971).

Johnson v. De Grandy, 114 S. Ct. 2647 (1994).

Johnson v. Transportation Agency, Santa Clara County, Calif., 480 U.S. 616 (1987).

Jones v. Alfred H. Mayer, Co., 392 U.S. 409 (1968).

Katzenbach v. McClung, 379 U.S. 294 (1964).

Katzenbach v. Morgan, 384 U.S. 641 (1966).

Keyes v. School District No. 1, Denver, Colo., 413 U.S. 189 (1973).

Korematsu v. United States, 323 U.S. 214 (1944).

Larry P. by Lucille P. v. Riles, 793 F.2d 969 (9th Cir. 1984).

Lau v. Nichols, 414 U.S. 563 (1974).

League of United Latin American Citizens v. Clements, 999 F.2d 831 (5th Cir. 1993).

Local 53 of the International Association of Heat and Frost Insulators and Asbestos Workers v. Vogler, 407 F.2d 1047 (5th Cir. 1969).

Marbury v. Madison, 5 U.S. (1 Cranch) 137 (1803).

Martin v. Wilks, 490 U.S. 755 (1989).

Mayor of Baltimore v. Dawson, 350 U.S. 877 (1955).

McCabe v. Atchison, Topeka & Santa Fe Railway, 235 U.S. 151 (1914).

McCleskey v. Kemp, 481 U.S. 279 (1987).

McDaniel v. Barresi, 402 U.S 39 (1971).

McDonald v. Santa Fe Trail Transportation Co., 427 U.S. 273 (1976).

McDonnell Douglas Corp. v. Green, 411 U.S. 792 (1973).

McGhee v. Granville County, 860 F.2d 110 (4th Cir. 1988).

McLaurin v. Oklahoma State Regents, 339 U.S. 637 (1950).

Metro Broadcasting, Inc. v. FCC, 497 U.S. 547 (1990).

Miller v. Johnson, 63 U.S.L.W. 4726 (U.S. June 27, 1995).

Milliken v. Bradley, 418 U.S. 717 (1974).

Milliken v. Bradley, 433 U.S. 267 (1977).

Missouri v. Jenkins, 495 U.S. 33 (1990).

Missouri v. Jenkins, 63 U.S.L.W. 4486 (U.S. June 12, 1995).

Missouri Ex Rel. Gaines v. Canada, 305 U.S. 337 (1938).

Mobile v. Bolden, 446 U.S. 55 (1980).

Monroe v. Board of Commissioners, 391 U.S. 450 (1968).

New York City Transit Authority v. Beazer, 440 U.S. 568 (1979).

North Carolina State Board of Education v. Swann, 402 U.S. 43 (1971).

Officers for Justice v. Civil Service Commission of San Francisco, 979 F.2d 721 (9th Cir. 1992).

Palmer v. Thompson, 403 U.S. 217 (1971).

Patterson v. McLean Credit Union, 491 U.S. 164 (1989).

Planned Parenthood v. Casey, 112 S. Ct. 2791 (1992).

Plessy v. Ferguson, 163 U.S. 537 (1896).

Podberesky v. Kirwan, 38 F. 3d 147 (4th Cir. 1994), *cert. denied*, 63 U.S.L.W. 3832 (U.S. May 22, 1995).

Regents of the Univ. of California v. Bakke, 438 U.S. 265 (1978).

Reitman v. Mulkey, 387 U.S. 369 (1967).

Reynolds v. Sims, 377 U.S. 533 (1964).

Richmond v. J.A. Croson, Co., 488 U.S. 469 (1989).

Richmond v. United States, 422 U.S. 358 (1975).

Roe v. Wade, 410 U.S. 113 (1973).

Rogers v. Lodge, 458 U.S. 613 (1982).

Rome v. United States, 446 U.S. 156 (1980).

Runyon v. McCrary, 427 U.S. 160 (1976).

School Board of Nassau County v. Arline, 480 U.S. 273 (1987).

Shaw v. Reno, 113 S. Ct. 2816 (1993).

Sheet Metal Workers' International Association v. EEOC, 478 U.S. 421 (1986).

Sipuel v. Board of Regents, 332 U.S. 631 (1948).

Slaughter-House Cases, 83 U.S. (16 Wall.) 36 (1873).

Smith v. Olin Chemical Corp., 555 F.2d 1283 (5th Cir. 1977).

Southeastern Community College v. Davis, 442 U.S. 397 (1979).

South Carolina v. Katzenbach, 383 U.S. 301 (1966).

Spallone v. United States, 493 U.S. 265 (1990).

State v. Russell, 477 N.W.2d 886 (Minn. 1991).

St. Francis College v. Al-Khazraji, 481 U.S. 604 (1987).

St. Mary's Honor Center v. Hicks, 113 S. Ct. 2742 (1993).

Strauder v. West Virginia, 100 U.S. (10 Otto) 303 (1879).

Sullivan v. Little Hunting Park, 396 U.S. 229 (1969).

I N D E X